INTERPRETING
THE WISDOM
BOOKS

HANDBOOKS FOR OLD TESTAMENT EXEGESIS
David M. Howard Jr., series editor

Interpreting the Pentateuch: An Exegetical Handbook
Peter T. Vogt
Interpreting the Historical Books: An Exegetical Handbook
Robert B. Chisholm Jr.
Interpreting the Wisdom Books: An Exegetical Handbook
Edward M. Curtis
Interpreting the Psalms: An Exegetical Handbook
Mark D. Futato
Interpreting the Prophetic Books: An Exegetical Handbook
Gary V. Smith
Interpreting Apocalyptic Literature: An Exegetical Handbook
Richard A. Taylor

INTERPRETING
THE WISDOM
BOOKS

An Exegetical Handbook

Edward M. Curtis

David M. Howard Jr.
SERIES EDITOR

Kregel
Academic

Interpreting the Wisdom Books: An Exegetical Handbook
© 2017 by Edward M. Curtis

Published by Kregel Publications, a division of Kregel, Inc., 2450 Oak Industrial Dr NE, Grand Rapids, MI 49505-6020.

The Greek font GraecaU and the Hebrew font New JerusalemU are from www.linguist-software.com/lgku.htm, +1-425-775-1130.

ISBN 978-0-8254-4230-8

Printed in the United States of America
17 18 19 20 21 / 5 4 3 2 1

*This volume is dedicated to my sons
Ed and Matthew and their wives.*

*My wife Joy and I are deeply grateful
to God for the gift of these two boys,
and that gratitude has been increased
by adding Ed's wife Tamara
and Matthew's wife Amy to our family.*

*Our prayer is that our sons and their wives
will continue to grow in their experience of
God's gracious love and that God's purposes
for them may be fully realized.*

CONTENTS IN BRIEF

Series Preface 15
Preface 17
Abbreviations 21

1. Interpreting Old Testament Wisdom Literature 23
2. Primary Themes in the Wisdom Books 57
3. Preparing for Interpretation 87
4. Interpreting the Wisdom Books 115
5. Proclaiming the Wisdom Books 141
6. Putting It All Together: From Text to Sermon 167

Appendix: Computer and Internet Resources for
           Old Testament Exegesis—by Austen M. Dutton
Glossary 199

CONTENTS

Series Preface 15
Preface 17
Abbreviations 21

1. Interpreting Old Testament Wisdom Literature 23
   Introduction to Old Testament Wisdom 23
   Wisdom's Perspective and Worldview 25
   Wisdom Literature and the Rest of the Old Testament:
   *   A Complementary Relationship* 28
   Wisdom's Goal and the Pedagogy of the Sages 30
   Wisdom's Genres: Poetry and Proverb 32
       The Nature of Poetry 32
           The Characteristics of Poetry 33
           The Way Poetry Describes Reality 34
           The Power of Metaphors and Images 36
           How Metaphors Work 36
           Interpreting Metaphors 38
           Parallelism 41
           Other Literary Features 45
       The Nature of a Proverb 47
           A Proverb Captures a Tiny Cross-Section of Truth 49
           Proverbs Are Characterized by Ambiguity 50
           Proverbs Describe the Way Things Usually Work 50
       The Authority of a Proverb 51

2. Primary Themes in the Wisdom Books 57

Job.. 58

Job Explores the Relationship between God
and Humanity 58

Job Shows Humanity's Limited Understanding
of God's Work and Purposes 60

Job Shows That God Accepts the Honest Cries
of His Hurting People 60

Job Shows That People Should Serve God for Who
He Is Rather Than for Benefits He Provides 61

Job Teaches Important Lessons about God 61

Job Shows How God's People Should Respond
to Circumstances That Call into Question
God's Justice and Goodness 62

Proverbs.. 63

Biblical Wisdom Begins with the Fear of the Lord 63

Proverbs Sees both General and Special Revelation
as Wisdom from God.. 64

Proverbs View of Life: Cause–Effect and Complexity 65

Important Values in Proverbs 66

Proverbs Values Moral and Ethical Behavior 66

Proverbs Values Humility 66

Proverbs Values Discretion 67

Proverbs and the Two Ways 68

Proverbs and the Importance of Application 69

Ecclesiastes 70

Ecclesiastes Declares That All Is *hebel* 70

Ecclesiastes Emphasizes Perplexing Realities about Life 72

Ecclesiastes Affirms the Reality of Human Limits............... 73

Ecclesiastes Affirms the Importance of Fearing God
and Keeping His Commandments.............................. 75

Ecclesiastes Affirms the Importance of Wisdom
and Living Wisely 75

Ecclesiastes Affirms the Importance of Enjoying Life
as God Gives Opportunity 76

Ecclesiastes Recognizes God's Sovereignty
and Providence 77

Song of Songs 78

Introduction 78

Some Approaches to the Song.. 79

Working Assumptions about the Song 80

Primary Themes 82

*The Song Sees Human Love, Sex, and Marriage
as Part of God's Design for Creation* 82

The Song Reveals Attitudes and Behaviors Important
  in Relationships between Men and Women 82
The Song Provides a Glimpse into How the One-Flesh
  Relationship Is Designed to Function 83
The Song Suggests That This Relationship Is a Gift
  of God That Cannot Be Forced or Manipulated 84
The Song Allows Us to More Fully Understand
  the Nature of God... 84

3. Preparing for Interpretation 87
    The Importance of Ancient Near Eastern Background
      in Interpreting Wisdom Literature 88
      Helpful Parallels 88
      Significant Differences 91
      Specific Parallels to Old Testament Wisdom Books 94
        Job 94
        Proverbs 95
        Ecclesiastes 96
        Song of Songs 98
      Basic Resources for Ancient Near Eastern Background 98
    Textual Criticism: Determining the Best Text 100
      Introduction 100
      The Task and Basic Principles 102
      The Hebrew Text of the Wisdom Books........................... 105
      Basic Resources for Textual Criticism............................. 106
    Translation and Developing a Sense of the Context................ 106
      Resources for Translation and Exegesis 107
        Concordances.. 107
        Language Tools.. 107
        Lexicons... 108
        Word Study Tools 109
        Other Resources.. 109
    Considering the Contribution of Others 110
      General Introductions 110
      Commentaries and Related Studies 110
        Job 110
        Proverbs 111
        Ecclesiastes... 112
        Song of Songs 113

4. Interpreting the Wisdom Books.. 115
    Wisdom Literature: General Guidelines for Interpretation 115
    Guidelines for Interpreting Individual Wisdom Books................... 118
      Job 119

Interpret Individual Passages in the Context
of the Entire Book 119
Interpret the Book Recognizing That It Is Poetry 121
Interpret the Book in Its Broader Ancient
Near Eastern Context 121
Proverbs 123
Interpret Passages in the Context of the Book and the
Fear of the Lord 123
Interpret Proverbs in the Light of Genre
and Wisdom's Purposes 124
Interpret Proverbs in Light of the Book's Total
Teaching on a Topic 125
Interpret Proverbs Recognizing the Wide Diversity
of Sayings in the Book 127
Considering the Claims of Proverbs 129
Ecclesiastes 131
Interpret Ecclesiastes as a Unified Composition 132
Recognize the Tensions and Lack of Coherent Structure
as Part of the Book's Design 133
Interpret the Book in the Light of Its Dominant Themes 134
Seek a Balanced Understanding of All That Qoheleth Affirms .. 135
Interpret Ecclesiastes in the Broader Context of Scripture 135
Song of Songs 136
Interpret Song of Songs as Poetry 137
Exegesis of Song of Songs Requires Careful Analysis
of the Poetry 137

5. Proclaiming the Wisdom Books 141
The Value of Proclaiming Wisdom 143
Preparing a Sermon 145
Gaining Familiarity with the Passage 145
The Importance of Context and Literary Analysis 147
Proverbs 2 147
Job 28 148
Organizing the Presentation 149
Proverbs 2 149
Job 28 149
General Guidelines for Proclaiming Wisdom Literature 150
The Nature of Wisdom 150
The Realities of Life under the Sun 151
The Goals of Wisdom and the Importance of Application 152
The Potential of Wisdom 154
The Power of Rhetorical Devices and Examples 155
Guidelines for Proclaiming Individual Books 157

Job 157
    Proclamation Should Do Justice Both to Job's Struggle
       and His Faith 157
    Proclamation Should Reflect the Book's Poetic Genre 158
    Proclamation Should Use Examples to Connect
       the Ancient Text to Today's World 158
    Proclaim Job with a Broad Awareness of How People Suffer 158
Proverbs 159
    Proclamation Should Reflect the Big Picture
       and Recurrent Themes 159
    Proclamation Should Reflect the Book's Genre 160
    Proclamation Should Emphasize the Need for Application 160
Ecclesiastes 161
    Proclamation Should Do Justice to Qoheleth's Tensions 161
    Proclamation Should Point to Further Light
       on Qoheleth's Unanswered Questions 162
    Proclamation Should Instruct God's People How to Live
       with Unanswered Questions 162
Song of Songs 163
    Proclaim Song of Songs as Love Poetry 163
    Proclamation Should Celebrate the Marriage Relationship
       Between a Man and Woman as Reflecting God's Order 163
    Proclamation Should See Song of Songs as Congruent
       with the Rest of Scripture 164
    Proclamation of Song of Songs Should Reflect
       Wisdom's Pedagogy 164
    Proclamation of Song of Songs Should Emphasize
       the Importance of Application 165

6. Putting It All Together: From Text to Sermon 167
   Step One: Focusing on the Topic 168
   Proverbs and Friendship 168
   An Example of Friendship in Job 4–6 169
   Step Two: Recognizing Genre and Exegetical Details 170
   Proverbs and Friendship 170
   Job 4–6 and the Practice of Friendship 171
   Step Three: Organizing the Material 172
   A Topical Study on Friendship in Proverbs......................172
       Building Up the Image: Benefits and Liabilities
        of Friendship...172
       Building Up the Image: Friends, Relatives, and Needs 173
       Building Up the Image: Companions Can Either Build
        Us Up or Tear Us Down.......................................174
       Building Up the Image: Finding Good Friends 175

A Case Study on Friendship from Job 4–6........................176
 The Prologue and the Narrative Context..........................176
 Job's Outburst (Job 3:3–26) 177
 Job's Experience and Contemporary Relevance 177
 Eliphaz' Response: A Resort to the Doctrine of
  Retribution (Job 4–5) 178
 Eliphaz and Knowing What Is True 179
 Application and the Reality of Human Limits 179
 Defining Key Words and Allowing
  the Narrative to Develop...180
 Proverbs, Metaphors, and the Importance
  of Ḥesed in Friendship 180
 Step Four: Applying the Text 182
 Applying Proverbs to Life 182
 Applying Job 4–6 to Life 183

Appendix: Computer and Internet Resources for
  Old Testament Exegesis—by Austen M. Dutton 187
 Introduction 187
 Using Bible Software for Searches..188
 Downloadable Software 190
 Bible Works..191
 Accordance...191
 Logos 192
 Olive Tree 192
 TheWord..192
 Other Software 193
 Kindle Resources..193
 Online Resources 193
 English Bible Resources...194
 Hebrew Resources...194
 Septuagint Resources 195
 Up-and-Coming Resources 195
 Conclusion..196

Glossary 199

SERIES PREFACE

AN APPRECIATION FOR THE RICH DIVERSITY of literary genres in Scripture is one of the positive features of evangelical scholarship in recent decades. No longer are the same principles or methods of interpretation applied across the board to every text without regard for differences in genre. Such an approach can lead to confusion, misunderstanding, and even wrong interpretations or applications. Careful attention to differences in genre is a critical component of a correct understanding of God's Word.

The Handbooks for Old Testament Exegesis series (HOTE) offers students basic skills for exegeting and proclaiming the different genres of the Old Testament. Because there is no one-size-fits-all approach to interpreting Scripture, this series features six volumes covering the major genres in the Old Testament: narrative, law, poetry, wisdom, prophecy, and apocalyptic. The volumes are written by seasoned scholar-teachers who possess extensive knowledge of their disciplines, lucid writing abilities, and the conviction that the church and the world today desperately need to hear the message of the Old Testament. These handbooks are designed to serve a twofold purpose: to present the reader with a better understanding of the different Old Testament genres (principles) and provide strategies for preaching and teaching these genres (methods).

These volumes are primarily intended to serve as textbooks for graduate-level exegesis courses that assume a basic knowledge of Hebrew. There is no substitute for encountering God's Word in its original languages, even as we acknowledge the limitations of language in plumbing the depths of who God is. However, the series is also accessible to those without a working knowledge of Hebrew, in that an English translation is always given whenever Hebrew is used. Thus, seminary-trained pastors for whom Hebrew is a distant memory, upper-level college students, and even well-motivated laypeople should all find this series useful.

Each volume is built around the same six-chapter structure as follows:

1. The Nature of the Genres
2. Viewing the Whole: Major Themes
3. Preparing for Interpretation
4. Interpreting the Text
5. Proclaiming the Text
6. Putting It All Together: From Text to Sermon

Authors are given freedom in how they title these six chapters and in how best to approach the material in each. But the familiar pattern in every volume will serve students well, allowing them to move easily from one volume to another to locate specific information. The first chapter in each handbook introduces the genre(s) covered in the volume. The second chapter covers the purpose, message, and primary themes in the individual books and canonical sections under consideration. The third chapter includes such diverse matters as historical and cultural backgrounds, critical questions, textual matters, and a brief annotated bibliography of helpful works. The fourth chapter sets forth guidelines for interpreting texts of the genre(s) under consideration. The fifth chapter details strategies for proclaiming such texts. The final chapter gives one or two hands-on examples of how to move through different stages of the interpretive process, in order to demonstrate how the principles discussed previously work out in practice. Each volume also includes a glossary of specialized terms; these terms are boldfaced at their first occurrence in each chapter.

The Scriptures themselves remind us in many ways about the importance of proper interpretation of God's words. Paul encouraged Timothy to "do your best to present yourself to God as one approved by him, a worker who has no need to be ashamed, rightly explaining the word of truth" (2 Tim. 2:15 NRSV). In an earlier day, Ezra the scribe, along with the Levites, taught God's Word to the postexilic community: "So they read from the book, from the law of God, with interpretation. They gave the sense, so that the people understood the reading" (Neh. 8:8 NRSV). It is my prayer, and that of the authors and publisher, that these handbooks will help a new generation of God's people to do the same.

Soli Deo Gloria.

—DAVID M. HOWARD JR.
Series Editor

PREFACE

OLD TESTAMENT WISDOM LITERATURE IS A DIVERSE and somewhat bewildering body of material. It often confronts us with tensions and disturbing questions and describes life in ways that we must admit are quite realistic, but sometimes perplexing. It often raises more questions than it answers, and Ecclesiastes even posits conclusions occasionally that seem to be skeptical, cynical, and the antithesis of hope and positive Christian thinking. In addition, these books are dominated by poetry and proverb—genres with which our culture is largely unfamiliar. And then there is the perception that the claims of some of this material are something of an overreach because they sometimes fly in the face of our own experiences in the world. We know that godly people do not always enjoy good health, abundant wealth, and success in the community. We see too many examples of godly people suffering and dying young while evil people die at a ripe old age rich, prosperous, and with their children dancing around their feet, as Job puts it.

At the same time, these books do emphasize things like the fear of the Lord and obeying his instruction, the importance of seeking wisdom and living wisely, and the awareness of God's sovereignty and overarching providence. At the end of his struggle Job declares that his still unexplained experience has resulted in great spiritual growth. He says, "I had heard of you by the hearing of the ear, but now my eye sees you" (Job 42:5). Proverbs claims that the diligent and persistent search for wisdom will lead, not just to more wisdom and knowledge, but to "understand the fear of the Lord and find the knowledge of God" (Prov. 2:5). Ecclesiastes indicates that it is only a life that is centered in God that has ultimate meaning; he may even imply that it is in remembering God from one's youth and in fearing God and keeping his commandments that a person can gain a profit that death cannot erase—something that the New Testament clearly confirms. Such general observations about the wisdom literature reveal a spiritual and theological value in this material that is often missed by the church.

The wisdom literature, of course, is filled with practical, though often somewhat secular-seeming principles that have to do with everyday matters of life—things like civil speech, honesty, integrity, self-control, diligence, and other useful values. While some are deterred by the secular character of many of these principles, it seems likely that these practical guidelines for living are as integral to God's purposes for his people as is the explicitly theological material that dominates many other parts of Scripture. The wisdom literature ties these two streams in God's revelation together in a way that affirms the importance of both for the church, and one suspects that the neglect of the practical stream has done particular damage to the witness of the church in the world.

The goal of this volume is to provide a general discussion of the background and perspective that characterizes the wisdom material along with suggestions and guidelines for interpreting and proclaiming this part of Scripture. I hope the book will be a useful resource for pastors and teachers in the church to help them navigate the sometimes bewildering waters of the wisdom literature. The claim of wisdom is that those who choose the path of wisdom and persist on it will demonstrate to the people around them what God's grace is capable of doing in a person's life. The result will be that God will be glorified. Wisdom will help us significantly as we seek to be salt and light in a fallen world. My hope is that this volume will provide useful tools for engaging in that task.

I would like to thank a number of people for their help with this book. Each has brought insight and made the book a better product. I want to thank the series editor, Dr. David Howard, first for asking me to do the volume, and then for his patience and helpful suggestions along the way. I also want to thank Kregel and the various people who have worked to bring this volume to its conclusion. I am deeply grateful for all the students at Biola University and Talbot School of Theology who have taken my classes on the various wisdom books. They have stimulated my thinking and helped me to refine many ideas related to these books. I also want to thank the members of the various Sunday School classes with whom I have interacted on this material. I want to thank Talbot student Austen M. Dutton for preparing the excellent appendix on Internet and computer resources for this volume. His outstanding work is both acknowledged and greatly appreciated. I also want to thank the administration and deans at Talbot for giving me a one-course reduction and reduced committee assignments for one academic year during the time I worked on this project.

Finally, I want to single out two people in particular for their help. The first is my good friend Dr. John Brugaletta. John read this material and made many helpful suggestions about wording, grammar, etc., with the insight that only a seasoned poet and wordsmith possesses. The second is my wife Joy. She encouraged me to do the project when Dr. Howard asked me to write the volume, and she continued to encourage me throughout the project. She read various drafts of each chapter and made many helpful suggestions that made the book more concise and understandable. She is truly an excellent woman (Prov. 31:10) and a gracious gift from God for whom I am deeply thankful.

—EDWARD M. CURTIS

ABBREVIATIONS

AB	The Anchor Bible
AEL	Miriam Lichtheim. *Ancient Egyptian Literature*. 3 vols. Los Angeles: University of California Press, 1975, 1976, 1980.
ANET	*Ancient Near Eastern Texts Relating to the Old Testament*. Edited by James B. Pritchard. 3rd ed. Princeton, NJ: Princeton University Press, 1969.
AOTC	Apollos Old Testament Commentary
AUSS	*Andrews University Seminary Studies*
BCOTWP	Baker Commentary on the Old Testament Wisdom and Psalms
BDAG	W. Bauer, F. Danker, W. Arndt, and F. Gingrich. *Greek-English Lexicon of the New Testament and Other Early Christian Literature*. Chicago: University of Chicago, 3rd edition, 2001.
BDB	Brown, F., S. R. Driver, and C. A. Briggs. *A Hebrew and English Lexicon of the Old Testament*. Oxford: Clarendon Press, 1907.
BHQ	*Biblia Hebraica Quinta*
BHS	*Biblia Hebraica Stuttgartensia*
Bib Sac	*Bibliotheca Sacra*
BST	The Bible Speaks Today
BWL	W. G. Lambert. *Babylonian Wisdom Literature*. Oxford: Oxford University Press, 1960.
CBQ	*Catholic Biblical Quarterly*
CEJ	*Christian Education Journal*

COS	*The Context of Scripture.* Edited by William Hallo. 3 vols. Leiden: Brill, 1997–2000.
DOTWPW	*Dictionary of the Old Testament Wisdom, Poetry & Writings.* Downers Grove, IL: InterVarsity, 2008.
DSS	Dead Sea Scrolls
EBC	*Expositor's Bible Commentary*
EQ	*The Evangelical Quarterly*
ESV	English Standard Version
HALOT	*Hebrew and Aramaic Lexicon of the Old Testament*
HOTE	Handbooks for Old Testament Exegesis
INT	Interpretation Commentary
JBL	*Journal of Biblical Literature*
JPS	Jewish Publication Society
JSNTSup	Journal for the Study of the New Testament: Supplement
JSS	*Journal of Semitic Studies*
LXX	Septuagint
NAC	New American Commentary
NAS	New American Standard
NET	*New English Translation* (netbible.org)
NETS	*New English Translation of the Septuagint*
NICOT	New International Commentary on the Old Testament
NIDOTTE	*New International Dictionary of Old Testament Theology & Exegesis.* Edited by Willem VanGemeren. 5 vols. Grand Rapids: Zondervan, 1997.
NIVAC	NIV Application Commentary
NKJ	New King James
MT	Masoretic Text
OTL	Old Testament Library
SBLDS	Society of Biblical Literature Dissertation Series
TB	*Tyndale Bulletin*
TCC	The Communicator's Commentary
TDOT	*Theological Dictionary of the Old Testament.* Edited by G. J. Botterweck and H. Ringgren. Translated by J. T. Willis, G. W. Bromiley, and D. E. Green. 15 vols. Grand Rapids: Eerdmans, 1974–2006.
TOTC	Tyndale Old Testament Commentary
TTC	Teach the Text Commentary
TWOT	R. L. Harris, G. L. Archer Jr., and B. K. Waltke, eds. *Theological Wordbook of the Old Testament.* 2 vols. Chicago: Moody, 1980.
WBC	Word Biblical Commentary

1

INTERPRETING OLD TESTAMENT WISDOM LITERATURE

The Chapter at a Glance

Introduction to Old Testament Wisdom

Wisdom's Perspective and Worldview

Wisdom Literature and the Rest of the Old Testament: A Complementary Relationship

Wisdom's Goal and the Pedagogy of the Sages

Wisdom's Genres: Poetry and Proverb

- The Nature of Poetry
- The Nature of a Proverb
- The Authority of a Proverb

INTRODUCTION TO OLD TESTAMENT WISDOM

THE OLD TESTAMENT WISDOM BOOKS are Job, Proverbs, Ecclesiastes, and Song of Songs. They are so designated because wisdom is a prominent theme in this literature, and they are characterized by a common methodology and **epistemology**.[1] They are inspired and authoritative in the same sense as the rest of Scripture but are characterized by differences in perspective and worldview which must be taken into account for correctly interpreting and teaching this material.

Wisdom in the Old Testament regularly involved the ability to do something or accomplish a desired objective as opposed to the accumulation of information or theory formation. The terms חָכָם, "wise" and חָכְמָה, "wisdom" are used to describe the skilled craftsmen who took Moses' plans and constructed the Tabernacle and the furnishings associated with it.[2] Sailors who could successfully reach their destination despite the dangers of ocean travel are described in Ezekiel 27:8 as "wise." Psalm 107 describes a storm so intense that the sailors' skill/ wisdom "was swallowed up" (v. 27),[3] and they survived only because of God's gracious intervention. The term is used of military strategists and political leaders (Isa. 10:13) and of women skilled in lamenting for the dead (Jer. 9:17).[4]

Israel recognized the presence of wisdom in other cultures such as Egypt (Isa. 19:11–13), Phoenicia (Ezek. 28; Zech. 9:2), Persia (Esth. 1:13; 6:13), and Babylon (Dan. 2:12–13; 5:7). Sometimes the wisdom associated with other nations was viewed negatively because of their **pride**,[5] or because the wisdom was associated with divination and magic,[6] but generally their wisdom was recognized as legitimate. First Kings 4:29–34 compares Solomon's wisdom with the wisdom of the "sons of the East" and Egypt. Ancient readers would have been impressed that Solomon's wisdom surpassed that of people renowned for their wisdom.

There are similarities in form and content between the wisdom literature of Egypt, Mesopotamia,[7] and Israel. Themes such as the problem of inexplicable suffering or traits that contribute to success or failure are dealt with in each culture's wisdom literature. Similar forms such as **proverb**s, **acrostic**s, and riddles are also found. Similar proverbs ex-

---

1. In addition, a dozen or so psalms are recognized as wisdom psalms; see Mark Futato, *Interpreting the Psalms*, HOTE (Grand Rapids: Kregel, 2007), 171–73.

2. E.g., Exod. 28:3; 31:3–6; 36:1. The artisans who constructed the temple are described in a similar way in 1 Chron. 22:15–16 and 2 Chron. 2:7, 13–14 [Heb. 2:6, 12–13].

3. Author's translation.

4. Probably professional mourners.

5. For the biblical perspective on pride and **humility**, see below chapter 2.

6. For example, Exod. 7:11; Isa. 10:13; 44:25; Jer. 50:35.

7. Literature from Mesopotamia is designated "wisdom literature" because its content and form are similar to the biblical material that we call wisdom literature. W. G. Lambert (*Babylonian Wisdom Literature* [Oxford: Oxford University Press, 1960], 1–2) points out that the Babylonians and Assyrians applied the term "wisdom" (*nemequ*) to their magic and divinatory traditions.

isted in Mesopotamia and Egypt as early as 2600 B.C., and some may even have been borrowed by the biblical authors.[8]

WISDOM'S PERSPECTIVE AND WORLDVIEW

Several biblical passages state that wisdom is a gift from God, but when the content of some biblical and extrabiblical wisdom literature (certain proverbs, for example) is examined, it appears that some of this material comes from God in what appears to us to be a secondary sense. Many proverbs articulate principles that can be identified by any insightful person who carefully observes the world, and Israel and her neighbors recognized many of the same principles as contributing to a person's success. It does not require direct revelation from God (what theologians call "**special revelation**") to realize how diligence contributes to success or the problems that a bad temper can cause for a person.

This kind of wisdom comes from God in the same sense as is affirmed in Isaiah 28:23–29.[9] There the farmer's knowledge of how to plant and cultivate his crops is said to come from God. Such skill and understanding, however, does not normally come as the result of special revelation: rather, the farmer carefully observes and calculates; he tries various techniques in order to improve his agricultural production. His own experience with planting and harvesting supplements and refines traditions that have been passed down by past generations. A similar process is described in Proverbs 24:30–34, where a person walking down the road observed the overgrown and unproductive field of the sluggard. This person reflected on what he saw and made the connection between the sluggard's behavior and the outcome. He received instruction (v. 32) from the experience and presumably went on his way determined to avoid the behavior that produced such unfortunate results for the sluggard.

This kind of knowledge is possible for anyone who carefully observes the world because God has designed order and regularity into it. Wisdom presupposes the existence of "an all-embracing cosmic order . . . which served as the cohesive force holding together the various components of created order in a well-integrated, harmonious whole."[10] Israel recognized that this order was created and maintained

---

8. See chapter 3, "Proverbs."

9. Theologians often refer to this as "**general revelation.**" It is sometimes referred to as "horizontal revelation" to distinguish it from the "vertical revelation" that came to the prophets or the revelation on Mt. Sinai that came directly from heaven.

10. Leo G. Perdue, *Wisdom and Cult*, SBLDS 30 (Missoula, MT: Scholars Press, 1977), 135. Bruce Waltke ("The Book of Proverbs and Ancient Wisdom Literature," *Bib Sac*, 136 [1979], 135) also notes that the "notion of a fixed, eternal righteous order does compare

by **Yahweh**, and it is this order that provides the basis for systematic and repeatable observations about the world.

The order that is part of God's design constitutes an essential aspect of wisdom. Crenshaw points out that "God has embedded truth within all of reality. The human responsibility is to search for that insight and thus learn to live in harmony with the cosmos . . . [and] being wise meant a search for and maintenance of order."[11]

This wisdom is practical in nature rather than philosophical or academic, and as Estes has pointed out, "In the thought of Proverbs, wisdom is skill in living according to **Yahweh's order**. Folly is choosing to live contrary to the order he embedded in the universe."[12] People can discover many of the principles by which the natural world operates; they are able to identify attitudes and behaviors that contribute to people's success and others that detract from it. This appears to be the way many of the principles in biblical wisdom literature had their origin, and this probably accounts for the parallels in content between biblical wisdom and that of other nations.

The wisdom literature reflects a somewhat different perspective from other biblical literature. It rarely touches on theological themes such as covenant or God's choice of Israel or the Exodus, though Waltke has demonstrated the theological consistency between the wisdom literature and other biblical material.[13] Wisdom literature reflects the human struggle to understand how things work in the world that God created, and the search generally proceeds without special revelation. The struggle for answers takes place the way we normally experience life in the world.

Living according to the principles God designed into the world can help a person and contribute to his or her success. As Ross says, "The wisdom that directs life is the same wisdom that created the universe; to surrender to God's wisdom is to put oneself in harmony with creation, the world around one."[14]

---

favorably with the biblical meaning of 'wisdom.' . . . [Wisdom] is an eternal order existing for man's good. . . . Wisdom is God's fixed order for life, an order opposed by chaos and death." Note the similar statement of H. J. Hermisson, ("Observations on the Creation Theology in Wisdom," in *Israelite Wisdom: Samuel Terrien Festschrift,* ed. John Gammie, et al. [New York: Scholars Press, 1978], 44).

11. James Crenshaw, *Old Testament Wisdom* (Atlanta: John Knox, 1981), 18–19.

12. Daniel Estes, *Hear, My Son*, New Studies in Biblical Theology (Grand Rapids: Eerdmans, 1997), 26.

13. Bruce Waltke, "The Book of Proverbs and Old Testament Theology," *Bib Sac* 136 (1979), 302–17. See also Bruce Waltke, *Proverbs 1–15*, NICOT (Grand Rapids: Eerdmans, 2004), 64–65 and 65–133, where the congruence between Proverbs and the rest of the Old Testament is apparent. Also see the discussion below on "Wisdom Literature and the Rest of the Old Testament: A Complementary Relationship."

14. Allen Ross, "Proverbs," *EBC* 5 (Grand Rapids: Zondervan, 1991), 919.

Much of the wisdom material reflects humanity's search for Yahweh's order. Often, however, the **sages**' search brings them face to face with enigmatic and anomalous experiences that cause them to acknowledge the limited ability of human beings to understand the world. Such experiences make it clear that the world is far too complex for even the wisest person to come to a comprehensive understanding of this order. The world is full of things that people can never fully understand or control, and an important part of wisdom involves understanding human limits and living in the light of them.

All the observations in the biblical wisdom literature (including those that may have had their origin in human observations of the world) have, through the process of inspiration, been incorporated into sacred Scripture.[15] The inclusion of what appear to be largely common-sense principles in the canon affirms the legitimacy and truth of these particular bits of wisdom. It likely affirms the importance of the enterprise that led to these observations, thus commending the human search for wisdom when it is pursued in faith and dependence on God.

Scripture recognizes that human beings are not God; they are creatures, and their finitude establishes limits to what they can discover as they seek to understand the work of God and their world. Humanity's inability to gain a comprehensive understanding of the world or of the work of God is evident throughout the Bible.

Human wisdom is also limited because people are fallen, and the human propensity to go their own way rather than acknowledge the truth of God's revelation is clear. Ways that seem right to people often end in death and disaster (Prov. 14:12). Scripture's many exhortations to trust God rather than people emphasize the vital need to supplement and test human discovery with the special revelation that God gives his people. Even so, the value of such observations is emphasized throughout the wisdom literature.

Biblical wisdom, in contrast to that of Israel's neighbors, reflects **Yahwistic** theology through its regular use of terms like "**fear of the Lord**," its affirmation of God's providence, and its recognition that wisdom ultimately comes from God. Proverbs 1:7 insists that the fear of the Lord is where the search for knowledge/wisdom must begin.[16] This

---

15. As Waltke (*Proverbs 1–15*, 78–83) emphasizes, and as Proverbs 2:6 makes clear, the wisdom that results from the human search for wisdom described in Proverbs 2 comes from God; it is not the result of human effort exerted independently of God. The presence of these principles in Scripture clearly affirms their inspired and authoritative nature.

16. This essential principle occurs a number of times throughout the wisdom literature, usually at crucial points in those texts. For example, Job 1:1; 28:28; Prov. 1:7; 9:10; 15:33; 31:30; Eccl. 3:14; 12:13. See below in chapter 2, and Edward Curtis and John Brugaletta, "The Fear of the Lord and the Knowledge of God" in *Discovering the Way of Wisdom* (Grand Rapids: Kregel, 2004), 122–35.

means that a person recognizes who God is and who he or she is, and then lives in the light of that understanding. It means that the search for truth in **general revelation** must take place in the knowledge that Yahweh is the Creator and sustainer of all things, and it must be done in dependence on God. This involves recognizing the instruction of God in Scripture as authoritative on any matter. As von Rad notes, "The search for knowledge can go wrong because of one single mistake at the beginning. . . . Israel was of the opinion that effective knowledge about God is the only thing that puts a man into a right relationship with the objects of his perception."[17]

The methodology of wisdom—**empiricism**, carefully observing life, and struggling with its anomalies and enigmas—can produce many accurate and helpful conclusions about God's order. At the same time, such methods have no power to answer crucial questions like, "What is the meaning of life?" The methods of wisdom apart from God's special revelation allow people to see that life ends with death, but cannot discover what—if anything—lies beyond the grave. Human discovery has little power to understand what God is like or his purposes for creation. Nor can people discover anything about redemption, the nature of sin, or any number of other things having to do with the spiritual, the moral, or the theological.

WISDOM LITERATURE AND THE REST OF THE OLD TESTAMENT: A COMPLEMENTARY RELATIONSHIP

The methods of wisdom and the fact of human finitude establish significant limits on the knowledge that can be discovered by people seeking to understand the order that God designed into the world. Many spiritual, moral, and theological questions are beyond the boundaries where wisdom's methods can function effectively, and answers to such questions will not be forthcoming unless God reveals those answers directly to his people, as he has done through special revelation.

What is not clear to many in the church today is why such common-sense principles as are found in the wisdom material would be needed to complement the great redemptive truths revealed elsewhere in Scripture. Many people today are also put off by the fact that wisdom focuses on the way things usually work rather than on universal and invariable principles, and they have trouble understanding

---

17.   Gerhard von Rad, *Wisdom in Israel,* trans. James D. Martin (New York: Abingdon, 1972), 67. The New Testament also affirms that the effective search for truth must begin with submission to God's truth. Unbelievers are characterized by their refusal to acknowledge God (Rom. 1:28), and their minds are said to be defiled (Titus 1:15). It is clear that this attitude affects their ability to perceive truth, especially in the moral and spiritual realms.

why general statements of truth should have authority over life. For the biblical authors, living according to Yahweh's order included the ordinary and mundane as well as the more spiritual dimensions of life. The activity of God was not confined to the miraculous and spectacular but embraced all of life, and God's providence overshadowed and impacted every part of life. Kidner captures the perspective of the sages when he says, that the function of the book of Proverbs in Scripture is:

> To name business and society as spheres in which we are to acquit ourselves with credit to our Lord, and in which we are to look for his training. . . . If we could analyze the influences that build up a godly character to maturity, we might well find that the agencies that we call natural vastly outweighed those that we call super-natural. [Wisdom] reassures us that this, if it is true, is no reflection on the efficiency of God's grace; for the hard facts of life, which knock some of the nonsense out of us, are God's facts and His appointed school of character; they are not alternatives to His grace, but means of it.[18]

The major themes in wisdom literature are generally non-theological. They come out of peoples' daily experience in the world and deal with areas of life not emphasized in the Law and the Prophets. The importance of principles such as self-control, compassion toward the poor, the dangers of pride, inappropriate trust in one's own judgment, and various virtues related to the development of responsible character is not reduced because they deal with the ordinary affairs of life and are generally confined to the wisdom books. As Kidner says, "there are details of character small enough to escape the mesh of the law and the broadsides of the prophets, and yet decisive in personal dealings. Proverbs moves in this realm, asking what a person is like to live with, or to employ."[19]

Finally, the example of Job, the enigmatic dilemmas of Proverbs, and the unanswerable questions of Ecclesiastes show us aspects of life that believers often ignore. The sages believed that a biblically informed worldview must recognize the realities of life in a fallen world. They believed that acknowledging such realities is important in developing skills for coping with the experiences of life in the world. This awareness, along with an appropriate knowledge of our own limitations in controlling life, can also drive us toward the trust in God that reflects God's purpose for his people.

---

18. Derek Kidner, *Proverbs*, TOTC (Downers Grove, IL: InterVarsity, 1964), 35.

19. Ibid., 13.

WISDOM'S GOAL AND THE PEDAGOGY OF THE SAGES[20]

The goal of biblical wisdom is practical, and its focus is application and skill.[21] The pragmatic perspective of the Old Testament demands that a person act on this knowledge rather than just processing it cognitively. A passage like Proverbs 2 emphasizes upright behavior, integrity, justice, and righteousness, and indicates that the goal of biblical wisdom is not just about what works, but what is right as well. This chapter is also set in a context that emphasizes the central importance of fear of the Lord,[22] and this makes clear that wisdom also involves what is consistent with the order that God designed into the world. Such considerations support the idea that wisdom involves the sort of competence that allows a person to live in harmony with God's design. The skill that is wisdom's goal must flow out of observations and traditions that are true, but the central intent of wisdom involves the appropriate application of knowledge to a task.

Wisdom's goal is to produce people who can skillfully apply wisdom principles to life in a complex world, but the goal goes beyond that to the development of mature and godly character.[23] Wisdom's methods reflect the idea of an old anonymous **aphorism**: "Sow a thought, reap a deed. Sow a deed, reap a habit. Sow a habit, reap a character." To accomplish these goals the sages used a wide variety of methods, ranging from the authoritative teacher who expected the student to accept the instruction and do it (as is typical in Proverbs 1–9) to the teacher who provided few answers to the students and challenged them to find answers for themselves (as we see throughout the book of Ecclesiastes). Estes has suggested that "The teacher's progression from expert authority to facilitator parallels the intellectual and moral development of the learner. When the learner is a novice, the teacher must exert a higher degree of direction, but as the learner grows in wisdom, the teacher is able to become more of an enabler to assist the learner as he or she makes their own decisions."[24] The goal of this is "that the learner will develop independent competence in living in Yahweh's world."[25]

Sometimes the sages simply wanted to communicate bits and pieces of information that reflect components of Yahweh's order. Examples include straightforward aphorisms like the one found in Proverbs 10:19, which says, "When words are many, transgression is not lacking,

---

20. See Edward Curtis, "Learning from the Sages," *CEJ*, Series 3, vol. 2 (2005): 113–28.
21. See "Proverbs," chap. 2.
22. See above, n. 16.
23. For more on this, see William P. Brown, *Character in Crisis* (Grand Rapids: Eerdmans, 1996).
24. Estes, *Hear, My Son*, 134.
25. Ibid.

but whoever restrains his lips is prudent." Or Proverbs 10:4: "A slack hand causes poverty, but the hand of the diligent makes rich." These sayings occasionally include more overtly theological insights, such as Proverbs 16:9: "The heart of man plans his way, but the LORD establishes his steps." These sayings make up the bulk of Proverbs 10–31, but they are found throughout the wisdom books and elsewhere in the Old Testament. They were part of a body of tradition that was shared in order to build into people a growing knowledge of how God designed things to work in the world. The expectation was that the person hearing the instruction would respond in ways that facilitate the development of skills for living wisely in the world.

Not even the wisest teacher can teach such skills; the learner must develop them through long and arduous practice. The mental challenge of dealing with the tensions and ambiguities[26] set forth by the sages can help a person in that quest. Several proverbs make observations that touch on issues of ethics and morality without affirming any moral values.[27] Such proverbs require a person to consider the morality of a behavior even though the proverb makes no mention of moral values. This requires the learner to reflect on the proverb and draw from sources outside the proverb to make judgments about wise and appropriate behavior. The sages apparently believed that such mental exercises facilitated the development of wisdom.

Ecclesiastes 12:11 describes the words of the wise as "like goads," or pointed sticks used to move cattle in the direction they should go. Statements that seem conflicting or contradictory often work like goads. One proverb pushes the student in a certain direction, and then a contrasting principle modifies his or her direction toward the balance that reflects mature wisdom. Proverbs 26:4–5 illustrate the technique. Verse 4 instructs the budding sage to "Answer not a fool according to his folly, lest you be like him yourself." Verse 5 appears to give the opposite instruction as it says, "Answer a fool according to his folly, lest he be wise in his own eyes."

The tension of apparently contradictory advice is meant to show that a wise response to a fool depends on the circumstances. Sometimes it requires answering the fool in kind while in other situations that kind of response must be carefully avoided. Implicit in this is the understanding that the appropriate rejoinder may involve a creative response between the two extremes. While such challenges may be frustrating to those learning wisdom, the process moves the learner toward a more accurate understanding of God's order and facilitates the development of skill in living wisely and effectively in a complex world.

---

26. See discussion in "Proverbs" and "Ecclesiastes," chap. 4.

27. See examples in "Interpret Passages in the Context of the Book and the Fear of the Lord" in chapter 4.

The wisdom teachers challenged their students and were willing to take the risk of allowing them to reach their own conclusions. They saw questions and tension as important teaching devices that would challenge and provoke students to discover appropriate answers. Such methods reflect confidence in those who are seeking to grow in wisdom, and suggest that something important can be gained in these struggles. While the sages obviously believed that tradition is important, they also understood that the search for wisdom does not involve simply accepting other people's answers to standard questions. It is likely that the most important contribution of a book like Ecclesiastes lies in the questions it raises rather than the answers it provides.

The realities of life are far more varied than the paradigm questions might suggest, and it is only as people forge answers in the complex experiences of life that genuine wisdom is acquired. Wisdom is not mastery of a body of knowledge; it is skill for living in a world filled with significant tensions—sometimes even polar opposites. True wisdom consists in the skill to respond appropriately to experiences different than we expected we would encounter. A book like Ecclesiastes both alerts us to this fact, and through its methodology begins to equip learners for these realities, thus preparing them for living wisely. It forces them to deal with tensions and polarities as they seek to understand God's activity in the world, and provides them with essential grist for the mill that produces spiritual maturity.

Wisdom teachers like **Qoheleth** saw life as an integrated whole and believed that true wisdom—a full understanding of the way things really work—would result in coherence between experience and other aspects of God's revelation such as **Torah**. They struggled with the tensions generated by disconnects between the world we experience and that which the religious (or any other) tradition tells us is true. They struggled with the **ambiguity** they saw in the world and the impossibility of fitting all the data of experience into patterns that reflect the order they assumed was a fundamental part of God's creation. They also struggled to understand and incorporate into their paradigms how God works in the world and in history. Sages like Qoheleth realized that in the presence of such realities the essential thing is trusting God and dependence on him.

WISDOM'S GENRES: POETRY AND PROVERB

The Nature of Poetry

An Arabic proverb says, "He is the best speaker who can turn ears into eyes," and poetry has the power to do that in a particularly effective way. This power is illustrated by the poem "The Daffodils" by William Wordsworth. The poet describes the scene, the delight he experienced on a particular day, and the way that scene continues to bring him pleasure long after the experience ended.

The Daffodils[28]
I wandered lonely as a cloud
That floats on high o'er vales and hills,
When all at once I saw a crowd,
A host, of golden daffodils,
Beside the lake, beneath the trees,
Fluttering and dancing in the breeze.

Continuous as the stars that shine
And twinkle on the Milky Way,
They stretched in never-ending line
Along the margin of the bay:
Ten thousand saw I at a glance,
Tossing their heads in sprightly dance.

The waves beside them danced, but they
Outdid the sparkling waves with glee;
A poet could not but be gay
In such a jocund company.
I gazed, and gazed, but little thought
What wealth the show to me had brought;

For oft, when on my couch I lie
In vacant or in pensive mood,
They flash upon that inward eye
Which is the bliss of solitude;
And then my heart with pleasure fills,
And dances with the daffodils.

The way the poet describes his experience resonates with us, allows us to feel his pleasure, and, in a sense, participate in that experience. At the same time it captures better than most of us could ever articulate what happens when we experience delightful things that have nothing to do with flowers or walks around a lake.

The Characteristics of Poetry
Virtually all Old Testament wisdom literature consists of poetry, and proper interpretation of this material must begin with a basic understand-

---

28. The version of the poem cited here is Wordsworth's revised version from 1815. This text is taken from the website poetryfoundation.org.

ing of what poetry is and how it functions. Poetry has largely fallen on hard times today in American culture, but its power can occasionally be seen. I often read to one of our grandchildren, while the other one is occupied with something else. When I read poetry, it is not unusual for the play to stop and for me to find myself with both children listening intently. That seldom happens when I am reading a prose story. It is also interesting to hear our three-year-old granddaughter walking around the house reciting a poem or rhyme that we have read to her several times. Again, she almost never does that with the prose stories she hears.

A central purpose of the wisdom literature is to bring people's thoughts and behavior into congruence with the way God designed the world to work. Focusing attention on God's truth in ways that foster ongoing thought and reflection plays a significant role in accomplishing that goal. Poetry as the vehicle for God's revelation to his people seems to be especially appropriate for the goals of wisdom. As Brown points out, however, "The appreciation of poetry, like music appreciation, requires a *cultivated* receptivity on the part of the reader,"[29] and that receptivity begins with an understanding of how poetry works.

The Way Poetry Describes Reality

There are many different ways of describing reality. An engineer or scientist would likely describe a mountain range or a swiftly flowing river or a field of flowers in a different way than would a poet or artist. Recently, scientific research has focused on the process by which people fall in love. These studies measure what happens in the brain during various interpersonal encounters and describe those experiences in terms of the release of chemicals and hormones. While such studies identify certain aspects of falling in love, a scientific report on this research will have a much different impact on a reader than would a sonnet by Elizabeth Barrett Browning dealing with the same reality. A scientist fully conversant with the latest scientific findings regarding love and passion, but who has never personally experienced falling in love, will have a very limited knowledge about the reality.

Charles Dickens' novel, *Hard Times*, describes Thomas Gradgrind as "a man of realities. A man of facts and calculation," and Dickens describes a conversation between Mr. Gradgrind and a group of young students. His intimidating interaction with "girl number twenty" left her speechless when he sought her definition of a horse. He concluded that she was unable to define a horse, and that "girl number twenty possessed no facts, in reference to one of the commonest of animals." He then turned to another student in the class named Bitzer.

---

29. William Brown, *Seeing the Psalms: A Theology of Metaphor* (Louisville: Westminster John Knox, 2002), 9 (emphasis in original).

"Bitzer," said Thomas Gradgrind. "Your definition of a horse."

"Quadruped. Graminivorous. Forty teeth, namely twenty-four grinders, four eye-teeth, and twelve incisive. Sheds coat in the spring; in marshy countries, sheds hoofs, too. Hoofs hard, but requiring to be shod with iron. Age known by marks in mouth." Thus (and much more) Bitzer.

"Now girl number twenty," said Mr. Gradgrind. "You know what a horse is."

As John Ciardi points out, from Bitzer's description, girl number twenty would know what a horse is in a very limited way. She would not, however, know what a horse is in the same sense as would an artist or poet or a person who rides and trains horses. While there is a place for Bitzer's dictionary definition of a horse, it falls far short of the knowledge of a horse possessed by anyone who has spent time actually interacting with horses. Such a person may not know "how many incisors a horse has, nor how many yards of intestines. . . . He is concerned with a feel, a response-to, a sense of the character and reaction of the living animal. And zoology cannot give him that."[30] There is a world of difference between the knowledge resulting from experience and that which results from processing textbook facts and definitions. Poetry captures realities about human experience and communicates them in ways that connect with the reader's emotions and causes him or her to feel (and even participate in) the poet's experience rather than just providing additional information about it. While the scientist will provide technical measurements, the poet will use such imagery as the horse's hairy muzzle and its expressive ears.

Biblical poetry was likely written by and for ordinary people, but poetry has become, in our day, "part of high art, an elite activity for the contemplation of a privileged few."[31] A major contributor to this was the rise of **Rationalism** and **Enlightenment thinking**, which typically value as true and important only those things that are empirically demonstrable or logically irrefutable. Such thinking often dismisses the significance of ordinary human experience and devalues any understanding of reality that emerges out of aesthetic or emotional perception as too subjective to be taken seriously.

The focus on scientific study as the only path to truth and knowledge has also impacted biblical studies and given rise to a sort of technical

---

30.   John Ciardi, *How Does a Poem Mean?* (Cambridge, MA: The Riverside Press, 1959), 665–66.
31.   Craig Bartholomew and Ryan O'Dowd, *Old Testament Wisdom Literature: A Theological Introduction* (Downers Grove, IL: InterVarsity, 2011), 51.

analysis that can short-circuit the original intent and purpose of some biblical texts, especially poetic ones. Such methods, applied to the neglect of allowing biblical poetry to function as it was designed to, can easily lead to analysis that produces, "Quadruped, graminivorous—and now you know what the poem means" kinds of interpretations. As a result of largely analytical approaches, the power of the poetry is often lost and an important aspect of the revelation is destroyed. The medium for much of God's revelation in the Old Testament is poetry, and exegesis that does not capture the affective dimensions of these texts and connect people with the experience of the author falls short of the goal of exegetical excellence to which we should aspire.

The Power of Metaphors and Images

The power of poetry is illustrated by hymns such as "It Is Well With My Soul" or "Immortal, Invisible, God Only Wise." These poems/songs were written out of intensely personal experiences, but the power of the compositions lies in the fact that the experiences of these authors capture universals of human experience. We feel each author's emotion and relate to it; each writer's words quickly become our words and can be applied to a variety of experiences that may be quite different from the specific circumstances that inspired the hymns. **Metaphors**[32] such as "when sorrows like sea billows roll" or the description of the work of God in the world as "silent as light" capture the feelings of our specific experiences.

The language and structure of poetry contribute to its impact on a reader or hearer, and biblical poetry shares many literary features with poetry in general. It is characterized by an economy of words in comparison to prose, with few lines of Hebrew poetry consisting of more than four or five words, and it has a metrical quality about it, though attempts to discover a theory of meter in Hebrew poetry have produced little consensus.

How Metaphors Work

Hebrew poetry makes extensive use of images drawn from human experience and this contributes to its power to stir the emotions and connect with readers/hearers far removed from the author in time, place, and culture. Images resonate with us in a different way than even the most carefully articulated propositions. They are also easier to remember and they keep us thinking and reflecting on a point long after a proposition has left our conscious awareness. Images can be especially effective in communicating truth about abstract concepts. Comparing love or beauty or the providence of God with concrete examples drawn from the world of ordinary experience can make the abstract seem

---

32. Metaphors differ from similes in that similes use "like" or "as," while metaphors do not. For simplicity's sake, no distinction is made between the two in this book.

more real. It certainly makes such concepts more understandable to ordinary people than would theological or philosophical propositions. Leland Ryken argues that "the prevalence of images in poetry requires us to read poetry with what psychologists call the right side of the brain. This is our mental capacity to think in pictures. We first need to experience poetry with our senses and then become analytic in determining the connotations and logic of the images in their context in a poem."[33]

The poet often compares an abstract or lesser-known concept with a concrete or better-known one with which it has something in common. For example, Song of Songs 4:12–5:1 compares the woman's beauty and sexuality with a garden. Isaiah 40:31 compares the rejuvenating power that comes from trusting God to "mounting up with wings like eagles." Ecclesiastes compares life that is not centered in God and does not trust in him to a puff of air (הֶבֶל),[34] or to trying to catch the wind.[35] The interpreter "sees" the poet's image and is impacted by it. The way he or she experiences the image will, of course, be influenced by that person's knowledge/experience, but the image will become the lens through which the text is understood. Many of the images have to do with concrete or sensory characteristics such as appearance or smell or some other sensory quality, but sometimes they involve things like value or the intensity of pain or delight.

Sometimes the way the reader responds has to do more with what the example connotes or evokes rather than what it denotes, and those associations are generated by experiences of the reader. An unmarried person who reads Song of Songs will be impacted by the metaphors in the book quite differently than will a married person, and the way a married person is impacted will depend on that person's own experience of marriage. An image like "Father," while positive to most people, can be very negative to some.

While many factors influence how someone understands and experiences the metaphors used by the biblical authors—what Brown calls the **source domain**[36]—the somewhat open-ended nature of some metaphors does not necessarily lead to a kind of subjective interpretation that amounts to little more than "this is what the text means to me."

---

33. Leland Ryken, *Words of Delight: A Literary Introduction to the Bible* (Grand Rapids: Baker Academic, 1987), 162.

34. In Eccl. 1:2; 12:8, and numerous times in between.

35. For a fuller discussion of this word see the section "Ecclesiastes Declares That All Is *hebel*" in chapter 2. Common glosses for the word *hebel* are "vanity" or "meaningless."

36. Brown, *Seeing the Psalms*, 6. The source domain is the example or metaphor that the poet is using to explain a concept. The **target domain** is the concept the poet is explaining. In Psalm 23, "the Lord/Yahweh" is the concept that is being explained (the target domain) while "shepherd" is the source domain.

The meaning of a metaphor is tied to the source domain and it is essential that serious exegetical effort be directed toward determining as much about the source domain as possible. When the man compares his lover to a dove,[37] it is necessary to know what a dove is like as opposed to some other kind of bird like a parrot or vulture.

Context provides significant clues to the point of a metaphor and the source domain. For example, both Job 1:10 and 3:23 use the metaphor of Job being hedged in, but the point is quite different in each case. In Job 1:10 the point is that God has hedged Job in to protect him from difficulty and trouble. In 3:23, Job in his suffering feels as if God has him hedged in so he cannot escape from the pain and frustration. Even in a difficult Hebrew text like Job, the book tells a story that is generally clear, and the context established by that story often helps to understand the point of an obscure metaphor.

Interpreting Metaphors

But while context is important, often more is needed, and it is important to learn as much as possible about what the image would have meant to the poet and to those who originally heard it. As Brown says, "For a metaphor to work, an understanding of both [the source and target] domains is presupposed. There must be correspondence between the metaphor and its target domain that is recognized by both poet and reader. Accurate interpretation and appropriate application come only when the poet's understanding of the metaphor and that of the reader are generally congruent."[38]

Our distance in history and culture from the original context of the words sometimes makes our conclusions tentative, and it is essential to use resources that can help us understand the culture and perspective of the world out of which the texts originated.[39] It is essential for the exegete to move beyond the analytical assessment of the text and personally experience the text in the full and robust way that poetry makes possible. Understanding the source domain as accurately as possible is essential in this. Experiencing the text without analysis causes the poem to function as little more than a Rorschach test, and analysis without experiencing the text merely dissects the text and leaves it in pieces.

---

37. Song of Songs 2:14; 6:9.

38. Ibid.

39. Helpful resources include: Leland Ryken, J. C. Wilhoit, and Tremper Longman, III, eds. *The Dictionary of Biblical Imagery* (Downers Grove: InterVarsity, 1998); Othmar Keel, *The Symbolism of the Biblical World: Ancient Near Eastern Iconography and the Book of Psalms* (repr. Winona Lake, IN: Eisenbrauns, 1997 [1972]); Tremper Longman III and Peter Enns, eds. *DOTWPW*; John Walton, ed. *Zondervan Illustrated Bible Backgrounds Commentary* (Grand Rapids: Zondervan, 2009); and commentaries on specific biblical books.

Many ancient images are perfectly understandable (apart from symbolic and connotative aspects that we will likely never fully appreciate). The image of an eagle soaring in the sky, or the refreshing effect of water on a hot day, or the protection of shade are common metaphors that we experience in our culture in essentially the same ways as they were in antiquity. Such metaphors reflect common human experiences and are understood across time and cultures. Comparing the woman of Song of Songs to a beautiful flower—even if we are unable to determine the exact flower being referred to—still communicates clearly enough to make an effective point today. Some metaphors are clarified by understanding ancient Near Eastern culture and background. The book of Job contains many legal metaphors, so an understanding of how legal disputes were handled and the terminology used in rendering verdicts clarifies details in certain passages.

Sometimes biblical images are so tied to the ancient Near Eastern context out of which they came that a modern reader would likely never understand them apart from extrabiblical material that explicates them.[40] In a few instances the cultural distance is so great that we can do little more than guess what the point of the comparison might be. When the man in Song of Songs 4:1 compares the woman's hair to a flock of goats descending from Mt. Gilead, we know it is a compliment, but few women today would take those words as a welcome description of their beauty.

Sometimes the images used in biblical poetry are open ended. When the man in Song of Songs 4:1 describes the woman's eyes as doves behind her veil, it is not clear whether the point of his comparison is color, texture, softness, the bird's peaceable nature, or some other quality of the dove. In many instances in Song of Songs such ambiguity is reflective of the playful nature of the lovers' conversation. In other instances it probably illustrates wisdom's propensity for setting before us ambiguities designed to stimulate contemplative reflection on the part of those who read or hear the poet's words. Such metaphors allow the reader to relate more than one of the dove's qualities to the woman's eyes, thus enriching the experience.

The interpreter must also determine the points of correspondence between the source domain and the target domain, and unless this is done "the metaphor remains idiosyncratic and indecipherable."[41] Often this connection is clear. The meaning of the woman's comparison of her beloved's love to the exhilarating and intoxicating effects of wine in Song of Songs 1:2 is fairly transparent, as is the man's comparing her to a delicate and beautiful flower among brambles (Song 2:2). Others are

---

40. See examples in "Helpful Parallels," chap. 3.
41. Brown, *Seeing the Psalms*, 6.

not so clear, as when he compares her to a mare among Pharaoh's chariots in 1:9. When the woman describes her beloved in Song of Songs 5:10–16 in terms of gold, spices, jewels, ivory, sapphires, and alabaster, she is describing him not in terms of appearance but in terms of his strength and his value in her eyes.

As Ryken says, "When a biblical poet states his meaning in the form of a metaphor or simile, he entrusts his utterance to the reader's ability to discover the meaning. . . . The process of interpretation involves discovering the nature of the similarities between the two halves of the comparison. More often than not the comparisons are multiple. . . . The meanings moreover are affective and extraverbal as well as intellectual and conceptual."[42] This certainly requires more of the interpreter than a legal or scientific text or an essay that offers three easy steps for solving a particular problem. While there is risk in poetry, with its emotional impact on readers/hearers, somewhat open-ended metaphors, and its multiple connections, there are also substantial benefits given poetry's more holistic impact on people.

The graphic and concrete images attract our attention in ways that other kinds of words rarely do. Images, especially those with significant affective components, enable us to see things from a different perspective and understand abstract concepts in ways that the intellect alone cannot bring about. The way images impact us emotionally and affectively causes them to stick in our minds, and this often provokes the kind of contemplative reflection that generates transformation. Images slow us down as we read the text and encourage us to reflect on connections and consider various possibilities that hopefully enable us to refine our understanding and come to a more accurate interpretation. The fact that metaphors are often open-ended makes it easier for us to make the metaphors our own and apply them to our own specific situation.

Our culture is dominated by powerful images that shape the thinking and behavior of the people in our world, but many of these images are the antithesis of God's wisdom. The images in the wisdom literature have the power to counter those cultural images and replace them with God's truth.

Poetry seems particularly well suited for the topics dealt with in the wisdom books, whether the passion and delight of Song of Songs, the struggles with pain and suffering in Job, or the frustrations of dealing with enigmatic and unpredictable realities in Ecclesiastes. This poetry shows us important aspects of what living wisely looks like in a world where evil and oppression abound and where anomalies abound. It shows us people struggling in a world where righteous people suffer and face injustice and where many painful things that occur remain beyond

---

42. Ryken, *Words of Delight*, 168.

their ability to understand or change. And it shows us these things in ways that impact us more holistically than prose could ever do.

Living by faith involves mystery and waiting confidently for what we know God has promised, even when we see little evidence of God's activity around us. Details about God's governance of the world remain unclear to us, and yet we must respond to an uncertain present and move into a future that we are unable to predict. According to Bartholomew and O'Dowd, "Poetry . . . is at its best an ethical way of preserving the mystery, ambiguity, power, tragedy and sublimity of our world. It should be clear to us that our modern preference for the concrete, certain and measurable hardly matches with our daily experiences of God, life and reality."[43] Equipping us for the realities of life in the world, and developing in us skill in living according to the order God designed into the world is more effectively accomplished through means that engage the whole person and not just the intellect.

Parallelism

Hebrew poetry is characterized by **parallelism**, which involves two (occasionally three or more) complementary lines. The lines relate to the same idea and each line looks at the idea in a slightly different way. This has been likened to stereophonic sound in which slightly different sounds come to each ear, but they combine to provide a single effect.[44] There are many different ways in which this is done, but the key thing is that the lines have to do with a single idea, and it is the combination that communicates the author's point. For example, Song of Songs 5:3 says,

> I had put off my garment; how could I put it on?
> I had bathed my feet; how could I soil them?

Taking off a garment and bathing one's feet are different activities, but the correspondence between the lines has to do with the focus of the poet's interest. The two lines work together to make the single point that the woman had already retired for the night and was reluctant to be disturbed; each line looks at the central point from slightly different perspectives.

The older understanding of parallelism identified three categories: *synonymous* where the idea of the first line is repeated in different words in the second; *antithetical*, where the idea of the first line is expressed in contrasting terms in the second; and *synthetic*, where the idea of the first line is simply continued in some way. Today parallelism is understood

---

43.   Bartholomew and O'Dowd, *Old Testament Wisdom Literature*, 69.

44.   Ronald Allen, *Praise! A Matter of Life and Breath* (Nashville: Thomas Nelson, 1980), 51.

in much broader terms.[45] Berlin describes it as "the pairing of a line (or part of a line) with one or more lines that are in some way linguistically equivalent. . . . The second line of a parallelism rarely repeats exactly the same words or exactly the same thought as the first; it is more likely to echo, expand, or intensify the idea in the first line in any one of a number of ways."[46] The insight of Kugel that most scholars today would affirm is that the relationship between the two parallel lines should no longer be seen as exactly synonymous (that is, "A=B"), but rather "A, and what's more, B."[47] The point made in the first line is further clarified or amplified in some way in the second line.

This correspondence between lines can occur in numerous ways, only a few of which will be pointed out here. Examples of parallelism that a previous generation of scholars would have viewed as saying the same thing in different words is found in Job 5:9, where Eliphaz describes God as the one

> who does great things and unsearchable,
>   marvelous things without number:

Today's understanding recognizes that the second parallel member of the verse both reinforces our understanding and advances it by noting the nature and the extent of the great things that God does. His works are נִפְלָאוֹת, "marvelous things," things that to people appear to be impossible to accomplish, and there are so many of these marvelous works that they cannot be counted. In Job 5:10 the poet continues the idea of the poem by giving us specific examples of these amazing and innumerable acts of God:

> he gives rain on the earth
>   and sends waters on the fields.

In the first parallel member of the verse, the poet makes a general statement and in the second explains this in more precise terms. In so doing,

---

45.   The major discussions of parallelism are: Robert Alter, *The Art of Biblical Poetry*, 2nd ed. (New York: Basic Books, 2011), 19; Adele Berlin, *The Dynamics of Biblical Parallelism* (Bloomington: Indiana University Press, 1985); and James Kugel, *The Idea of Biblical Poetry: Parallelism and Its History* (Baltimore: Johns Hopkins University Press, 1981). Among the useful shorter discussions are: Allen Ross, *A Commentary on Psalms 1–41*, Kregel Exegetical Library (Grand Rapids: Kregel, 2012), vol. 1, 81–91; J. M. LeMon and B. A. Strawn, "Parallelism" in *DOTWPW*, 502–15; Futato, *Interpreting the Psalms*, 33–41; Adele Berlin, "Reading Biblical Poetry," in *The Jewish Study Bible*, 2nd ed. (New York: Oxford University Press, 2014), 2184–2191; J. P. Fokkelman, *Reading Biblical Poetry* (Louisville: Westminster/John Knox, 2001), 61–86; and Tremper Longman III, *Literary Approaches to Biblical Interpretation* (Grand Rapids: Zondervan, 1987), 122–28.

46.   Berlin, *Jewish Study Bible*, 2185–86.

47.   Kugel, *Idea of Biblical Poetry*, 13, 42.

he makes it clear that the general beneficence of God expresses itself in specific ways that bring practical benefit to people in the world. It is possible, as well, that the author is emphasizing two different ways that God sends water to the earth.

A third example is found in Job 3:3, as Job begins an entire chapter in which he expresses his wish that he had never been born, since that would have spared him the suffering he is experiencing. Job said,

> Let the day perish on which I was born,
>   and the night that said, "A man is conceived."

Job's point is clear: he is saying, "I wish I had never been born," but as Kugel says, "He does not mean the second half [and the night said . . .] to be merely an independent version of the first, but something more emphatic. . . . Blot out the day of my birth, *in fact* go back to the very night I was conceived and destroy it."[48]

Another pattern, especially common in Proverbs, is one in which the correspondence between lines involves contrast, with an idea being presented in one line with a contrasting perspective in the second line. The way in which this type of parallelism carries forward the idea expressed in the first line is evident. Proverbs 10:1 illustrates this type of parallelism:

> A wise son makes a glad father,
>   but a foolish son is a sorrow to his mother.

Again, the proverb makes a single point that a child's behavior has an effect on the parents. It is not intended to suggest that mothers and fathers are affected in different ways by a child's behavior.

A third common type of pattern in parallelism involves a correspondence where the second line simply continues the idea begun in the first line and advances the thought. For example, Proverbs 31:11–12 says about the excellent wife,

> The heart of her husband trusts in her,
>   and he will have no lack of gain.
> She does him good, and not harm,
>   all the days of her life.

In both verses the second parallel member simply advances the thought of the first by describing the results and outcomes of the husband's trust in her (v. 11) and the duration of the benefit (v. 12), rather than restating the idea. In addition, verse 12 also further develops the idea of verse 11.

---

48. Kugel, *Idea of Biblical Poetry*, 9.

The possibilities for correspondence between the lines are many, and this can make interpretation rather complex. There are, though, several rather obvious ways in which parallelism contributes to the effect of biblical poetry. As Berlin points out, it binds together the short lines of poetry which in Hebrew are normally connected only by the conjunction *waw* (usually translated "and" or "but"), and parallelism creates a relationship between the lines that is otherwise unexpressed in the grammar.[49]

Parallelism also contributes to a rhythmic quality to the poetry. Berlin suggests that "the ancient Hebrew poets embraced a system in which many lines of a poem are more or less the same length and partake of the rhythm of their parallelism, but without the requirement of precise measurement."[50] There is something aesthetically pleasing about biblical poetry and, in part, because of the parallelism, it is easier to remember and reflect on than prose. Bartholomew and O'Dowd suggest that the brevity of the poetic lines "limits the words surrounding the main idea, thus adding intensity to the parallel structures and making them memorable in the process."[51] Proverbs 1:20–21 provides an example of the clarifying and intensifying power of parallelism.

> Wisdom cries aloud in the street,
>   in the markets she raises her voice;
> at the head of the noisy streets she cries out;
>   at the entrance of the city gates she speaks.

The determination of wisdom to get her message out is evident as she proclaims it wherever the people are. This introduction to a longer poem amplifies the point that wisdom is readily available to anyone who chooses to seek it. As is the case with images in poetic literature, parallelism also calls the reader to slow down and reflect on the relationship between the poetic lines. While such careful analysis can sometimes be tedious, this sort of contemplative reflection on the poetry can also bring us to a deeper understanding of the text, which "enriches our experience of hearing God speak to us through [his Word]."[52]

God chose to reveal himself to his people through poetry, and the holistic impact of poetry is a part of the revelation. To omit either the careful analysis of the text or its **affective** power us from experiencing God's revelation in the fullest way. Bartholomew says, "We must remember that poetry is an encounter with an imaginative new world of sights, sounds and meaning. As readers, therefore, we must develop

---

49. Berlin, *Jewish Study Bible*, 2186.

50. Ibid., 2186–87.

51. Bartholomew and O' Dowd, *Old Testament Wisdom Literature*, 64–65.

52. Futato, *Interpreting the Psalms*, 41.

powerful habits of expecting God to speak through the variety and richness of poetic language."[53] Brown laments the loss of reading religiously in our culture and says, "To read religiously, however, is to read the text as a lover reads, with a tensile attentiveness that wishes to linger, to prolong, to savor."[54] A part of that is to linger over the metaphors, the parallelism, the figures of speech and all the other things that make poetry what it is. This is an essential task for every person who is committed to interpreting and teaching God's truth. It is also an attitude and a practice that we must strive to instill in our students and congregations as we seek to motivate them to personal engagement with God's saving and transforming word.

Other Literary Features[55]

While there are many literary features and devices used in the wisdom literature, we will note only a few that are often missed by readers of this material:

- **Acrostic:** Several poems in the Old Testament are structured so that the first letter of consecutive lines, half-lines, or even stanzas follows the order of the letters in the Hebrew alphabet. Several psalms (25, 34, 37, 111, 112, 119, and 145), along with the poems in Lamentations 1–4, reflect this structure. Proverbs 31:10–31 is also structured in this way. The structure makes the poem easier to memorize, and likely suggests that it describes the excellent woman from A to Z.

- **Chiastic order** involves a change in word order in which the second line reverses the order of the elements in the first line. This creates variety and is done largely for aesthetic reasons. It normally has minimal interpretive significance. Chiastic order is not always evident in English translations, where word order is sometimes rearranged for the sake of readability. An example of chiastic order is found in Job 28:15, where the author says about wisdom:

> It cannot be bought (A) for gold (B),
> and silver (B') cannot be weighed as its price (A').

Sometimes entire poems are arranged in chiastic order where the lines in the first half are mirrored in the second half. In this structure the main point of the poem is often found at the midpoint of the poem

---

53. Ibid., 67.

54. Brown, *Seeing the Psalms*, 13.

55. Useful summaries of these features can be found in Ross, *Commentary on the Psalms, Vol. 1: 1–41*, 81–109; Futato, *Interpreting the Psalms*, 23–55; and Ryken, *Words of Delight*, 159–85.

where it begins to fold back on itself. Duane Garrett points out an example of this in Proverbs 26:6–10:

> A: Committing important business to a fool (v. 6)
>   B: A proverb in a fool's mouth (v. 7)
>   C: Honoring a fool (v. 8)
>   B': A proverb in a fool's mouth (v. 9)
> A': Committing important business to a fool (v. 10)[56]

The literary structure suggests that the main point of this unit is the lack of wisdom reflected in honoring a fool. Each proverb makes clear the consequences that are likely to result from such an unwise practice.[57]

- **Ellipsis** is the omission of a word or words in one line with that element assumed in the other line. While the word is normally explicit in the first line and assumed in the second, occasionally the omission is in the first line. Proverbs 3:9 provides an example of ellipsis:

>   Honor the LORD with your wealth
> and   with the firstfruits of all your produce.

- **Hyperbole** involves exaggeration in order to emphasize a point. For example, Job says in Job 6:2–3:

> Oh that my vexation were weighed,
>   and all my calamity laid in the balances!
> For then it would be heavier than the sand of the sea.

He describes his situation in such terms to make a point about the enormity of his pain and suffering. Proverbs 26:15 describes the sluggard in exaggerated terms in order to underscore the absurdity of his behavior.

> The sluggard buries his hand in the dish;
>   it wears him out to bring it back to his mouth.

- **Inclusio** involves the repetition of words at the beginning and the end of a passage, often to emphasize the theme of the section. Ecclesiastes

---

56. Duane Garrett, *Proverbs, Ecclesiastes, Song of Solomon*, NAC (Nashville: Broadman, 1993), 212.

57. The consequences may take many forms, but the project in which the fool was involved will almost surely misfire (a stone tied to a slingshot in v. 8). Harm will likely come to the person who sent the fool on an important mission (v. 6) and sometimes to others as well (v. 10). Failure will almost always result when a fool is given a responsible role in an important project.

(apart from the prose epilogue: 12:9–14) begins and ends with the words, "Vanity of vanities, says the Preacher. . . . All is vanity" (Eccl. 1:2; 12:8), thus establishing a major theme for the book.

- **Personification** involves attributing to an abstract entity the characteristics of a human being. Both wisdom and folly are depicted as women (Prov. 1:20–33; 8:1–36; 9:13–18).

- **Merism** involves the use of two opposites or extremes to indicate everything in between. Proverbs 6:22 is part of a section exhorting a young man to embrace his parents' teaching. The father says to his son, "When you walk, they will lead you; when you lie down, they will watch over you." What he means is that obeying the parents' teaching will benefit him at all times.

The Nature of a Proverb

The proverb is another literary form that is not highly valued in our culture. This is not so much apparent in the number of proverbs encountered today—they are frequently heard in conversations, in movies and television programs, in popular songs, and, of course, their popularity on greeting cards and in advertising remains high. What has changed is the lack of authority that our culture attaches to these popular sayings.

I once taught Proverbs at a small seminary in the Netherlands, and began by asking if anyone had experience with proverbs. A student from Africa said that she had grown up in a small rural village where her parents used proverbs to teach her and to correct her. They were used in conversations at home and with relatives, and at the market she heard dialogue and negotiations peppered with proverbs. Her father even told her about legal disputes in the community that were settled on the basis of proverbs. All this changed when she went to the university. Proverbs were rarely mentioned there and when they were, it was usually in a derogatory and dismissive way.

A student from a village in the Alps indicated that he had great respect for people who use proverbs and said that the wisest people he knew often use them. He also said that he would rarely use a proverb and that he associated their use with old people. His wife, from a different village, concurred with her husband's assessment. Finally, a young man from a small European city said that he had little respect for people who use proverbs—at least nonbiblical ones—because he viewed proverbs as the best that uneducated people could come up with.

Over my teaching career, I have encountered few students like the woman from Africa. I have, though, interacted with many whose opinions mirrored the others who responded in that class. Few Christians would dismiss the biblical proverbs as irrelevant because they know that "All Scripture is breathed out by God and is profitable" (2 Tim. 3:16). At the same time, most do not understand what a proverb is or how proverbs function in culture. As a result, proverbs have little impact on the way many believers think and behave—and that even includes many who read a chapter from the book of Proverbs each day. Unfortunately, when proverbs are ignored or misused, it is to the detriment of both the believer and those around him or her.

The Hebrew word for proverb, מָשָׁל, *mashal*, has a broad range of meanings that includes literary forms such as allegories, parables, and taunts. The short aphorisms that we call proverbs are very common throughout the wisdom literature. As Thompson points out, proverbs are found virtually everywhere in the world and from every period in human history. They are found in Sumerian and Egyptian literature as early as the third millennium B.C. and were almost certainly used by people long before writing was developed. Proverbs are common in most preliterate cultures and play a significant role in those cultures.[58] The great diversity found in proverbs makes it difficult to formulate a precise definition of the **genre**. Such efforts range from Lord Russell's aphoristic definition of a proverb as "The wisdom of many, the wit of one"[59] to Mieder's definition of a proverb as "A short generally known sentence of the folk which contains wisdom, truth, morals, and traditional views in a metaphorical, fixed and memorable form and which is handed down from generation to generation."[60]

Proverbs are usually brief, have a form that resonates with those who hear them, and are memorable. In addition, their content strikes those who hear them as true. Thompson says,

> It is impossible to state exactly what it is that happens in the human mind when it perceives the "truth" of a poem or "poetic proverb," but that it happens few would deny. It is as though, within the depths of human consciousness, we perceived the proverb's content to be true, not because of logical demonstration or even just its appeal to "common sense," but by the way in which it says what it has to say.[61]

---

58. John Mark Thompson, *The Form and Function of Proverbs in Ancient Israel* (The Hague: Mouton, 1974), 20–21, 35–58. Thompson's discussion is dated, but it remains useful. See also Ted Hildebrand, "Proverbs, Genre of," in *DOTWPW*, 528–39.

59. Noted in Taylor Archer's article, "The Wisdom of Many and the Wit of One," in *The Wisdom of Many*, ed. by W. Mieder and A. Dundes (New York: Garland, 1981), 3.

60. W. Mieder, *Proverbs: A Handbook* (Westport, CT: Greenwood, 2004), 3.

61. Thompson, *Form and Function*, 23–24.

In most instances the origin of an individual proverb remains uncertain or unknown. Somewhere, someone expressed a common-sense principle in a particularly memorable way. The saying caught on, began to circulate more broadly, and finally became part of a tradition that was transmitted to succeeding generations. Typically, proverbs circulate orally among ordinary people, and the tradition that preserves them is informal and unofficial. As economic and social conditions create the leisure for more formal literary pursuits, they are put into written collections where sages and scholars often bring a literary and artistic sophistication to the sayings. Proverbs are quite diverse, and it is difficult to categorize them; at the same time, the characteristics of this genre must be understood in interpreting and applying proverbs.[62]

A Proverb Captures a Tiny Cross-Section of Truth

A proverb makes a focused observation about life, and its claims are rarely complete or comprehensive. It often uses hyperbole and exaggeration to make its point more emphatically. It states the point in a concise and memorable way and normally does not qualify it in any way. "A soft answer turns away wrath, but a harsh word stirs up anger" (Prov. 15:1) makes a single important point about using words in dealing with angry people. In reality, a variety of other principles may also be necessary in responding wisely and effectively in such situations.

The truth of the proverb normally depends on a specific set of circumstances, but those circumstances are presupposed by the proverb. For example, the secular proverb, "Early to bed, early to rise, makes a man healthy, wealthy, and wise," implies a setting where useful work can be done only in daylight hours.[63] It also assumes that the person described will sleep when he retires and will diligently follow a wisely laid out plan of action when he gets up. None of those things are explicit in the proverb—both the speaker and hearer must recognize them without their being stated. In a world where proverbs are commonly used, the one hearing the aphorism will intuitively identify the required givens. This does not always happen with people who rarely use proverbs, and their response is often to try to construct a set of circumstances where the proverb is not true and then dismiss it. Clearly, the interpreter must correctly identify the appropriate conditions under which the saying is true in order to ascertain the point the proverb is making.

Because of the narrow focus of each proverb, it is often useful to put together a larger mosaic about what wisdom teaches about a topic. An awareness of the breadth of wisdom's teaching about a topic contributes

---

62. See examples in "Proverbs," chap. 4.

63. This proverb is attested as early as the fifteenth century in England, so this assumption would have been a given. Benjamin Franklin apparently popularized the proverb in America.

to a balance that reduces the risk of misapplication that a more narrow view can sometimes generate. This is why a topical approach to teaching from Proverbs is often beneficial.[64]

Proverbs Are Characterized by Ambiguity

Proverbs are often characterized by ambiguity both in terms of their exact meanings and their appropriate applications. Proverbs 17:9 says, "Whoever covers an offense seeks love,[65] but he who repeats a matter separates close friends," and the meaning of the word translated "repeats" (שׁנה), is equally ambiguous in Hebrew and most English translations. One can repeat a matter by continuing to engage in an offensive behavior; one can do it through gossip[66] or breaching a confidence; one can keep reminding a repentant offender of his or her past words or actions, and the list of possibilities could easily be lengthened. The ambiguity stimulates thinking and plays a significant role in developing the skill in living that constitutes wisdom. The ambiguity in application gives these aphorisms the potential for being used for quite different purposes. Proverbs that connect a parent's emotional state with a child's behavior (10:1 and 17:25) can either be applied in ways that affirm good parenting or warn a parent who is moving in a problematic direction; they can also be used to motivate children to obedience and good behavior or upbraid them for unwise behavior.

In interpreting proverbs the expositor should recognize the ambiguity and explore possibilities rather than seeking to eliminate the ambiguity and offer only one option as the correct one. Not every option will be appropriate, but thinking about the limits of legitimate meaning and application is one mechanism by which wisdom is developed.

Proverbs Describe the Way Things Usually Work

Proverbs 20:29 says, "The glory of young men is their strength, but the splendor of old men is their gray hair." While it is generally true that young people have physical strength and endurance going for them, that is not always the case. Older people often have wisdom that comes from life experience—something that many young people have not yet acquired—but there are old people who are remarkable exceptions to this general principle. Such exceptions give rise to the saying, "There is no fool like an old fool." And there are young people who have a remarkable grasp of wisdom.

---

64. See the topical study from Proverbs in chapter 6.

65. There is ambiguity in what "covering an offense (פֶּשַׁע)" means. In the proverb it almost certainly means to overlook a fault rather than focusing on every minor irritation, but one could imagine a situation where "covering a transgression" could amount to obstruction of justice.

66. Proverbs 16:28 also talks about "separating close friends," and attributes this to a "whisperer."

Many proverbs recognize the connection between diligence, hard work, and wealth, and the connection between laziness and poverty. Proverbs 10:4 says, "A slack hand causes poverty, but the hand of the diligent makes rich." There are, though, people who, as the saying goes, "were born with a silver spoon in their mouth," and live in luxury their entire lives without ever doing any useful work. Proverbs 10:2 says, "Treasures gained by wickedness do not profit, but righteousness delivers from death," and while it generally works that way in life, there are evil people like those described in Job 21:7–15 who die at a ripe old age with their children dancing around their feet and with their wealth intact. And there are righteous people who die at a relatively young age.

The Authority of a Proverb

The problem with making lists of activities that are right or wrong is that you can never make the list long enough. The Bible is certainly interested in right and wrong, but usually discusses such matters in terms of principles rather than lists. Fathers are told, "do not provoke your children to anger, but bring them up in the discipline and instruction of the Lord" (Eph. 6:4). Husbands are told to "love your wives, as Christ loved the church and gave himself up for her" (Eph. 5:25). Elders are told to exercise leadership in the church "not under compulsion, but willingly, as God would have you; not for shameful gain, but eagerly; not domineering over those in your charge, but being examples to the flock" (1 Pet. 5:2–3).

Often biblical principles are clear but general, and those seeking to live them out will have to determine exactly what that looks like in widely disparate times and circumstances. An individual proverb contributes to our understanding by presenting a tiny snippet of truth, which must then be integrated with other bits of truth to give us a more complete picture of God's order. God's people must then apply those principles to the various situations that confront them in life.

A central difficulty in interpreting, teaching, and applying proverbs in our culture has to do with their authority, and this relates to modern perceptions about the truth claims of proverbs. Few people will live under the authority of something they do not really believe is true. Today's dismissive attitude toward proverbs reflects a radical shift in thinking since the days when they were regularly used even in legal contexts. Enlightenment thinking and Rationalism have successfully promoted the idea that only things that are empirically demonstrable or logically irrefutable should be embraced as true, and proverbs do not fall into either category. Bartholomew and O'Dowd recognize the divide between practical and scientific knowledge that characterizes post-Enlightenment Western culture. They say, "In general, this approach distrusts everyday, lived experience and insists that true *truth* about the world is attained through scientific analysis rooted in the human ego."[67]

Our culture has been trained to disregard the truth claims of folk observations, since they are derived by methods far less rigorous than is required by modern scientific research. Many would say that proverbs amount to little more than anecdotes, and anecdotes have little value or credibility among most scholars today. We have been trained to think that if we can falsify a statement we can generally dismiss its truth claims, and counter examples can easily be constructed for most proverbs. In addition, proverbial authority has been eroded by the fact that some proverbs make claims that sometimes seem contradicted by the experiences of life.

Throughout history, proverbs have been recognized as authoritative, and even the form of a proverb seems to contribute to its authoritative feel to those who hear it.[68] Proverbs reflect common sense, and multiple generations have found the principles to work. As Norrick says, "Proverbs carry the force of time tested wisdom. . . . The weight of traditional or majority opinion inculcates utterances of proverbs with authority."[69]

Jesus regularly used proverbs in his teaching,[70] and he used them in a variety of ways. Proverbs 25:6–7 says,

> Do not put yourself forward in the king's presence
>   or stand in the place of the great,
> for it is better to be told, "Come up here,"
>   than to be put lower in the presence of a noble.

---

67. Bartholomew and O'Dowd, *Old Testament Wisdom Literature*, 280. They cite Brian Greene (*The Fabric of the Cosmos, Time, Space and the Texture of Reality* [New York: Vintage, 2004, 5] who says, "*The* overarching lesson that has emerged from scientific inquiry over the last century is that human experience is often a misleading guide to the true nature of reality." Most academics would affirm this general truth, as would those who have been educated by them. The problem lies in reducing everything to this general truth and thereby dismissing many important insightful common sense observations in the process. It appears to me that a better balance is needed.

68. Mieder (*Proverbs*, 81–88, 244–51) notes that advertisers often use proverbs (or create their own) because they "express a message with a certain claim of traditional authority and wisdom" (82).

69. Neal Norrick, *How Proverbs Mean: Semantic Studies in English Proverbs* (Berlin: Walter de Gruyter, 2011), 28.

70. Kim Dewey ("*Paroimai* in the Gospel of John," *Semeia* 17 [1980], 81–99) identifies 34 proverbs used by Jesus in the Gospel of John. Charles Carlston ("Proverbs, Maxims, and the Historical Jesus," *JBL* 99 [1980], 91) has identified 102 such wisdom sayings in the Synoptics.

Jesus almost certainly draws from these ideas in Luke 14:8–11.

> When you are invited by someone to a wedding feast, do not sit down in a place of honor, lest someone more distinguished than you be invited by him, and he who invited you both will come and say to you, "Give your place to this person," and then you will begin with shame to take the lowest place. But when you are invited, go and sit in the lowest place, so that when your host comes he may say to you, "Friend, move up higher." Then you will be honored in the presence of all who sit at table with you.

In Luke 14:11 Jesus reinforces the point with a proverb:

> For everyone who exalts himself will be humbled, and he who humbles himself will be exalted.[71]

Jesus's proverb is similar to Proverbs 29:23 which says, "One's pride will bring him low, but he who is lowly in spirit will obtain honor" and reflects an idea found throughout the Old Testament.[72] It is unclear; however, whether Jesus is quoting a traditional proverb or created one for this occasion, but he regularly alludes to ideas that were well known from Old Testament wisdom literature.

Jesus sometimes cited traditional proverbs. In John 4:35 he introduced the proverb "There are yet four months, then comes the harvest," with the words, "Do you not say." In John 4:37 he introduced a proverb ("One sows and another reaps") with the words, "For here the saying holds true." In these instances Jesus cited traditional proverbs rather than originating them. It is rarely possible to trace a proverb to its origin, and this is certainly the case with the sayings of Jesus. His use of a saying gives it a unique authority and guarantees its ongoing use. His words are particularly memorable to his followers, and the proverbs used by him have become familiar sayings in virtually every language spoken by Christians. As the ultimate teacher, he probably originated many proverbial sayings, but he also used proverbs taken from the traditional sayings of first-century Judea.[73] He taught using proverbs because of their effectiveness in teaching and because he knew their truth and authority would be recognized by his audience.

---

71. Jesus applied the same proverb to a different situation in Luke 18:14.

72. Ps. 10:4; 31:18 (Heb. 31:19); Prov. 11:2; 16:18; Isa. 2:11, 17.

73. Alan Winton, *The Proverbs of Jesus*, JSNTSup 35 (Sheffield: Sheffield Academic Press, 1990), 32.

This does not mean that every nonbiblical proverb is true. Proverbs have their origins in human observation, and human observations are not always true or accurate. They are limited by human finitude and human sinfulness. As Waltke points out,

> None can know the real world objectively. That which is known is inescapably relative to the person who does the knowing. The way we see is colored by a mix of previous experiences and stereotypes perpetuated by our families, friends, peers, movies, and television. Moreover, unaided human reason cannot come to absolute truth . . . to come to absolute meanings and values, one must know all the facts. . . . Moreover, facts are known only in relation to other facts. . . . To see any object "truly," one must see all objects comprehensively. Unaided rationality cannot find an adequate frame of reference from which to know.[74]

Limits to human discovery become especially apparent when they touch on moral or ethical values. Proverbs do, however, reflect a culture's values and understanding of how things work, but as Proverbs 14:12 recognizes, "There is a way that seems right to a man, but its end is the way to death." When human discovery fails to operate in ways that are consistent with Proverbs 1:7,[75] false conclusions will often result and given the right circumstances the edifice that is built on the observations will come crashing down.

Some proverbs turn out not to be true because the observations that generated them did not take into account sufficient data. In Ezekiel's day a popular proverb said, "The days grow long, and every vision comes to nothing" (Ezek. 12:22). God rebuked Ezekiel's generation for prematurely passing judgment on the validity of prophetic warnings about judgment. He told them that they had not waited long enough; the judgment would take place—and in their generation.

Every proverb must pass the test of experience to be verified, and those that do not work do not make it into the tradition that continues from generation to generation. While the truth of every proverb has been pragmatically verified over many generations, some, especially those that reflect ethical, moral, or theological values, may still be rejected by later generations or cultures that hold to different values or discover new things that invalidate or modify the observation.

---

74. Bruce Waltke, "Does Proverbs Promise Too Much?" *AUSS* 34 (1996), 335.
75. That is, in the fear of the Lord.

Biblical proverbs, irrespective of whether they originated from insightful human discovery or from special revelation, come to us in the canon of Scripture, and reflect the process of divine inspiration. They are "God-breathed" (2 Tim. 3:16) and come to us from God himself (Prov. 2:6). Their truth is assured by their presence in Scripture, but this does not lessen the need to understand what a proverb is[76] and how proverbs function in a culture. It is also important to begin with the understanding that these biblical proverbs are true.[77] We must then determine the set of circumstances in which the proverb is true in order to determine the point that is being made by the text.

We must also determine the function of the particular proverb.[78] Good exegesis requires that we understand the individual proverb in the context of the literary unit in which it occurs, in the context of the collection of which it is a part, in the context of the entire book of Proverbs,[79] in the context of the Old Testament wisdom literature, and in the context of the rest of Scripture. In addition, we need to look for examples of the principle applied or neglected from history or contemporary experience as we seek to appropriately apply these truths in life. These proverbs identify principles that work and they are principles that God wants his people to embrace and apply.

---

76. For example, they are not promises; they are not invariable laws; they are not comprehensive statements of reality.

77. Apart from those such as Ezekiel 12:22 that God's revelation affirms are wrong; or apart from those like Ezekiel 18:1 or Jeremiah 31:29 that were misunderstood and misapplied by many Judeans. The "truth" of a proverb requires both that it be understood correctly and applied appropriately.

78. For example, is it a statement of universal validity? Does it affirm an important value about how God's people should live? Is it a non-moral observation about how things work?

79. This means that we consider other passages that deal with the same topic. See the topical study on Proverbs in chapter 6.

2

PRIMARY THEMES IN THE WISDOM BOOKS

The Chapter at a Glance

Job
- Relationship between God and Humanity
- Humanity's Limited Understanding of God's Work
- God Accepts the Honest Cries of His Hurting People
- Serve God for Who He Is Rather Than for Benefits
- Important Lessons about God
- How God's People Should Respond to Circumstances

Proverbs
- Biblical Wisdom Begins with the **Fear of the Lord**
- General and **Special Revelation** as Wisdom from God
- Proverbs View of Life: Cause–Effect and Complexity
- Important Values in Proverbs
- Proverbs and the Two Ways
- Proverbs and the Importance of Application

The Chapter at a Glance

Ecclesiastes
- All Is *hebel*
- Perplexing Realities about Life
- Reality of Human Limits
- Fearing God and Keeping His Commandments
- Wisdom and Living Wisely
- Enjoying Life as God Gives Opportunity
- God's Sovereignty and Providence

Song of Songs
- Introduction
- Primary Themes

JOB

Job Explores the Relationship between God and Humanity

The book of Job sets in relief the tension that often occurs at the intersection of faith and human experience as people deal with suffering that appears to be undeserved and unfair. Job was a "blameless and upright [person], who feared God and turned away from evil" (Job 1:1, 8; 2:3), and he illustrates the reality of righteous suffering. The book describes the struggle of Job and his friends in a context where they had limited knowledge about the complexities of life and the work of God in the world. The reader knows that Job's sin did not cause his suffering, but neither Job nor his friends knew that with certainty. Nor did they know about the events in heaven that constituted the broader context for Job's suffering. They had to interpret Job's experience in the same way as each of us must do in life.

Job's friends evaluated his experience through a theological paradigm that consisted primarily of the doctrine of **retribution**, and they never considered that God sometimes works in ways unrelated to this idea. They perceived this as a dispute between Job and God, and they believed that the fundamental principle by which God works is retribution. In their paradigm, Job's innocence, would mean that God was unjust, and that obviously could not be. Thus they denied Job's claim that he was innocent and that any explanation besides retribution could explain Job's experience. As far as they were concerned, Job had brought all this on himself by his sin. From the friends' perspective, the justice of God was at stake here!

Job began with a similar paradigm, but as he struggled with what had happened to him, he became more confident about his innocence. Job never maintained that he was sinless, but argued that he had done nothing that would, on the basis of the doctrine of retribution, account for this great calamity. The theological implications of Job's claim of innocence caused his friends to react vigorously. They argued that retribution had been proved in a variety of ways and had been established by the observations of many **sages** from the past. They told Job that the moral order of the universe would have to be overturned for him to be right (18:4). They argued that his interpretation of his experience was wrong, and that only his sinfulness could account for what he was experiencing.

Job was also troubled by the theological implications of his innocence, but he could not confess sins about which he was unaware. His friends could not point them out to him, nor would God. Job was not comfortable with a conclusion that suggested that God might be unjust, though in his emotional struggle he clearly considered that possibility (27:2; 34:5; 40:8). In Job 42:1–6, Job repents, and it seems likely that he reached the point where he was ready to deny God's justice and goodness before he would deny his own innocence.

Job's experience forced him to consider alternatives that took him beyond familiar theological categories, and he contemplated the possibility that he might be vindicated after death (14:13–22; 19:23–29). As he reflected on the difficulty of arguing his case before God, he expressed the desire for an advocate or mediator who could stand with him in that encounter (9:23; 33:23). Neither idea plays a role in the solution given in Job or elsewhere in the Old Testament, but the New Testament reveals that both possibilities imagined by Job are true,[1] though the mediatorial work of Christ goes far beyond anything that Job could have imagined.

The intense suffering of pious people often creates tension between faith and experience, and people struggle with these issues in much the same way as Job did. Such experiences have the power to call into question the goodness and justice of God. They bring confusion and disorientation to one's theology and ideas about how God works, and even with the additional revelation of the New Testament, the struggle is little different than that experienced by Job and his friends. People must struggle in the absence of knowledge about what might be going on in the heavenly arena and must relate to the experience without knowing why things are happening as they are or how they fit into the broader purposes of God.

---

1. Verses like Matthew 5:12, Luke 6:23, and 1 Peter 1:4–6 teach the idea of rewards in heaven after death.

Such tensions are not normally resolved through more information and better theological paradigms. Answers to why a person suffers or even how his or her suffering fits into God's broader purposes are rarely forthcoming. Speculating about such questions may be intriguing for the scholar, but scholarly answers are rarely helpful to people who are suffering. The awareness that "God is greater than we are and may be doing something really amazing outside our understanding," while true, is seldom therapeutic for a person in deep pain and emotional turmoil. The solution that the Old Testament regularly presents[2] is found in a deep relationship with God that allows a person to live in trusting dependence on him in the midst of suffering and in circumstances where cognitive answers are not forthcoming.

Job Shows Humanity's Limited Understanding of God's Work and Purposes

Job's friends knew something about **Yahweh** and the way he works, but their knowledge about God—and about Job as well—was far from comprehensive. Their arrogance in failing to recognize how little they actually knew about God resulted in even more pain for Job. While much that the friends said was true in general, their failure to apply their theology appropriately to Job added to his misery and ultimately led to a rebuke by God.

Elihu's role is more difficult to determine because the book provides no evaluation of him, but his arrogance is evident from the beginning of his speech (32:1–33:7). Perhaps he did bring additional insight into the debate, and he clearly provides a literary transition into the Yahweh speeches in chapters 38–41. At the same time, he did not identify the reason for Job's suffering and never thought beyond the idea that Job's sin caused his suffering.

Job also failed to realize how little he knew about God and the world he created, and his **pride** led him to imagine that he could pass judgment on Yahweh's moral governance of the world. Clearly, **humility** in recognizing the limits of human understanding about God and his ways is an important theme in this book and is at the heart of good discipleship and effective ministry.

Job Shows That God Accepts the Honest Cries of His Hurting People

Job's words in chapter 3 involved cursing the day of his birth and wishing for something that might have spared him such intense suffering.

---

2. For example, Ps. 73, Job 40:8; 42:1–6; Hab. 3:15–19.

His friends, likely expecting words like those in chapters 1 and 2, were shocked and reminded him that rash words like he had just uttered are characteristic of foolish people. Job conceded in chapter 6 that his words had been rash, but maintained that the friends had misunderstood their significance. They supposed that his words reflected his folly and bad theology, but Job argued that his words were simply cries of pain. He said that what a person in such pain needs from a friend is not theological arguments but kindness and compassion (*ḥesed*). While the friends and Elihu found Job's words offensive and off putting, God's response in 42:7 was that Job had spoken about him "what is right," and God rebuked the friends for not speaking about him as Job had. It appears that God accepts bold and honest responses from his hurting but trusting people.[3]

Job Shows That People Should Serve God for Who He Is Rather Than for Benefits He Provides

This theme is introduced in the first chapter when God pointed out Job to "the Accuser"[4] as an example of great piety. The Accuser responded by asking, "Does Job fear God for no reason?" and his question impugned both Job's piety and God's intrinsic worth. He implied that no one ever serves God apart from self-serving reasons. People invest in God rather than love and worship him. The Accuser's claim was that if Job's blessings were removed, his piety would end as well, and his question implied that God is not innately worthy of worship apart from the gifts he gives. A central point of the book has to do with this issue. The test to which Job was subjected was to show the Accuser and all who read this book that disinterested piety does exist. There are people who serve God because they see in him one who is innately worthy of their trust and worship rather than serving God for what they get in return for their piety.

Job Teaches Important Lessons about God

Job and his friends recognized that God is the Creator of all things and oversees the workings of the universe by his power and wisdom. God's sovereignty over the cosmic Accuser is clear in chapter 1, as God must grant him permission before he can touch Job. The friends and Elihu affirmed God's power and wisdom with examples that focus on

---

3. Similar responses are found in Jeremiah 20:7–18, and in laments such as Psalm 44:9–26.

4. The Hebrew suggests that the expression is not a proper name because it is used with the definite article. It seems best to understand it in the generic sense of "accuser" or "adversary" rather than translating it "Satan" and running the risk of having people import all sorts of ideas from the New Testament into the text—ideas that an Old Testament reader would not have understood. On this, see John Walton, "Satan," *DOTWPW*, 714–17.

God's beneficence and justice (Job 5, 12:7–25, 36:22–37:24). Job also recognized God's power and wisdom (Job 9:4–13), but his examples focus on judgment and calamity rather than goodness and justice.

Job never doubted God's power and wisdom, but his suffering did cause him to question God's goodness and justice. Yet an even greater concern for Job had to do with his relationship with God. The things that happened to him were things that according to retribution happen to evil people who are God's enemies, and a major part of Job's struggle had to do with what caused the change in God's treatment of him. Had he become an enemy of God rather than his friend?

The Yahweh speeches (Job 38–41) constitute the climax of the book and bring resolution to many of these issues. Yahweh appeared to Job and took him into the world he created and oversees. He asked Job one question after another about the workings of the world. Job is unable to answer the questions, and this brings Job to realize his own limits and the absurdity of passing judgment on God's moral governance. The Yahweh speeches also make it clear that Yahweh is sovereign in the universe and that he does things for purposes of his own. It is a theocentric universe rather than an anthropocentric one.

Finally, the Yahweh speeches assured Job that his relationship with God was intact and that his suffering was not indicative of a loss of God's favor. This experience made it clear that Job was right in vigorously affirming his innocence through his suffering; at the same time it is clear that Job must continue to affirm God's goodness and justice even when his innocence and God's justice seemed like mutually incompatible ideas. There is mystery at the intersection of faith and experience, and wisdom does not always provide a way to explain away such tensions.

Job Shows How God's People Should Respond to Circumstances That Call into Question God's Justice and Goodness

Most people in the face of deep pain and seeming injustice cry out as Job, Jeremiah, and many psalmists did, and the book of Job affirms the legitimacy of such cries of pain and confusion. Job makes it clear that our perception of a situation rarely exhausts reality, and seeing the entire picture can sometimes radically change our understanding. This book allows us a brief glimpse into the heavenly realm, a realm that, while real, exists apart from our normal perception. The Yahweh speeches show Job the extent of the gap between God's wisdom, knowledge, and power and ours.

The book of Ruth shows that God sometimes works out his purposes in ways that are hidden from those through whom he is working. Our limited awareness of a circumstance should encourage patience as we wait to see what God might be doing in a situation. It is easy to focus on our suffering to the neglect of other realities like God's steadfast love and faithfulness which are also a part of the total reality. Job also shows us the importance of holding on to God's revealed truth even when faith assertions seem to stand in irreconcilable tension with human experience.

Job 28 makes it clear that the wisdom required to unravel mysteries like why people suffer belongs to God, and he does not always choose to reveal it to people. Job 28 also points us to a different perspective on wisdom and how people should respond to difficulty and suffering. Job 1 makes it clear that God's desire for people in their prosperity is to fear God and turn from evil; Job 28:28 affirms that in times of difficulty where no explanations are forthcoming God's desire for people is still to fear God and turn from evil.

Job shows us that the answer to suffering does not lie in understanding why it happened or how it fits into God's broader purposes in the world. Instead it lies in a deep and intimate relationship with God. Even the **theophany** (Job 38–41) did not reveal to Job why he suffered or what the ordeal was about. It did show him that his relationship with God was intact and that he remained in God's favor. The experience also brought Job into a more intimate knowledge of God, and he says in 42:5, "I had heard of you by the hearing of the ear, but now my eye sees you." This knowledge of God was sufficient for Job, and in the light of that deeper intimacy, answers about his suffering were no longer needed.

Few people experience the kind of theophany that Job did, and our knowledge of God must come from God's revelation of himself in Scripture and the experience of living by faith in God. Scripture proclaims God as the sovereign Creator of all things, affirms his providence, declares him to be just, gracious, and holy. In times of difficulty and pain these truths about God must be embraced, even when they are called into question by circumstances that seem incongruent with such truths. The biblical answer to suffering is relational rather than cognitive or propositional. People in their suffering will regularly have to endure difficult experiences without being given any answers to the "Why?" or "What does it mean?" questions, but God, even in those experiences where faith and life stand in irreconcilable tension, still gives evidence of his goodness and justice.

PROVERBS

Biblical Wisdom Begins with the Fear of the Lord

Traditional wisdom is often generated from a methodology that appears to be secular and humanistic.[5] Many insights in wisdom literature

---

5. See "Wisdom's Perspective and Worldview" and "Wisdom's Goal and the Pedagogy of the Sages" in chapter 1.

appear to be the result of human observations about the world and the people in it, and often the principles identified in Proverbs are little different from the natural cause-effect relationships acknowledged by Israel's neighbors.

Biblical wisdom, however, is set apart from its non–Israelite counterparts by the insistence that genuine wisdom must begin with the trust and dependence on God that the Old Testament calls the fear of the Lord (Prov. 1:7; 9:10), and this insistence defines the way Proverbs understands wisdom and the world. As Kidner points out, in these verses "beginning" signifies "the first and controlling principle, rather than a stage which one leaves behind."[6]

One must begin the search for wisdom by recognizing who God is and who we are as human beings. Any attempt to gain knowledge that proceeds without this foundation is in danger of suffering the fate of the person described in Matthew 7:24–27: He built his house on a foundation of sand rather than on rock, only to discover that it could not withstand a powerful storm. People using their intellectual abilities and powers of observation can produce impressive results in their search for knowledge, but from the perspective of Old Testament wisdom, any approach that does not begin with the fear of the Lord rests on an unstable and insecure foundation. When it comes to questions of ultimate reality, the meaning of life, truth about God, the basic nature of humanity, or any number of other vital issues, the vicissitudes of life will often reveal the flawed nature of the foundation, and the structure set on it will begin to slip and collapse.

Proverbs Sees both General and Special Revelation as Wisdom from God

Wisdom in Proverbs consists of many common-sense principles dealing with civil behavior, moral and ethical values, as well as more theological principles about human limits, and Yahweh as Creator and sovereign over the world. No distinction is made between the secular and sacred; it all comes from God (Prov. 2:6) and is one of God's gracious gifts to humanity. Living in harmony with this wisdom minimizes the difficulties people experience as they function in the world. The people of God, to whom this material is directed, are called to live out God's truth before the people around them.

The more theological and moral/ethical principles in Proverbs obviously contribute to this, but even the common-sense values show what Yahweh is like and how he designed the world to work. Compassion for those in need and protecting widows and orphans from oppression

---

6. Derek Kidner, *Proverbs*, TOTC (Downers Grove, IL: InterVarsity, 1964), 59.

show others who God is, but civil and responsible behavior in the community and avoiding harsh and disrespectful words also convey something about the values that God designed into creation. As Estes puts it, "The modern dichotomy between secular life and religious faith, or between the profane and the sacred, is foreign to the worldview of biblical wisdom. In Proverbs, the juxtaposition of the routine details of daily life with reminders of Yahweh's evaluation of those activities (cf. Prov. 3:27–35) reveals that all of life is regarded as a seamless fabric."[7]

Proverbs View of Life: Cause–Effect and Complexity

Most proverbs describe typical outcomes that result from certain attitudes or behaviors,[8] and the emphasis throughout the book is to live in ways that contribute to desired outcomes. At the same time Proverbs recognizes that many other variables are at work in determining what happens in life. People are limited in terms of what they can discover about how things work in the world, and human ignorance often contributes to undesirable outcomes. Proverbs identifies several things that contribute to our inability to control outcomes in the world; only two will be noted here.

Wicked people can create significant problems for the righteous. Some use bribes to pervert justice (Prov. 17:23), and righteous victims of such evil often experience outcomes quite different than they deserve. Sometimes people suffer because they are oppressed by the rich and powerful in the community. Proverbs 13:23 says, "The fallow ground of the poor would yield much food, but it is swept away through injustice." An entire community can suffer adverse results because of the presence of worthless people like those described in Proverbs 6:12–14. A sluggard can do irreparable harm to anyone who has him as an employee or family member. Such proverbs illustrate what can happen to righteous people when others disregard God's instruction.

A number of proverbs also make clear the role of God's providence in determining outcomes. Among the more striking is Proverbs 21:30–31: "No wisdom, no understanding, no counsel can avail against the LORD. The horse is made ready for the day of battle, but the victory belongs to the LORD." Much in Proverbs affirms the limited ability of people to understand the complexities of life and the various elements that ultimately influence outcomes in human activities.

---

7. Estes, *Hear, My Son*, 25.

8. For example, diligence usually results in prosperity while laziness results in poverty; rash behavior usually results in disaster while carefully determined plans usually contribute to beneficial results.

Important Values in Proverbs

These sayings that through inspiration were included in Scripture represent important principles for equipping God's people to represent him in a fallen world. They identify patterns of thinking and acting that should characterize people who fear God, and their importance is evident since they occur repeatedly in Proverbs.[9] The following are among the high priority values emphasized in Proverbs.

Proverbs Values Moral and Ethical Behavior

Proverbs recognizes the importance of sexual morality and provides focused warnings on this in Proverbs 5:1–23, 6:20–35, and 7:1–27. The value of moral and ethical integrity is found through the book. Proverbs 11:1 says, "A false balance is an abomination to the LORD, but a just weight is his delight." This proverb asserts the importance of just dealings, honesty, and integrity in business transactions. At the same time it is clear that these values are to be applied and practiced more broadly. The skill in living comes as a person thinks about what justice, honesty, and ethical behavior mean in the family, in politics, in one's leisure, and even in one's religious life.

Proverbs Values Humility

Proverbs 11:2 says, "When pride comes, then comes disgrace, but with the humble is wisdom." While this proverb affirms the importance of humility and the dangerous nature of pride, the wise person again recognizes the importance of reflecting on what pride and humility look like in every area of life. Proverbs describes the fool as proud and arrogant while the wise person is humble. Proverbs 12:15 says, "The way of a fool is right in his own eyes, but a wise man listens to advice."

The creation narrative in Genesis describes God as the Creator and people as creatures, and this appropriately defines the relationship between God and human beings. Creatures are dependent on the Creator; the Creator is the sovereign and creatures are servants under his authority. Submission to the Creator is the essence of humility.

The prohibition of eating the fruit in the garden became a test for the man and woman, and the central issue was whether they would rely on the Creator's instruction to them or act independently of his commandment. The man and the woman chose to act autonomously, and according to von Rad, "Man has stepped outside the state of dependence, he has refused obedience and willed to make himself independent. The guiding principle of his life is no longer obedience but

---

9. For an expanded discussion of these topics and others, see Edward Curtis and John Brugaletta, *Discovering the Way of Wisdom* (Grand Rapids: Kregel, 2004).

his autonomous knowing and willing, and thus he has ceased to understand himself as creature."[10] It is this human refusal to submit to God that is the essence of pride in the Old Testament.

Pride and humility are also important in human relationships. People are not designed to function independently, but to live in relationships with others. Adam needed a helper (Gen. 2:18), and the man and woman were designed to complement each other.[11] It seems that this pattern should also operate in other relationships. People are different, and individuals have both strengths and weaknesses. Families, communities, and churches function best when each person uses his or her unique strengths to help others at their points of weakness and need. Proverbs insists that people need correction, advice, and even discipline both from God and from other people.

Throughout Proverbs this difference between the fool's pride and arrogance and the wise person's humility is evident. It is seen in the wise person's openness to painful rebuke while the foolish person hates even gentle correction. Proverbs 12:1 says, "Whoever loves discipline loves knowledge, but he who hates reproof is stupid." Proverbs 9:7–9 indicates that the fool's hatred of reproof is so strong that he often reacts violently toward the one bringing the correction. This person sees no need for advice or counsel because he thinks he knows everything and insists on pursuing the path that appeals to him, oblivious to the reality that the path which seems so right to him will likely lead to destruction, as Proverbs 16:25 insists. Humility involves a proper self-understanding that includes the recognition of both one's strengths and weaknesses and an openness to learn from others and benefit from their strengths. Humility is essential both to functioning well in society and to growing in godliness.

Proverbs Values Discretion

Another quality emphasized in Proverbs is **discretion**. The wise person responds calmly and deliberately to every situation and waits until he or she has sufficient information to make a good decision. In contrast, the foolish person recklessly forges ahead only to encounter difficulties or discover unanticipated aspects of the task. The discreet person knows that "The one who states his case first seems right, until the other comes and examines him" (Prov. 18:17), and withholds judgment until sufficient information

---

10.   Gerhard von Rad, *Genesis*, OTL (Philadelphia: Westminster, rev. ed., 1972), 97.

11.   I understand the word עֵזֶר, "helper," in the sense of one who brings strength to assist another at a point of weakness and see the man and woman as having both strengths and weaknesses by design. They were supposed to depend on and help each other. See Allan Harman, עזר, *NIDOTTE*, 3, 378–79; E. Lipiński, עָזַר *TDOT*, 11, 12–17. God is often described as an *'ezer*, and in those instances the idea is certainly not that of a subordinate. It is rather one who brings strength to help another person who has a need. For God as helper see Ps. 10:14; 72:12; 87:17;107:12; and 121:1–2.

is available. He seeks out others for counsel and guidance to secure needed information and insight. In contrast, the fool, quite unaware of his limited understanding, is quick to pronounce judgment and express his opinion as to what should be done. His rash response often leads to embarrassment (Prov. 18:2, 13). A prudent person recognizes danger and takes appropriate action while fools rush ahead to their detriment. As Proverbs 21:5 makes clear, careful planning combined with diligence leads to success while rash commitments lead to trouble and poverty.

A person with discretion listens, then carefully thinks about what to say. As a result, he is able to communicate in ways that make words of truth acceptable. The foolish person speaks impulsively and often "pours out evil things" (Prov. 15:28) in ways that tarnish his reputation or that result in even more painful consequences. Proverbs has much to say about the positive and negative potential of words, and the wise person's discretion plays a major role in his or her ability to frame words that are timely and appropriate.

Proverbs warns about the danger of allowing passion or strong emotion to cloud one's judgment, and this passion can take many forms. Drunkenness, romantic passion, or a covetous desire for something can cause people to make irresponsible choices that bring unfortunate consequences. Responses that are driven by anger are another example of a lack or discretion and self-control and are regularly warned against. As Proverbs 29:11 puts it, "A fool gives full vent to his spirit, but a wise man quietly holds it back." The fool reacts instantly and aggressively to any affront, while a wise person knows how to overlook an insult. The fool's rash behavior often causes strife to escalate to the point where disastrous and even fatal consequences occur.

Discretion and self-control are essential for wise living, and these principles must be applied in every area of life.

Proverbs and the Two Ways

Proverbs regularly sees life as a choice between the way of wisdom and the way of folly. The way of wisdom involves submission to God and trust in him at every point; the way of folly involves autonomy, independence, and self-direction, and each person must regularly choose between these two paths. Wisdom results in blessing from God and the benefits that come from living life in harmony with the way it was designed to function. These blessings include *shalom* and abundant life.

The way of folly, however, leads to trouble, distress, and destruction. What Proverbs leaves open is the question of when and how these results will occur. In some instances the consequences are physical and immediate; in many others they are not readily apparent. Sometimes God's purposes are best served by blessings that do not involve full barns and overflowing wine vats (Prov. 3:10), but rather by the prayer in Proverbs 30:8–9. The New Testament makes it clear that the ultimate realization of both the blessings of wisdom and the judgments of folly and unbelief will be fully realized beyond the grave.[12]

Proverbs and the Importance of Application

The importance of application is recognized in Proverbs 26:7 and 9. Verse 7 reads "Like a lame man's legs, which hang useless, is a proverb in the mouth of fools," and "useless" seems to be what is common to both situations. Neither legs on a lame man nor a proverb in the mouth of a fool can accomplish what it was designed to do. Verse 9 makes the point in an even stronger way. It says, "Like a thorn that goes up into the hand of a drunkard is a proverb in the mouth of fools," and in this scenario "useless" has become "danger" and "threat." Van Leeuwen uses the term "fitting" to describe the kind of application that was the goal of the sages. Fitting has to do with what is appropriate to a specific situation and it relates to the order that characterizes that particular situation.

According to Van Leeuwen, this order "includes the aspects of time and place, of contingent situation and context."[13] As he further points out, "That is fitting which corresponds to the divinely instituted order of things."[14] Proverbs 15:23 describes the result of an appropriate word when it says, "To make an apt answer is a joy to a man, and a word in season, how good it is!"[15] A principle that is true must be applied appropriately to a context in order for "good" outcomes to result, and this is a skill that must be acquired through practice.

The various sections in Proverbs 2–4 emphasize the importance of putting the sage's advice into practice and then persisting on that course. The old adage "practice makes perfect" applies to most endeavors in life, and certainly that is how the book of Proverbs views the acquisition of wisdom. Skill in living according to God's order requires knowledge of the principles by which the world works and instruction from those who have mastered the skills. What is also required is a lifetime of practice in applying wisdom to the complex and varied circumstances of life.

---

12. For example, Matt. 6:19–20; Rom. 8:12–25; 1 Cor. 3:12–15; 1 Pet. 1:3–9; 5:10. It should also be noted that Jesus used the **metaphor** of the two ways in Matthew 6:13–14.

13. Raymond C. Van Leeuwen, *Context and Meaning in Proverbs 25–27*, SBLDS, 96 (Atlanta: Scholars Press, 1988), 100.

14. Ibid., 99.

15. The proverb is ambiguous; it is not clear whether the benefit comes to the person hearing the word or the person delivering it. In this instance both parties may benefit from a fitting remark.

Proverbs describes a process similar to the way skill is developed in sports, in music, or any art or craft. A world-class tennis player does not develop a two-handed backhand by reading books and watching videos. She must practice the technique over and over and develop the strength and accuracy necessary to make it effective in competition. A champion must persist until the skills become second nature. And she must develop a feel for the game that enables her, in the heat of competition, to instinctively know which shot or strategy increases the chance of winning the point and the match. Becoming wise requires significant commitment and resolve, but its benefits are enormous.

ECCLESIASTES

Ideas in Ecclesiastes circle around and around in ways similar to the poem with which the book begins in Ecclesiastes 1:2–11. There are discernible themes, but no clear linear structure, and **Qoheleth** likely makes a point through this lack of coherence. Garrett says that disorder in a collection of proverbs can serve a didactic purpose by demonstrating that "while reality and truth are not irrational, neither are they fully subject to human attempts at systemization. The proverbs are presented in the seemingly haphazard way we encounter the issues with which they deal."[16] This point is equally appropriate for Ecclesiastes. Some of life can be understood fairly well (though unexpected outcomes still occur), but the real difficulty comes in trying to identify all the pieces and fit them together into a comprehensive structure. The design of Ecclesiastes likely contributes to this point, though certain themes do recur throughout the book.

Ecclesiastes Declares That All Is *hebel*

Ecclesiastes begins and ends by declaring that all is **hebel**[17] and this Hebrew word occurs some forty times in the book. While the word is used concretely of a puff of air or smoke, it is used as a **metaphor** throughout Ecclesiastes, and the interpreter must determine in each instance which aspect of "puff of air" is in view. Suggestions for translating the word into English include "vanity," "absurd," and "meaningless." According to Seow, the term "refers to anything that is superficial, ephemeral, insubstantial, incomprehensible, enigmatic, inconsistent, or contradictory. Something that is *hebel* cannot be grasped or controlled."[18] *Hebel* is often used in parallel with shepherding wind

---

16.   Duane Garrett, *Proverbs, Ecclesiastes, Song of Songs,* NAC (Nashville: Broadman, 1993), 46.

17.   Eccl. 1:2 and 12:8.

18.   C. L. Seow, *Ecclesiastes,* AB (New York: Doubleday, 1997), 47.

or striving after wind,[19] a metaphor that describes trying to do something impossible like catching the wind. Qoheleth uses *hebel* of tasks that are beyond our ability to fully understand or accomplish, and the word is used to describe the short-lived nature of something.

Hebel describes the length of an individual's life within the continuum of human history (1:2–11), and is used of the limited duration of youth (11:10). Often the focus has to do with pursuits undertaken to give meaning to life or to produce satisfaction and fulfillment (1:14; 2:1, 11; 4:16). Ecclesiastes takes us down paths that look promising only to conclude that the pursuit was *hebel*. People often succeed in achieving some difficult and long-sought-after goal only to find the outcome far less fulfilling than they imagined. They open their hand to examine their prize and find nothing of real substance—it is like a puff of air or smoke.

Sometimes *hebel* describes the futility that results from recognizing the dysfunction and difficulty of life in a fallen world; sometimes it is realizing how little one has to show for their hard work and toil (2:11). Sometimes a person realizes that there is little he or she can do to straighten what is crooked in the world (1:14–15). The sage recognizes that death is inevitable and will rob every person of all their accomplishments on earth (2:12–17). He realizes that few will remember those accomplishments and knows that there is nothing anyone can do to change this. The sage sees such realities as *hebel*.[20]

The fact that "all is *hebel*" regularly gives rise to the question, "What does a person gain?" or "What is the profit/advantage?"[21] Sometimes the sage is asking the question of how a person should live to the best advantage; at other times he is asking, whether life has any meaning for people living **under the sun.**

Qoheleth recognizes that certain ways of living provide advantages over other ways (2:12–17). Living wisely is better than living foolishly. He is frustrated, however, by the realization that both the wise person and the fool die. Death appears to rob the wise person of any advantage, and the sage's **epistemology** of self-discovery provides him with no way to look past the grave. His frequent references to death throughout the book[22] suggest that Qoheleth is seeking a profit/advantage that death cannot destroy, and this suggests that his

---

19. For example, Eccl. 1:14; 2:11, 17, 26; 4:4, 16; 6:9.

20. For a brief discussion of *hebel*, see Edward Curtis, *Ecclesiastes and Song of Songs*, TTC (Grand Rapids: Baker, 2013), 11. For a more complete discussion see any of the major commentaries on Ecclesiastes, such as Seow or Longman. See also Gordon Johnston, הבל (2038), *NIDOTTE*, vol. 1, 1003–5; D. C. Fredericks, הֶבֶל (2039), *NIDOTTE*, vol. 1, 1005–6; and Victor Hamilton, הבל, *TWOT*, vol. 1, 204–5.

21. These questions are raised ten times in Ecclesiastes (for example, 1:3; 2:11; 3:9; 10:11).

22. These include Ecclesiastes 1:4; 2:13–16; 3:2, 19; 4:2; 7:2; 12:1–7.

all-encompassing judgment that everything is *hebel* is focused on life in the world as we experience it.

Ecclesiastes Emphasizes Perplexing Realities about Life

Qoheleth struggled with the tensions generated by disconnects between our experience and what the religious (or any other) tradition affirms is true. Qoheleth believed that human observations and experiences, while limited by human finitude, are significant and can lead to a true, though incomplete, understanding of wisdom. He likely assumed the coherence of knowledge in a world created by God and found little comfort in a faith that seemed incongruent with the experiences of life. Qoheleth believed that wisdom must be rooted squarely in reality, even when that reality includes **ambiguity** and elements that seem contradictory and irresolvable. While faith can take a person beyond the realities of life in the world, it must still be integrated into a context that faces those realities head on.

Ecclesiastes describes a world exactly like ours. There are beautiful and good things in life, and Ecclesiastes sees these as gifts coming from God and exhorts us to embrace them and enjoy them (2:24–26; 3:11–13; 5:18–20; 9:7–9). At the same time Qoheleth recognizes perplexing and unsettling things such as injustice and oppression. Evil people use their power to abuse others with apparent impunity (5:8; 10:5–7). He sees a world where unexpected reversals of fortune occur without explanation. Victory and success do not always go to those with the greatest skill or knowledge or to those who work the hardest (9:11–12; 10:5–7). It is a world where outcomes are often determined by factors that we cannot even identify much less control, and this world is far more complex than typical paradigms for life would lead people to believe. While Qoheleth does not provide a theological evaluation of the world, we recognize it as the same fallen world in which we live (7:20, 29; 9:3).

The sage emphasizes that there are few guarantees in life (11:1–6). Even the most carefully designed plan can be undermined by one small mistake or by factors outside the awareness of the plan's designer (9:18–10:1). He notes that most endeavors involve risk, in part because people cannot predict the future (6:12; 8:7; 10:8–11, 14). Qoheleth's advice is to assess the risk carefully, use wisdom to minimize it, and move forward with diligence (9:10; 11:1–6).

The sage sees little difference between what happens to the righteous and the unrighteous in the world—good and bad things happen to both (7:15; 8:14; 9:1–3; 11:5–7). He finds it especially perplexing when innocent people suffer from injustice or oppression and nothing is done to remedy the situation (4:1; 7:16; 8:10). He recognizes God's providence as an overarching **metanarrative** over all of creation. He knows that providence is related to all these anomalous, enigmatic, and inexplicable aspects of life in the world, but he cannot see how all the pieces fit together (3:1–13). He simply describes what he sees and leaves God's providence shrouded in mystery and uncertainty (2:22–26; 3:1–15; 5:18–6:2; 7:13–14; 9:1–3; 11:1–6; 12:9, 13–16).

Ecclesiastes Affirms the Reality of Human Limits

Ecclesiastes sees human limits as one of the important realities of life. This theme obviously relates to the points made above, but it is also related to the theme of fearing God. Qoheleth does not overtly connect his ideas to the early chapters of Genesis, but he deals with similar themes and does so in ways that closely resemble Genesis. While the relationship between Ecclesiastes and the early chapter of Genesis continues to be debated, Anderson says, "The Fall may provide the broader context of Qoheleth. The overlap of so many themes and concepts between Genesis 2–4 and Qoheleth is too great to be considered a coincidence."[23] Kruger does not see convincing literary connections but argues that the ideas of Genesis 1–11 are presupposed by Qoheleth as "commonly known and relevant."[24] Both Genesis and Ecclesiastes recognize that God created the world[25] and providentially oversees creation.[26] Given the many parallel themes, it is at least possible that ideas in Genesis lie underlie many things we see in Ecclesiastes.

As creatures we are dependent on the Creator for life and are designed to live in this relationship to him. God is infinite, and we are finite. God is not bound by time and space; as creatures we are bound by those limits (Eccl. 3:10–15).[27] The work of God is eternal (3:14), while even the most impressive human works are destroyed by death (2:14–16). Living in the **fear of God** means that we see ourselves as creatures and acknowledge our dependence on the sovereign Creator of all things. Embracing our human limits is an essential part of living wisely in the world.

Genesis sees death and the ongoing dysfunction in the world as a consequence of human rebellion,[28] and this accounts for the struggle

---

23. William Anderson, "The Curse Work in Qoheleth: An Expose of Genesis 3:17–19 in Ecclesiastes," *JSS* 70 (1998), 113.
24. Thomas Kruger, *Qoheleth*, Hermeneia (Minneapolis: Fortress, 2004), 25.
25. Gen. 1–2; Eccl. 11:5; 12:1, 7.
26. Gen. 1–4; Eccl. 3:9–18; 5:18–20; 9:1; 11:5; 12:14.
27. Eccl. 1:4; 2:13–16; 3:2, 12; 12:1–7, and all the passages in the book that talk about the inevitability of death, the inability of humans to understand the work of God or change many aspects of human experience.
28. Gen. 3:14–24.

and toil that is the lot of humanity in the world. While Qoheleth does not explicitly connect the world he describes with Genesis 3, his description strongly resembles the world that follows the fall in Genesis. This is reflected in the fact that everyone dies; it is also evident in Qoheleth's descriptions of evil (Eccl. 7:20, 29), injustice (Eccl. 3:16), and oppression (4:1, 5:8). As Qoheleth says in 7:20, "Surely there is not a righteous person on earth who does good and never sins."[29] Human sinfulness limits us as human beings and contributes significantly to the difficulties that people experience in the world.

The poem at the beginning of the book (1:2–11) sets the tone for this theme. People live only a short time in the world, and then die. We are faced not only with our limited life span, but with the nagging question of whether the repetitive and difficult toil that is a part of life in the world means anything in the continuum of human history. Was Macbeth correct when he said,

> Life's but a walking shadow, a poor player
> That struts and frets his hour upon the stage
> And then is heard no more: it is a tale
> Told by an idiot, full of sound and fury,
> Signifying nothing?[30]

It is apparent that human beings cannot answer such questions on the basis of the experiences of life alone. Apart from constructing an arbitrary answer by which to live, we are at an impasse—unless an authoritative answer comes to us from God. In Ecclesiastes, human limits confront us at every turn.

Qoheleth's teaching about human limits can be discouraging in a world that tells us we can do anything we are determined to do, but it can also motivate us to put our trust in God for his help in experiencing life as it was meant to be. It can also deliver us from spending immense amounts of time trying to straighten things that cannot be straightened or count things that are lacking (Eccl. 1:15; 7:13). Understanding who we are and how we fit into God's order can deliver us from the futility of spending a lifetime trying to find meaning and ultimate satisfaction in things that were never designed to provide that. Understanding our limits should also motivate us to abandon our autonomy and trust God for answers that he alone can provide through his special revelation.

---

29. Or Ecclesiastes 9:3 where he says, "Also, the hearts of the children of man are full of evil, and madness is in their hearts while they live, and after that they go to the dead."

30. William Shakespeare, *Macbeth*, Act 5, Scene 5.

Ecclesiastes Affirms the Importance of Fearing God and Keeping His Commandments

For Qoheleth the whole duty of human beings is summed up in fearing God and keeping his commandments (12:13). While some argue that fear of God has a different meaning in Ecclesiastes than it does elsewhere in the Old Testament,[31] Seow argues that "The concept of the fear of God here, as elsewhere in Israelite wisdom literature, stresses the distance between divinity and humanity. It is the recognition that God is God and people are human."[32] This summation connects the thinking of Qoheleth with the main trajectory of thought in the Old Testament and makes it clear that his ideas do not reflect a radical departure from Old Testament orthodoxy.

"Fear of the Lord" is a term for the life of faith throughout the Old Testament. As was the case in Job 28:28, Ecclesiastes calls us to live in the fear of God irrespective of the kinds of circumstances that we encounter in the world.

Understanding the *hebel*-character of human effort and accomplishment and our human limits that prevent us from knowing what will happen in the future should drive us toward fear of God. Recognizing our limited understanding of the work of God, and our inability to protect ourselves from the impact of evil and folly in the world should motivate us to trust God and move back into the relationship with God for which we were created. As Garrett points out, living in the fear of God "is the deepest expression of humble acceptance of what it means to be a human before God."[33]

Ecclesiastes Affirms the Importance of Wisdom and Living Wisely

Even as Ecclesiastes affirms human limits, the sage also emphasizes the importance of wisdom. He insists that "there is more gain in wisdom than in folly" (Eccl. 2:13), and points out that wisdom can sometimes deliver a city from a strong army (Eccl. 9:14–15). Qoheleth provides numerous examples of wisdom's usefulness in living in a fallen world. While wisdom does not constitute the meaning of life or allow us to always secure the results we desire, it is essential and can deliver us from the unnecessary consequences of foolish behavior.

---

31. For example, Tremper Longman, III (*Ecclesiastes*, NICOT [Grand Rapids: Eerdmans, 1998], 36) maintains that the fear advocated by Qoheleth "is that of fright before a powerful and dangerous being, not respect or awe for a mighty and compassionate deity."

32. Choon-Leong Seow, *Ecclesiastes*, AB (New York: Doubleday, 1997), 174.

33. Garrett, *Proverbs, Ecclesiastes, Song of Songs,* 345.

In 8:2–9 the sage describes a dangerous situation involving an official who disagrees with a king about some policy. Qoheleth warns the official not to get angry and storm off in a rage; nor should he participate in an evil matter (perhaps a coup attempt). In the earthly realm the king has absolute power, and it is risky to challenge his authority. In a very volatile and potentially dangerous situation the official is advised to remain calm, to be patient, and to wait for the proper time and the right way to address the issue. Patience, self-control, and a wisely formulated request can often deliver a person from a dangerous situation.

Finally, 7:21–22 advises a person who inadvertently overhears his servant cursing him to give the servant the benefit of the doubt and ignore the insult. The master has probably been guilty of the same thing. Ecclesiastes 10:20, though, warns against saying something bad about the king or a rich person, even in private. We are instructed to give other people the benefit of the doubt when they insult us, but we should not expect those with power over us to respond in the same way. Wisdom dictates that we say nothing that could cause us trouble if it got back to the person about whom the remark was made. These examples also illustrate the importance of application. Developing the skill to live wisely in a fallen and complex world requires a lifetime of reflection on wisdom principles and persistent practice.

Ecclesiastes Affirms the Importance of Enjoying Life as God Gives Opportunity

Life for Qoheleth is not characterized exclusively by toil, struggle, and difficulty, and in Ecclesiastes 2:24–25 he tells the reader that "There is nothing better for a person than that he should eat and drink and find enjoyment in his toil. This also, I saw, is from the hand of God." This is the first of several passages[34] commending enjoyment and delight in things such as food, drink, and relationships with friends and family. These are gifts from God and reflective of his goodness to humanity. Receiving and finding pleasure in them will contribute to our well-being and to a more positive perspective than focusing only on things that we think should be different. Recognizing these gifts and connecting them with God's goodness plays an important role in maintaining a balance that reflects both the difficult struggles that are part of life and the ongoing indications of God's steadfast love that according to Psalm 33:5 fill the earth. Such pleasures do not constitute the meaning of life nor should they become a central goal in life. They are, though, intended by God to be enjoyed.

---

34.   The others are 3:12–13, 22; 5:18–20; 8:15; and 9:7–10.

Ecclesiastes Recognizes God's Sovereignty and Providence

Qoheleth sees God as both creator of all things and as the one who, through his providence, oversees all of life.[35] The sage connects the work of God in the world with both the blessings that allow people to find enjoyment and delight, and with God's judgment on evil (3:17; 11:9; and 12:13). He also connects the providence of God with each person's lot[36] in life despite the huge disparities that exist there. He sees God's work reflected in situations where a person is allowed to become rich but then denied the opportunity to enjoy the benefits of the wealth (6:1–2). He sees God behind both days of prosperity and days of adversity (7:14–15). He recognizes that outcomes in life ultimately depend on God, and sees his governance operating over a world where there is injustice and oppression and where things happen to both righteous and wicked people in what appear to be random and arbitrary ways (3:16–17; 8:10–13; 9:1–3; 11:8–12:1). In the light of such realities, it seems evident that the world described by Qoheleth provides little unambiguous evidence that God's governance of human affairs is beneficent, just, and kind.[37]

Ecclesiastes does little more than confront us with these questions; it is the rest of Scripture to which we must turn for the answers. The book does make it evident that such questions cannot be answered on the basis of the experiences of life, and Qoheleth's occasional faith assertions[38] point us in the direction of those answers. The "better than" proverbs in chapter 7 also make it clear that even in the realm of human experience we lack the ability to know what is good and so we need to be patient in passing judgment on what the outcome of a matter may be. Clearly, we do not understand enough about the work of God to pass judgment on his moral governance of the world.

---

35. See "Ecclesiastes Affirms the Reality of Human Limits" above.

36. The word חֵלֶק , "lot," is used of allocating land to tribes or families after the conquest or of distributing spoil after a battle. In Ecclesiastes 3:22, 5:19, and 9:9 the word "refers to a person's circumstances in life and includes such things as when, where, and to whom one is born; health; abilities; wealth; status; educational opportunities; and the like. One's lot establishes both opportunities and limits for what a person can do in life" (Curtis, *Ecclesiastes and Song of Songs*, 56). Qoheleth sees these things as falling under the sovereign oversight of God. At the same time, Ecclesiastes 2:21 suggests that people have the power to change their lot in life through wisdom, knowledge, and hard work. In the instance described in 2:21, the person who worked hard and accumulated significant wealth died and left his חֵלֶק to someone who did not work for it.

37. Additional evidence is provided by oppression that is allowed to continue by corrupt officials (Eccl. 4:1; 5:8).

38. For example, his assertion that God will judge the wicked and the righteous (3:17; 11:9; 12:14) despite evidence of injustice that continues unchecked and his assertion in 12:7 that the grave may not be the end that human observation would suggest.

It is only in living the way Ecclesiastes commends that we understand the meaning of humanness and discover the true meaning of life. Living in the fear of God is the antithesis of self-fulfillment. Wisdom calls us to live according to God's instructions and leave outcomes with him, trusting in his providence to accomplish his purposes. Those who do this are the ones in whom God delights, and they are the ones God uses to accomplish his purposes. As Jesus makes clear, they are also the ones who lay up treasure for themselves in heaven that death cannot take away.[39]

SONG OF SONGS

Introduction

Identifying key themes in Song of Songs is difficult because of ambiguities and uncertainties related to virtually every aspect of this book. A casual reading of Song of Songs would lead most to conclude that the book consists of love poetry describing the relationship between a man and a woman and that the poetry includes suggestions of the physical and sexual aspects of the relationship.[40] Many interpreters throughout history have been put off by these explicit passages and have argued that such literature would never have been included in Scripture. As a result, the history of interpretation of Song of Songs is dominated by **allegorical interpretation**s that see the poetry as having little to do with actual relationships between men and women but is meant to describe the relationship between God and Israel or Christ and the church. While there is little to suggest that such an interpretation was intended by the author, this understanding of the book prevailed until a century or so ago, when scholars began to understand the book for what it appears to be: love poetry describing a relationship between a man and woman. Obviously, someone who concludes that the book is an **allegory** will identify the key themes of the book differently than will the person who sees the book as celebrating human love.[41]

---

39. Jesus answered Qoheleth's question about whether a person can live so as to gain a profit that death cannot wipe out in the Sermon on the Mount in Matthew 6:19–20. The New Testament makes it clear that a person enters into a relationship with God by faith in God/ Jesus (John 3:16; Acts 16:30–31) and that this life continues to develop by faith (Col. 2:6). The life that begins with regeneration continues to develop through the obedience of faith (John 14:21–24; 1 John 1:5–7).

40. We have a group of similar poems from Egypt and I am aware of no one who has suggested that they are anything except love poetry. On these poems, see Michael Fox, *The Song of Songs and the Ancient Egyptian Love Songs* (Madison: University of Wisconsin Press, 1985).

41. For examples of interpretations of those assuming that the book is an allegory, see the old but still useful essay by H. H. Rowley, "The Interpretation of the Song of Songs," in *The Servant of the Lord and Other Essays* (2nd ed.; Oxford: Blackwell, 1965), 195–246. Especially good

Most scholars today reject the allegorical understanding of the book because the text lacks indicators that it was written as an allegory. In addition, allegorical interpretation has produced little consensus among interpreters with conclusions often appearing to be subjective and imported into the text rather than flowing out of it. Most today also reject the premise that human love is an unworthy topic for inclusion in inspired Scripture, and with this shift a major reason for allegorical interpretation disappears.

While most interpreters today agree that Song of Songs is poetry describing love between a man and woman, major disagreements remain about the purpose of the book and the story—if any—that lies behind the poetry. The book provides insufficient clues for accurately reconstructing a background story, and widely diverse suggestions have been offered as to what the story might be. The speakers are not always identified and it is sometimes difficult to know who is speaking to whom.[42] Solomon's role in the book is problematic in that it is difficult to see how a man, who according to 1 Kings 11:1–8 had seven hundred wives and princesses and three hundred concubines, could be a role model for the way God designed relationships between men and women to function. The book does not clearly mention God, and while it describes the passion and physical desires of the couple, it does not explicitly address the question of appropriate sexual morality. Certain expressions like the exhortation directed to the daughters of Jerusalem in 2:7, 3:5, and 8:4 are repeated in ways that suggest that the book is a unified composition rather than an anthology of poems, but the exact story eludes us. The conversations and poetic descriptions of this relationship are like an impressionistic collage where only those familiar with this specific story would be able to put the snippets together and fill in the details between the pieces that we have. As frustrating as this may be to the interpreter, the ambiguity likely makes it much easier for people in different times, places, and cultures to apply the principles to their relationships.

Some Approaches to the Song

Theories about the background story of the Song are legion. Some of the more popular proposals include the following:

---

and extensive discussions of the history of interpretation can be found in Marvin Pope, *Song of Songs*, AB (Garden City, NY: Doubleday, 1977), 89–229; Duane Garrett, *Song of Songs/ Lamentations*, WBC (Nashville: Thomas Nelson, 2004), 59–97; and G. Lloyd Carr, *The Song of Solomon*, TOTC (Downers Grove, IL: InterVarsity, 1984), 21–41.

42. Many translations, both ancient and modern (for example, **LXX**, ESV, NIV, NASB), provide help for the reader by attempting to identify the speaker of each section of the Song.

1. The story is about Solomon's marriage to his first and favorite wife, who died young. Solomon's other relationships reflected his attempts to find another relationship like his first.[43]

2. Solomon met a young woman on a trip to the north and was captivated by her. He brought her back to Jerusalem intending to woo her and marry her. She, however, was in love with a young shepherd and rebuffed the king. She rejected all that would come with being queen, and returned to her true love. This view is sometimes referred to as the "Shepherd Hypothesis."

3. It is a story about a particular couple, but not king Solomon. Some see the relationship moving from courtship in the early chapters to marriage and consummation in chapters 4 and 5 and finally to the maturing of the relationship in the later chapters.

4. The story is not about an actual couple but an ideal one, described as king (Solomon) and queen (Shulamite).[44]

Conclusions about the kind of literature, the historical and cultural background,[45] the development of a story or argument, and the context of the passage should result from a careful study of the text itself. In the case of Song of Songs, these decisions cannot be made entirely on that basis, since the ambiguities of the text leave us with several scenarios that are possible and plausible rather than one that is highly probable. At the same time, the decisions made about these matters will inevitably be applied to the text to explicate difficulties encountered there. It is critical that each interpreter be aware of the way this works in Song of Songs and avoid, as much as possible, dogmatically teaching principles that actually flow more out of creative reconstructions than from the text itself.

Working Assumptions about the Song

As we attempt to identify key themes of Song of Songs, it is important to identify the assumptions that lie behind our choices, and ideally

---

43. This idea is sometimes heard in sermons and from popular Bible teachers. It is not an idea popular among scholars.

44. At many Jewish weddings today, the bride and groom are treated as king and queen during the wedding festivities. Many parents throughout history have spent money well beyond their resources to provide a "royal wedding" for their children.

45. One must be very careful about using cultural background to explicate a text. This often results in meaning being read into the text from extrabiblical sources rather than being generated by the biblical text itself.

this will enable a reader to evaluate how closely we have come to the goal of giving priority to principles actually taught by the text.

1. The book is poetry describing and celebrating love between a man and a woman. The descriptions include, but are not limited to, the physical and sexual dimensions of the relationship. It is a book about human love, in all its manifestations, rather than a book about sex.

2. The only context in which we have the book is Scripture, and we will assume that the moral values that are unstated in this book are those taught in the rest of the Old Testament. Thus adultery is viewed as wrong, as is premarital and extramarital sex. We will assume that the couple is committed to those values. Many today disconnect it from the rest of the canon and see it as a book celebrating passion and sexuality apart from considerations of biblical morality.[46] The consequences of such an assumption can be seen throughout our culture, though the problem is likely much older. Rabbi Akiba, in the second century A.D. said that "He who, at a banquet, renders the Song of Songs in a sing-song way, turning it into a common ditty, has no share in the world to come."[47] The context that one assumes for this book will significantly impact the meaning one finds in it.

3. Because the context of the book is the canon, we will assume that its teaching is consistent with the broad contours of **Yahwistic** theology and world view. Yahweh created the world and designed it to work in a certain way, and relationships are an important part of God's design. The book describes a generic, but properly functioning relationship, and this allows the reader a glimpse into the way the "one flesh" relationship in Genesis 2 is supposed to work. The identity of the man and woman is not the important thing; the way they relate and function in the relationship is.

4. The book introduces the reader to a relationship that is already established and it ends with presumably the same relationship still

---

46. For example, Pope, *Song of Songs*.

47. Mishna, *Tosefta Sanhedrin* 12:10. These comments come to us without context, and it is difficult to know exactly what Akiba meant. It is generally supposed that his point was directed toward those who interpreted the book literally rather than allegorically, since he played a significant role in making the allegorical interpretation normative in Jewish circles. His comment could have been directed toward those who applied the words of the Song to the bride and groom at a wedding. Akiba could also have had in mind "young men who used to sing them as erotic ditties in wine houses," as suggested by Alfred Sendrey, *Music in Ancient Israel* (New York: Philosophical Library, 1969), 465.

developing. While a marriage is described in the middle of the book, there is insufficient data to conclude that the book describes the relationship in a strictly chronological fashion, with the early chapters describing their courtship and the final chapters describing the later years of their relationship. The ambiguity is likely deliberate and suggests that no matter how a relationship begins—and most marriages in antiquity were arranged ones—the principles in this book can impact a relationship as it is and begin to move it in a direction that more closely resembles God's order. In addition, the ambiguities and the open-ended character of the relationship described in the book suggest that relationships can always grow toward maturity no matter where they happen to be in terms of time.

Primary Themes

The Song Sees Human Love, Sex, and Marriage as Part of God's Design for Creation

Human relationships, as the Bible affirms many times,[48] are a blessing from God and are meant to bring people benefit and delight. Human rebellion against God and his order had a particularly devastating effect on human relationships, and this book sets forth a more ideal picture of a relationship between a man and woman than the manipulative, self-serving, demeaning, and power-based examples that have characterized human culture throughout history.[49]

The Song Reveals Attitudes and Behaviors Important in Relationships between Men and Women

While time, place, culture, and personal circumstances will determine the characteristics of particular relationships, the Song identifies important aspects of **Yahweh's order**. The relationship is characterized by mutuality as both partners show respect and love for the other. They both initiate and participate in lovemaking and in expressing their praise for the other. Each values the other and expresses his/her thanksgiving and delight in having the other. They have a deep commitment to one another and find great delight in belonging to each other.[50]

---

48. For example, Gen. 2:18–25; Prov. 5:15–20; Eccl. 9:7–9.

49. Biblical examples include Lamech in Genesis 4:23–24, who seems to have begun the practice of multiple wives; Jacob and the family dysfunction that resulted from his several wives (Genesis 29–37); the Levite and his concubine in Judges 9; Solomon and his many wives; and the Persian king in Esther. The list could go on and on. In addition one could suggest Henry VIII, and many examples from today's world.

50. Examples of all these things are legion and are spread throughout this short book. Almost every verse shows one or the other of these things.

Their love is deep and filled with intensity and passion irrespective of how their relationship may have begun. Their love is not self-centered but reflects a deep concern for the desires and well-being of the other. Song of Songs 8:6–7 describes love—presumably, the love reflected in the relationship presented in the book—as "strong as death . . . [and] fierce as the grave." The passage goes on to say in verse 7 that "many waters cannot quench love, neither can floods drown it. If a man offered for love all the wealth of his house, he would be utterly despised." Their mutual love and commitment reflect the steadfast and loyal love that the Old Testament refers to as חֶסֶד (*hesed*).[51] Their relationship reflects the same kind of commitment to one another that is seen in Ephesians 5:20–33.

The Song Provides a Glimpse into How the One-flesh Relationship Is Designed to Function

Set in the broader context of Scripture, it seems likely that the book presupposes values such as purity and faithfulness, and the book may further explicate aspects of the "one-flesh" relationship in Genesis 2. God's relationship with his people is often described using the metaphor of marriage[52] and it would appear that fundamental to this image is the principle expressed in the first commandment: "You shall have no other gods before me" (Exod. 20:3). Israel's lack of trust in Yahweh and rebellion against him is regularly expressed in terms of adultery as they forsake Yahweh to pursue other gods.[53] The commitment of the man and woman in the Song appears to be central to their relationship and the foundation on which passion and delight can be appropriately built. God's provision of a suitable helper for Adam reflects the fact that God designed human beings to function in relationships rather than independently and autonomously. The idea of a helper in Genesis 2 is not that of an inferior partner, but rather of one who brings strength to complement a point of weakness in the other. In the Song we see both partners helping the other as the man's praise counters the criticisms of others and gives the woman a more accurate sense of her own worth and value.[54] The beauty that each sees in the other likely does not focus exclusively on external qualities, but on character and the kind of beauty celebrated in Proverbs 31:30.

Growth toward spiritual maturity is facilitated by relationships, and intimate relationships like marriage constitute a particularly effective

---

51. This is the sort of loving commitment that Ruth showed to Naomi (Ruth 1:8) and that she showed to Boaz (Ruth 3:10). It is used of God's persistent love for his people (for example, Psalm 136, Psalm 107, and Lam. 3:22). Also see the discussion of this word in chapter 6.

52. For example, Jer. 2:1, 3:20, Isa. 54:5–10; Hos. 2:14–20.

53. For example, Jer. 3:6–14, 5:7–8; Ezek. 23.

54. This is perhaps reflected in 1:15–2:3.

context for such growth to take place. The relationship that we see in Song of Songs is characterized by love, mutual respect, praise for and delight in one another. The power of the Song lies in its ability to draw readers into the experience of this couple and participate vicariously in their relationship. In the process God's people learn significant things about how the one flesh relationship designed by God is supposed to work.

The Song Suggests That This Relationship Is a Gift of God That Cannot Be Forced or Manipulated

The warnings to the daughters of Jerusalem (2:7, 3:5, 5:8–9) seem best understood as affirming this point. The kind of love that is seen in the Song cannot be bought with money (8:7); it cannot be coerced by power (8:11–12);[55] it cannot be brought about by sex (2:7; 3:5). It must be allowed to happen in the providence of God. At the same time we can infer that living according to wisdom and God's order creates an environment where this can occur.

The Song Allows Us to More Fully Understand the Nature of God

We have argued that the central focus of this book is on love between a man and woman and have rejected an allegorical interpretation of the book. Even as we reject that interpretive approach to the Song, it is important to recognize that reflection on human relationships—especially the relationship between a man and woman in marriage—does have significant potential for helping us develop a deeper understanding of God and how he works. To reduce the significant lessons from this book to only those having to do with male-female issues and marriage would be to miss an important feature of the text. As E. J. Young points out, recognizing the important lessons the book teaches about these matters "does not exhaust the purpose of the book. Not only does it speak of the purity of human love, but by its very inclusion in the Canon, it reminds us of a love that is purer than our own."[56]

The narrative of the Old Testament is regularly framed in terms of a relationship between God and individuals of faith (Abraham, David, Isaiah, the psalmists, etc.) or between God and his people Israel. The **Torah** makes clear God's basic desire for his people. Deuteronomy 10:12–13 says, "And now, Israel, what does the LORD your God require of you, but to fear the LORD your God, to walk in all his ways, to love him, to serve the LORD your God with all your heart and with all

---

55. These are perhaps the most difficult verses in the entire book. One wonders if they are contrasting the beloved's love freely given with the coercion that often forced women into marriage with a powerful person like the king.

56. E. J. Young, *An Introduction to the Old Testament* (2nd ed.; Grand Rapids: Eerdmans, 1960), 354.

your soul, and to keep the commandments and statutes of the LORD, which I am commanding you today for your good?" Jesus' response to the scribe in Mark 6:28–34 affirms the central importance of loving God with one's whole being, and adds that the second most important commandment involves loving others as ourselves. John presents loving God and others as a sort of litmus test of genuine faith in God,[57] and both the Old and New Testaments provide instruction about what this involves. Loving God means that we trust and worship him to the exclusion of other gods, and following false gods and idols is seen by every prophet as adultery.

Loving God also involves trusting him and keeping his commandments. Loving others means that we are to be kind and compassionate to them, respect them, and treat them justly and with integrity. It means that we are to avoid immorality and behave in ways that reflect God's character. The New Testament even provides us with lists that identify essential characteristics of this kind of love.[58] Certainly a marriage should be marked by such love.

At the same time, "love" is a rather abstract concept, and even a long list of attitudes and behaviors is insufficient for understanding exactly what it means in the various relationships that constitute life, including that most intimate human relationship between a husband and wife. Scripture regularly tells us about God's love for his people, and it becomes clear that God's love provides us with a paradigm for what love ought to look like in human relationships.

Marriage is used as a metaphor to make God's love for his people more understandable. Perhaps the classic example of this is the Old Testament story of Hosea. The prophet is instructed by God to marry a woman who became unfaithful to him. Her infidelity reached the point where she had left him and was living with one lover after another. God instructed Hosea to provide her with food and other necessities. When she reached the point where she was no longer desirable to any man she was put up for auction as a slave. Hosea went to the auction, bid against the others there, and bought back his unfaithful wife with a view toward restoring her. The egregious behavior of Hosea's wife and the profoundly unexpected behavior of Hosea toward his wayward spouse effectively showed the people of Israel the true nature of their rebellion against Yahweh and the nature of Yahweh's gracious love.

The New Testament often compares the relationship between Jesus and the church to marriage. It is Christ's self-sacrificing love for the church that is the model for how a husband is supposed to love his wife (Eph. 5:20–33), and the relationship between Christ and the church

---

57. For example, John 14:23–24; 1 John 4:7–12.
58. For example, 1 Cor. 13.

becomes a mysterious paradigm for how the marriage relationship is supposed to function. The description of the church as the "bride of Christ" further suggests that marriage and the relationship between Christ and the church are mirror images of one another in certain significant ways.

The New Testament emphasizes that an important part of the transformation effected by the new birth involves living out values that reflect God's truth and nature. Believers are to walk in love; husbands are to love their wives; and Christ's self-giving and sacrificial love is the paradigm for what this love involves. We learn about God's work and nature from his revelation in Scripture, and we are called to live out those values in the world. As we live out God's truth, we provide those around us with glimpses of who God is and what he is like and elevate God's reputation in the world. Relationships that function according to Yahweh's order provide an important context for doing this.

While it is true that we learn what God's love is like from Scripture and from experiencing it in our relationship with him, we also learn about it by doing it and by watching those around us live it out. I have learned much about what God's love is like by watching my wife practice it in her relationship with me, with our children, and with others. I have learned much about it by watching the people in our Sunday school class rally around members who are struggling and in need of God's gracious love. I have learned a great deal about God's love by seeing it in action through a colleague whose wife has been battling cancer. I have seen his self-sacrificing love as he ministers to her with deep compassion. What is even more striking to me is that his wife told me years ago that their marriage was an arranged one—but she quickly added, "But we learned to really love one another," and truly they have. My colleague's example has taught me an immense amount about God's gracious and persistent love.

Thus, while we have argued that the allegorical method used by interpreters through most of the history of the church is problematic and should be rejected, the insights of many of these interpreters were useful and reflect legitimate applications of the metaphor that the Bible itself often uses as it compares marriage to God's relationship with his people. As Murphy suggests, "God initiates and pursues a loving relationship with the community of faith. It is in terms of this grand metaphor that Jewish and Christian interpretive traditions understood the Song to express the communal 'bride's' response, her memories of the divine love that had first claimed her, and her longing to experience always the joys of the lover's sublime presence."[59]

---

59.   Roland Murphy, *The Song of Songs*, Hermeneia (Minneapolis: Fortress, 1980), 104.

3

PREPARING FOR
INTERPRETATION

The Chapter at a Glance

The Importance of Ancient Near Eastern Background in Interpreting Wisdom Literature

- Helpful Parallels
- Significant Differences
- Specific Parallels to Old Testament Wisdom Books
- Basic Resources for Ancient Near Eastern Background

Textual Criticism: Determining the Best Text

- Introduction
- The Task and Basic Principles
- The Hebrew Text of the Wisdom Books
- Basic Resources for Textual Criticism

Translation and Developing a Sense of the Context

- Resources for Translation and Exegesis

Considering the Contribution of Others

A NUMBER OF TASKS MUST BE DONE in preparation for exegesis of a biblical text, but we will limit our discussion here to several of the more important ones.

THE IMPORTANCE OF ANCIENT NEAR EASTERN BACKGROUND IN INTERPRETING WISDOM LITERATURE

In communication many things, such as a common language and culture and a common body of knowledge and experience, are shared by the author and the audience. These things are generally assumed and are often not explicit in the text, though they are essential for understanding the message the author meant to communicate. Background can sometimes help an interpreter, far removed from the original context in time, culture, or experience to discover some of these underlying givens.

An awareness of the context and worldview of the author and audience allows a distant reader[1] to identify certain shared worldview components that are helpful for bridging the gap between "then" and "now." An awareness of worldview differences also minimizes reading into a text meanings that are peculiar to modern culture. According to Tate, "The most effective safeguard against a wholesale imposition of the interpreter's world upon the world of the text is the diligent study of the world that produced the text."[2] Entering into the world of the author improves the accuracy and consistency of our interpretation, even if "more accurate" interpretation sometimes turns out to be less detailed and specific.

Helpful Parallels

Ancient Near Eastern culture rarely transforms our understanding of a biblical text, but sometimes broadens our understanding of things that are already generally clear in the Bible. In some cases, examples from the ancient Near East give us broader insight into how certain common elements in the culture functioned. The two examples noted below illustrate how this can work:

- Proverbs 22:28, 23:10, and Job 24:2 warn against moving boundary stones, and biblical passages like Deuteronomy 19:14, 22:28, and 27:16 connect these warnings with the protection of family land holdings

---

1. We are trying to understand a communication that was written in Hebrew and Aramaic and doing it in a culture separated by more than two millennia from the original text.

2. Randolph Tate, *Biblical Interpretation: An Integrated Approach*, 3rd edition (Grand Rapids: Baker, 2008), 38.

that were part of the allocation of land after the conquest. Several passages also connect this with the just treatment of the widow, the orphan, and the poor, and the abuse involves stealing land from people who lack the resources and political connections to protect their rights from others more powerful than they.

A similar warning is also found in the Egyptian text, *Instruction of Amenemope*, which says, "Do not move the markers on the borders of the fields, nor shift the position of the measuring cord. Do not be greedy for a cubit of land, nor encroach on the boundaries of a widow."[3]

A number of these boundary markers, called *kudurru* stones, have been found in Mesopotamia. Stone versions of these were deposited in temples while clay replicas were apparently used to identify property boundaries. The inscriptions on these stones often identify the land as property granted to someone by the king or by the court in settlement of a lawsuit. It is often specified that the property belongs to this family in perpetuity, and the inscriptions include a curse on anyone who challenges or denies the rightful ownership of the land or on anyone who moves the boundary marker.

Such background information does not significantly change our understanding of these biblical passages, but it does give us details that broaden understanding of how these boundary markers functioned in the ancient world.

- In Song of Songs 8:6 the woman says, "Set me as a seal upon your heart, as a seal upon your arm." Other biblical passages mention seals and provide a basic understanding of what she means by her statement. Seals were used by kings and other leaders to affirm the authority of a document (1 Kings 21:8; Esther 8:8). Jeremiah sealed the contract relating to his purchase of land from his cousin in order to establish proof about his ownership of the property and for future validation of his prediction regarding the coming exile and the return from Babylon (Jer. 32:10).

Archaeologists have found many seals and the impressions they left in clay, and this material has broadened our understanding of how seals functioned in antiquity. Seals were of two types: ring or stamp seals (more common in Israel) and cylinder seals (more common in Mesopotamia),[4] and they seem to have been used

---

3. Miriam Lichtheim, *AEL*, vol. 2, 151.

4. These were stone cylinders with a hole drilled through the length of the cylinder. A string was normally put through the hole and the cylinder worn around the neck. The name of the owner of the seal would be inscribed on the seal along with various designs. To use the seal a small stick would be inserted into the hole and the cylinder rolled across the wet clay.

by all classes throughout the ancient Near East. The seals were used to secure the contents of a container (oil, grain, etc.) and to indicate ownership of the item. It also guaranteed the authenticity of a document. It seems likely that the woman's request in Song 8:6 is related to her comments in Song 2:16 and 6:3, "My beloved is mine and I am his." They belong to each other, and she wants him to make the exclusive nature of their relationship clear to everyone.

Ancient Near Eastern background sometimes brings clarifying insight to meaning that would not be apparent to a reader today. This is especially the case with symbolism, associations, and connotations that help a modern reader understand the emotional impact the **metaphor** would have had on a reader. The two examples noted below show how this might work:

- In Song 2:3 the woman describes her beloved as "an apple tree among the trees of the forest," and in 2:5 she asks to be refreshed by apples because she is "sick with love." The Hebrew word used here is תַּפּוּחַ (*tappuah*) and its exact meaning is uncertain, though it likely does mean "apple."[5] As Garrett notes, evidence from both texts and artwork make it clear that in antiquity "the apple had sexual implications."[6] Thus in the mind of ancient readers the mention of apples would likely have provoked associations that do not come to the mind of most modern readers,[7] and the background material enables us to recognize that. Her desire for him has made her lovesick, and she asks for raisins and apples. Gordis says, "She is calling for concrete food, to be sure, but *at the same time*, by her choice of fruits that are symbolic of love, she is indicating that only the satisfaction of her desires will bring her healing."[8] In an Egyptian poem a young man says about the woman he loves, "She will make the doctors unnecessary because she knows my sickness."[9]

---

5. See, *HALOT*; Marvin Pope, *Song of Songs,* AB (Garden City, NY: Doubleday, 1977), 371–72; and Duane Garrett, *Song of Songs/Lamentations*, WBC (Nashville: Thomas Nelson, 2004), 149–50. Some identify it as the apricot.

6. Garrett, *Song of Songs*, 150.

7. The word is used in Song 7:8 (7:9 Heb.), where the context makes the sexual associations clear. This is not so evident in 8:5, where the word is used again, but it is likely that the sexual associations are present there.

8. Robert Gordis, *Song of Songs and Lamentations* (New York: KTAV, 1974), 38, italics in original.

9. John B. White, *A Study of the Language of Love in the Song of Songs and Ancient Egyptian Poetry* (Missoula, MT: Scholars Press, 1978), 105.

- In Song 2:1–2, the woman is described as a lily (שׁוֹשַׁנָּה, *shoshanah*). While the word שׁוֹשַׁנָּה in Song of Songs is usually translated "lily," it probably refers to a particular kind of lily, the lotus or water lily.[10] Keel argues that the capitals of the pillars in Solomon's temple were decorated with lotus flowers (1 Kings 7:19–22, 26) and that the large container for water outside the temple had lotus flowers around its rim.[11] Lotus flowers were a symbol of life and regeneration in Egypt, and scarabs and paintings from Palestine suggest that it was also viewed that way in Israel. When the man says that in comparison to the other young women she "is a lily among brambles" (2:2), he is obviously declaring that she is unique among the other women around them, but he is probably also alluding to her power to refresh and energize him. In 7:2 he describes her belly as "a heap of wheat, encircled with lilies," and Keel sees the image of these things surrounded by *lotus flowers* as a powerful symbol of regeneration and life.[12]

Perhaps the best example of the importance of background material from the ancient Near East has to do with biblical passages that use language and metaphors drawn from ancient Near Eastern myths. Some of these images are so tied to the ancient Near Eastern context out of which they came that a modern reader would likely never understand them apart from extrabiblical material that explicates them.[13]

Significant Differences

There are, however, important differences between the biblical wisdom texts and the ancient Near Eastern parallels. Perhaps the most striking difference has to do with the understanding of God/the gods and the relationship between people and deity in the two cultures. Apart from Israel, the cultures in the ancient Near East were polytheistic, and in contrast to **Yahweh**, all their gods had a beginning, and no deity was truly sovereign. The roles of each god often changed over time, and the interactions of the gods in many respects paralleled those that occur in human society. Sometimes the gods were promoted (as happened with Marduk in Babylon), and sometimes their function was reduced to a less significant role in the pantheon. The pantheon included a small group of gods functioning in authoritative roles over the rest.

---

10. See *HALOT* and any of the major commentaries.

11. Othmar Keel, *The Song of Song*, Continental Commentary, tr. Frederick Gaiser (Minneapolis: Fortress, 1994), 78–82.

12. Keel, *Song of Songs*, 78–80, 114–15, 234–35.

13. See the discussion in chapter 4 on "Guidelines for Interpreting Job."

There were gods who made up a council that issued decrees and made decisions that impacted both the heavenly and earthly realms. It appears that even the ruling gods were subject to these decisions and limited by them. The gods were limited by the functions assigned to them and were expected to act in their roles in ways that were consistent with the cosmic values to which all were subject.

There were major deities who functioned like powerful kings and others whose roles were more ordinary and limited, though they were still gods on whom people were dependent. The gods possessed the full complement of human traits, both good and bad, and these were magnified in the heavenly realm. The same conflicts and interpersonal challenges that occur in the human realm also took place in the cosmic realm, often to the detriment of people. The gods sometimes got drunk and were in bad moods; on occasion they acted rashly. They were sometimes driven by selfishness and anger. Some gods were generally kind and favorably disposed toward humans, while others were intent on throwing the world into chaos that would make human life impossible.[14]

Texts like *Atrahasis*[15] and *Enuma Elish*[16] describe a time before human beings were created when the lower-level deities had to maintain the temples and furnish offerings for the senior deities. According to these texts, people were created to relieve the minor deities from the drudgery of serving the other gods. As Schneider puts it, the texts "reveal really only one basic fundamental understanding of humans' role on earth: to serve the deities."[17] The gods were more powerful than humans, and people were subject to them in a variety of ways. They were dependent on the gods (including the minor ones) for health, prosperity, protection, and the like, and so had to please them and try to keep them happy. At the same time the gods needed people to supply them with offerings, keep the temples in good order, and do various things necessary for the well-being of the deities.

The gods were unpredictable and idiosyncratic, and given the rivalries and power struggles among the deities, knowing what they wanted from people was often difficult to determine. As one Mesopotamian poet put it, "I wish I knew that these things were pleasing to a god! What seems good to one's self could be an offense to a god, what in one's own heart seems abominable could be good to one's god. Where might human beings have learned the way of a

---

14. For a useful introductory summary of these matters, see Tammi Schneider, *An Introduction to Ancient Mesopotamian Religion* (Grand Rapids: Eerdmans, 2011).

15. *COS* 1, 450–52.

16. *COS* 1, 390–402.

17. Schneider, *Ancient Mesopotamian Religion*, 98–99.

god?"[18] At a practical level it seems that ordinary people had little access to the major deities, who were worshiped by kings and the rich and powerful. Ordinary people were devoted primarily to a personal god[19] to whom they would pray, bring offerings, and seek help in appeasing other deities whom the worshiper might have offended.

When people experienced trouble such as serious illness, financial reversal, or oppression, they immediately supposed this was the result of some offense they had committed. Often, though, they would be unaware of the offense and would seek help from a diviner to discover which god might be offended and what should be done to appease that deity.[20] In all probability, many found themselves in the situation of the poet who said, "My omens were confused, they were contradictory every day. The prognostication of the diviner and dream interpreter could not explain what I was undergoing."[21]

Sufferers in Mesopotamia described their plight much like Job described his situation, and in neither case does the one suffering discover the reason for the suffering. In both cases the one uttering the complaint claims to have done his religious duty in a careful and appropriate way. The doctrine of **retribution** played a significant role in Mesopotamia, but there is a profound difference between Job and the Mesopotamian texts. Job's friends affirmed the idea of retribution and insisted that he must have done something wrong to cause the suffering, and in this they espoused the view that was presupposed in Mesopotamia. In contrast, Job claimed to be innocent, and the book affirms that Job was correct.

There is more to the work of Yahweh than justice and retribution, but such thinking was foreign to those outside Israel. The possibility of disinterested piety, with which the book of Job begins, would have seemed absurd in the Mesopotamian paradigm. Humans were created to serve the needs and wants of the gods and this was their chief function in the world. The idea of a God who is intrinsically worthy of worship and trust would have seemed ridiculous. The gods in Mesopotamia

---

18. "The Poem of the Righteous Sufferer" (*Ludlul bel nemequi*), trans. by Benjamin Foster, *COS* 1, 486–92. The citation is found on 488.

19. On this see, Schneider, *Ancient Mesopotamian Religion*, 63–65.

20. Such practices are described in the biblical text. In Jonah 1:4–16 the sailors, caught up in a fierce storm at sea, each sought their respective gods and cast lots to find out on whose account the disaster had happened. In 1 Samuel 5–6 the Philistines began having serious problems after they captured the ark of the covenant from the Israelites. They called for priests and diviners to figure out why this was happening and what to do to stop the disaster (6:2). The priests came up with a plan to appease Yahweh, whom they suspected had been offended by the capture of the ark. A third example involves Laban and his efforts to recover the household gods that Rachel had stolen in Genesis 31:30–35.

21. *COS* 1, 487.

were the same mix of good and bad regularly seen in people from the king to the least significant commoner. Job struggled with how the sovereign and omnipotent Lord can be good and just in the light of what happened to him, but this question would have been dismissed by every polytheistic system, as would the idea of one God who was sovereign but also innately good and just. The book of Job, in addition to a much more sophisticated literary structure than is found in any of the compositions from the ancient Near East, breaks new ground as it explores questions that make little sense apart from the Bible's **Yahwistic** theology. In doing so, it presents a polemic against many of the ideas that were presupposed in the cultures around Israel.

Israel's theology was also unique in that Yahweh revealed himself to Israel and explained to them who he is and what he expected of the people he chose for himself. Thus Israel had a basis for morality and practice that was unique in the ancient Near East. Prohibitions against murder, stealing, and adultery were common well before Moses, but they came to Israel with a different sort of authority in that "thus says the Lord" stands behind these commandments.[22] Israel did not know everything about God and how he works—Job and Ecclesiastes make that abundantly clear. They did, though, have Yahweh's self-disclosure that he is good and just and that he is the sovereign Lord. Such claims meant that the struggle of Job or **Qoheleth** in times of difficulty and disorientation would be fundamentally different than would be the case for someone who suffered in Mesopotamia. And the acceptable answers in the two cultures would be quite different as well.

Specific Parallels to Old Testament Wisdom Books[23]

Job

Several Mesopotamian compositions recount the experiences of sufferers unaware of the specific nature of their guilt. The poets de-

---

22.   The Code of Hammurabi begins with a picture that shows Shamash, the sun god, giving this law code to the king, but such examples are rare in Mesopotamia and this kind of revelation does not play a significant role in Mesopotamia. In contrast Yahweh's revelation to his people Israel is fundamental to biblical religion. On this see Moshe Greenberg, "Some Postulates of Biblical Criminal Law," in *Studies in Bible and Jewish Religion Dedicated to Yehezkel Kaufmann on the Occasion of his Seventieth Birthday*, ed. by Menahem Haran (Jerusalem: Magnes, 1960), 5–28; and John Walton, *Ancient Near Eastern Thought and the Old Testament: Introducing the Conceptual World of the Hebrew Bible* (Grand Rapids: Baker, 2006), 295–302.

23.   A discussion of parallels to the biblical wisdom material can be found in most of the major commentaries. Excellent discussion of the Near Eastern parallels for each of the Old Testament wisdom books can be found in *DOTWPW*. Up-to-date translations of most of these texts can be found in *COS* 1, while older translations are available in *ANET*. The Egyptian texts are available in *AEL* as well.

scribe their suffering in ways similar to that of Job, but the nature of the struggle is quite different, largely because of the different theological paradigm within which they are working. The Mesopotamian sufferers never move from the idea that their suffering resulted because they offended a god. Little is offered in these poems beyond patient resignation and the possibility that at some point the gods might provide relief.

In the *Babylonian Theodicy*,[24] the poet dialogues with a friend who defends the traditional way of understanding things, and at points the friend's words resemble those of Job's friends. The sufferer complains about experiencing tragedy and injustice despite his piety while others who disregard the gods fare much better. He sees examples that suggest that a person's situation in life does not depend on piety but on factors that humans cannot understand. His experience suggests that retribution does not always work, and he complains that "Divine purpose is as remote as innermost heaven . . . people cannot understand it."[25] The sufferer wants to know how to ensure a happy life, but cannot figure out how to do that.

Proverbs

Proverb collections[26] from Mesopotamia and Egypt date back to approximately 2600 B.C.,[27] and some are instruction texts in which a father (sometimes a king) gives advice to his son in ways that resemble Proverbs 1–9. Similarities in both subject matter and form exist between these proverbs and the biblical ones. The **aphorism**s generally deal with the basic affairs of life, but a few proverbs include a religious dimension. For example, a Sumerian proverb dating to 1900–1800 B.C. says, "Coveting and reaching out (in greediness) are abominations to Ninurta."[28] Since some of these collections predate the biblical material by many centuries, it is clear that this kind of aphorism existed in the ancient Near East long before Israel existed.

Striking similarities exist between Proverbs 22:17–23:14 and the *Instruction of Amenemope* from Egypt. The question of the relationship between the two continues to be debated, and a final answer must

24. *COS* 1, 492–95. This **Akkadian** composition is known from texts from the neo-Assyrian period (ninth to seventh centuries BC).

25. *COS* 1, 494.

26. For a detailed summary of all the texts paralleling the book of Proverbs, see Kenneth A. Kitchen, "Proverbs 2: Ancient Near Eastern Background," *DOTWPW*, 552–66.

27. Bendt Alster, *Proverbs of Ancient Sumer*, 2 vols. (Bethesda, MD: CDL, 1997); W. G. Lambert, *Babylonian Wisdom Literature* (Oxford: Oxford University Press, 1960), 222–82; *COS*, 1, 563–68.

28. *COS* 1, 567.

await more precise dating of *Amenemope*. Given the close relationship between Solomon and the Egyptian court,[29] borrowing could have taken place in either direction, and studies based on the language of the two collections remain inconclusive. It is clear that there are significant theological differences between the two collections and some have argued that the Egyptian collection reflects a "higher" theology than one normally finds in Egypt. These kinds of arguments are seldom sufficiently objective to answer questions about borrowing. Even the words with which the book of Proverbs begins—"the proverbs of Solomon"—do not resolve the question, since at least some of the sections could have resulted from his collection of the proverbs rather than his authorship.

Irrespective of how those who put the biblical book together got each proverb, the significant and unique thing about the biblical material is the context in which the aphorisms (including Prov. 22:17–23:14) are set. From beginning (1:7 and 2:4–6) to end (31:30), the book affirms the revelatory oversight of God in giving this collection to his people. Throughout the book the providence of God is affirmed (for example, a number of proverbs in chapter 16), as is the importance of trusting in Yahweh. The goal of wisdom is only realized as a person thinks and lives in ways that are consistent with the principles found in this book, and that can only happen when people live in the **fear of the Lord**.[30]

Ecclesiastes

Qoheleth sets forth fundamental issues with which people struggle in the world. He asks questions like whether human life has any meaning or whether there is ultimate justice in the universe. Others in antiquity lived in the same world and wrestled with the same questions, and there are several parallels between Ecclesiastes and the literature of the ancient Near East. Few scholars, though, would argue that Qoheleth borrowed from any of these compositions.

Ecclesiastes makes it clear that such questions cannot be answered by human discovery and the methodology generally reflected in wisdom literature. If they are to be answered at all, it will have to be on the basis of revelation, and that is what sets Israel's religion apart from all the cultures around them.

The Babylonian *Epic of Gilgamesh* relates how Gilgamesh, the legendary king of Uruk, found little fulfillment and satisfaction in his great accomplishments. He and his friend Enkidu sought even greater accomplishments that could fill the void in his life. But nothing they ac-

---

29. According to 1 Kings 3:1, Solomon married one of Pharaoh's daughters.
30. See the discussion of the fear of the Lord in chapter 2 in "Ecclesiastes."

complished brought Gilgamesh the fulfillment he desired. His friend Enkidu was killed, and this set Gilgamesh on a quest to find the secret of immortality. Andrew George says that the story "tells of one man's heroic struggle against death—first for immortal renown through glorious deeds, then for eternal life itself; of his despair when confronted with inevitable failure, and of his eventual realization that the only immortality he may expect is the enduring name afforded by leaving behind some lasting achievement."[31]

Another parallel with Ecclesiastes comes from a song in a group of Egyptian tomb inscriptions known as *Harpers' Songs*. According to Lichtheim, this particular song "lamented the passing of life and urged enjoyment of life while it lasts!"[32] A final significant parallel comes from *Gilgamesh* and calls for the enjoyment of life even as Gilgamesh reflects on the death of his friend and searches for immortality. An alewife gives Gilgamesh advice about how to live in the light of such realities:

> When the gods created mankind
> they fixed Death for mankind,
> and held back Life in their own hands.
> Now you, Gilgamesh, let your belly be full!
> Be happy day and night,
> of each day make a party,
> dance in circles day and night!
> Let your clothes be sparkling clean,
> let your head be clean, wash yourself with water!
> Attend to the little one who holds onto your hand,
> Let a wife delight in your embrace.
> This is the true task of *mankind (?)*.[33]

The parallels with Ecclesiastes are clear, but they are too common to suggest Mesopotamian borrowing. Van der Toorn says, "Reflections on human mortality, the value of friendship, and the advantage of wisdom are the bread and butter of the **sage** all over the ancient Near East—and elsewhere."[34] He adds that Gilgamesh developed these themes in a distinctly Mesopotamian idiom, while Qoheleth developed them in ways consistent with Israel's Yahwistic perspective.

---

31. Andrew George, *The Epic of Gilgamesh* (New York: Barnes & Noble, 1999), xiii.

32. Lichtheim, *AEL*, 1, 193; *COS* 1, 49.

33. Maureen Kovacs, *The Epic of Gilgamesh* (Stanford: Stanford University Press, 1989), 85.

34. Karel van der Toorn, "Echoes of Gilgamesh in the Book of Qoheleth," *Veenhof Anniversary Volume*, ed. W. H. van Soldt, Publications de l'Institut historique-archeologique neerlandais de Stamboul 89 (Leiden: Nederlands Instituut voor het Nabije Oosten, 2001), 511.

Song of Songs

Love poetry[35] from Mesopotamia uses similar language and metaphors as those found in Song of Songs. It has limited value for explicating Song of Songs because it deals largely with sexual encounters between deities and was probably used in rituals intended to stimulate fertility and prosperity. The closest parallels to Song of Songs are Egyptian love poems[36] that date to between 1300 and 1150 B.C. They describe love, passion, and human sexual desire. They use many of the same metaphors found in the Song and deal with many of the same issues, such as fear of losing one's lover, parental and family opposition to the relationship, and fear that the person's beloved will not reciprocate. These poems describe the lover's beauty and the emotional disequilibrium that love for another sometimes creates. Some of the poems describe the delight of being together in a secret place under trees and surrounded by beautiful and fragrant vegetation that protects them from prying eyes.

Love poetry has a long history in the ancient Near East, and the Bible's celebration of human love is neither surprising nor unique. Song of Songs' treatment of romance and intimacy is devoid of the overt eroticism found in many of the other ancient Near Eastern examples. The similarities between Song of Songs and the love poetry of Egypt likely reflect the universals of human experience related to love and romance in most cultures and at most times in human history. As Hess suggests, "Many parallels that do exist do not provide much in the way of exegetical payoff. . . . The reason for this seems to be the universal nature of love poetry."[37]

Basic Resources for Ancient Near Eastern Background

Knowledge of ancient Near Eastern background is not something that one normally acquires in even the best college and seminary programs. Nor will gaining that knowledge be a top priority for a busy pastor or Bible teacher. Fortunately, scholars who specialize in such studies have made much basic information available to those not trained in these disciplines. The resources listed below enable one to develop at least a general understanding of these cultures, and almost all the relevant texts have been translated into English for those who want to delve more deeply into that world. In order to gain sufficient knowledge for preaching and basic Bible teaching, Bible dictionaries and encyclope-

---

35. For a survey of all the ancient Near Eastern parallels, see Gary A. Long, "Song of Songs 2: Ancient Near Eastern Background," *DOTWPW*, 750–60; and the major commentaries.

36. *COS* 1, 125–30; *AEL* 2, 181–93; Michael Fox, *The Song of Songs and the Ancient Egyptian Love Songs* (Madison: University of Wisconsin Press, 1985).

37. Richard Hess, *Song of Songs*, BCOTWP (Grand Rapids: Baker, 2005), 27.

dias will usually provide the basic information about historical or cultural topics. Many commentaries (for example, EBC, NAC, NICOT, NIVAC, WBC, and others) will discuss relevant background material for each passage they consider. Resources such as the NET Bible[38] often include basic information about these matters. While one must carefully check its veracity, a basic search of resources on the Internet will often turn up useful information about ancient Egyptian or Mesopotamian texts or ideas. For example one could search for "marriage contracts in Mesopotamia" or "customs regarding death in Mesopotamia" or "use of horses and chariots in Mesopotamia" and find much interesting information including several things written by reputable scholars.

Bottéro, Jean and Teresa Lavender Fagan. *Religion in Ancient Mesopotamia.* Chicago: University of Chicago, 2001.

Hallo, William, ed. *The Context of Scripture: Canonical Compositions from the Biblical World.* Leiden: Brill, 1997.
This volume provides up-to-date translations of most of the relevant ancient Near Eastern texts.

Keel, Othmar. *The Symbolism of the Biblical World: Ancient Near Eastern Iconography and the Book of Psalms,* Trans. Timothy J. Hallett. Winona Lake, IN: Eisenbrauns, 1997, reprint.
The major focus of the book is on Psalms, but there are many references to the wisdom books as well.

Lambert, W. G. *Babylonian Wisdom Literature.* Oxford: Oxford University Press, 1996.
This volume includes translations of many important wisdom texts from Mesopotamia along with a useful introductory essay about the texts, the thought world reflected in them, and a few comments on parallels with biblical texts.

Lichtheim, Miriam. *Ancient Egyptian Literature.* 3 vols. Berkeley: University of California Press, 1973–80.
These volumes include translations of many of the relevant Egyptian texts.

Nemet-Nejat, Karen. *Daily Life in Ancient Mesopotamia.* Peabody, MA: Hendrickson, 2002.
This is a helpful resource for understanding many aspects of life and culture in Mesopotamia.

---

38. See Appendix 1 on computer resources for the Web address.

Pritchard, James B., ed. *Ancient Near Eastern Texts Relating to the Old Testament*. Princeton, NJ: Princeton University, 3rd ed. with Supplement, 1969.
An older collection of relevant ancient Near Eastern texts .

Schneider, Tammi J. *An Introduction to Ancient Mesopotamian Religion*. Grand Rapids: Eerdmans, 2011.
This is a helpful book on religion in ancient Mesopotamia. It is well done and accessible to those who are not experts in Assyriology.

Silverman, David. *Ancient Egypt*. Oxford: Oxford University Press, 2003.

Van de Mieroop, Marc. *A History of the Ancient Near East ca. 3000–323 B.C.* Oxford: Blackwell, 2nd ed., 2007.

Walton, John. *Ancient Near Eastern Thought and the Old Testament: Introducing the Conceptual World of the Hebrew Bible*. Grand Rapids: Baker, 2006.
This is a helpful book for gaining a basic understanding of ideas and ways of thinking that characterized cultures that surrounded Israel and with whom they interacted.

_____, ed. *Zondervan Illustrated Bible Backgrounds Commentary*, vol. 5. Grand Rapids: Zondervan, 2009.
This commentary series puts a special focus on ancient Near Eastern background information. Volume 5 includes the Old Testament wisdom books.

TEXTUAL CRITICISM: DETERMINING THE BEST TEXT

Introduction

The first five books of the Bible are traditionally attributed to Moses who lived around 1400 B.C., and Old Testament books continued to be produced until approximately 350 B.C. We possess none of these **autograph**s, but only copies dating to many centuries after the original was penned. During the time between the composition of the biblical books and our earliest manuscripts, Scripture was copied by hand. Despite the care with which these scribes did their work, the manuscripts and translations that we have make it clear that the kinds of errors that are typical in any writing or copying of a text occasionally happened with the biblical material.

Several things contributed to occasional errors in copying these documents. The alphabet used to write the biblical texts changed from **paleo-Hebrew script**, to **Aramaic square script** sometime after the Babylonian exile. The Hebrew text was originally written with only consonants,[39] but over time certain consonants came into use to also represent vowels to reduce the possibility of misreading particular words. The use of these **vowel letters** increased over time, but their use was not consistent.[40] Languages change over time,[41] and we know that the geographical separation of the tribes produced dialect changes within Israel.[42] Such things increase the likelihood of errors in the copying process.

Textual criticism is the discipline that seeks to examine all the available evidence and determine the reading of the text that most likely reflects the original. The evidence used by textual critics consists of two kinds: external and internal. **External evidence** includes Hebrew manuscripts and ancient translations of the Old Testament into other languages. **Internal evidence** comes from the text itself and includes things like unexpected words, forms, or syntactical peculiarities. It also may also result from theological tensions or literary irregularities in the text.

The Hebrew text that we have today is excellent, but some textual differences do exist.[43] These involve only about ten percent of the Hebrew text, and most are minor differences like spelling that do not impact the meaning of a passage. There is never an instance where a major doctrine hinges on a disputed reading.

Unlike the situation with the New Testament, where abundant manuscript evidence exists, we possess few ancient manuscripts of the Hebrew Bible.[44] Until the discovery of the Dead Sea Scrolls in the 1940s and 1950s, the earliest extant Hebrew biblical texts dated to about A.D. 1000,[45] and textual criticism had to be done largely on the basis of ancient translations of the Hebrew Bible. The scrolls from **Qumran** and other ancient manuscript discoveries have now provided much-needed evidence for

---

39. The structure of Hebrew and other Semitic languages makes this possible, and anyone fluent in the language can easily supply the vowels needed to read and understand the text.

40. Originally these vowel letters were used to represent long vowels, but in many of the Dead Sea manuscripts they are used to represent even reduced vowel sounds.

41. Trying to read a passage from a 1611 version of the King James Bible makes this clear.

42. The *sibboleth/shibboleth* incident in Judges 12 illustrates this.

43. It is important to emphasize that these errors have to do with the copying and transmission of the text through the centuries rather than the authority and inerrancy of the original text.

44. According to P. D. Wegner ("Text, Textual Criticism," *DOTWPW*, 796) this includes about 222 manuscripts from Qumran, a few other early Hebrew manuscripts, and about 200 Hebrew manuscripts from medieval times or later.

45. A major reason for this seems to be that when a synagogue scroll had to be replaced, it was destroyed rather than simply discarded.

the history of the Hebrew text and its integrity in the period between the Qumran texts (about 300 B.C. to A.D. 350) and the **Masoretic text** (MT), which was completed some time around A.D. 950.

The consonantal text that served as the basis for the work of the **Masoretes** comprises the majority of biblical texts discovered there, and this text was recognized as authoritative by both Judaism and the Christian church. The Qumran manuscripts show remarkable congruence with the MT and attest to the care with which the scribes copied the biblical text. This clearly affirms the integrity of the text that has come down to us. While the MT is recognized as clearly superior to any of the other ancient witnesses, it does not always retain the best reading, and each case must be examined on its own merits. Thus textual criticism constitutes an essential task of exegesis.

The Task and Basic Principles

Decisions about the best Old Testament text must take into account the external evidence from the manuscripts and versions as well as internal evidence resulting from careful analysis of the text. Basic principles for evaluating all the evidence can be found in the books listed at the end of this section. In general the more difficult reading is to be preferred (assuming, of course, that the difficult reading makes sense). In general the shorter reading is to be preferred, but decisions must take into account the totality of the data (both external and internal), and most would argue that the preferred reading is the one that best explains how the other readings developed. The practice of textual criticism includes a scientific component, but it also involves creative intuition and common sense. A reading that brings a high level of confidence should be supported by both external and internal evidence.

A variety of scribal errors, both intentional and unintentional, are sometimes found in the text.[46] For example, the scribe's eye occasionally skipped from one occurrence of a word to a second nearby occurrence and left out the intervening words;[47] sometimes they copied a word or phrase twice,[48] and in a few instances they replaced what they saw as theologically inappropriate words in the text, though they noted when they did that. An awareness of the kinds of mistakes to which scribes were susceptible allows an exegete to better evaluate the possibilities for making text-critical decisions.

---

46. Examples of these can be found in most basic discussions of textual criticism. For example, see the section on "Scribal Errors" in Ellis Brotzman and Eric Tully, *Old Testament Textual Criticism: A Practical Introduction* (Grand Rapids: Baker, 2016), 117–29.

47. A practice known as **homoeoarcton.**

48. A practice known as **dittography.**

Occasionally it is very difficult to make sense of the text as we have it and none of the witnesses provide sufficient clarification to resolve the dilemma. Sometimes a conjectural **emendation** or reconstruction of the text may be necessary. It is, however, critical that we understand what we are doing in such instances and communicate this to those we are teaching. Our reconstructed text can never provide us with the same authoritative basis for teaching as those texts where the correct reading is undisputed.

While textual criticism involves a number of rather complex tasks, much of this work has been done for us by experts and is generally available to non-specialists. These resources make it possible for those without the technical knowledge of the expert textual critic to understand the issues in dispute and make informed decisions as they analyze, interpret, and teach passages from the Old Testament. Checking a number of English translations of a passage[49] will often enable a reader to identify textual issues and give a sense of the implications for understanding the passage. Notes in the translations can further clarify the issue and explain the basis for their translation.

The Masoretic notes relevant for textual criticism, along with the more important variants from the versions, are presented in the critical apparatus at the bottom of each page in **BHS**.[50] This will often help to clarify the issue sufficiently for exegetical purposes, and an important aspect of careful study involves examining the Hebrew text with the help of the notes in *BHS*. A very helpful resource for understanding textual issues is found in the NET notes provided with Lumina's *NET Bible* software.[51] Often these resources provide enough information to allow an exegete to make an informed decision about the text. The critical commentaries[52] also discuss text critical issues and explain the commentator's rationale for a decision about the text. Sufficient resources are available to enable any serious student of Scripture to understand these textual issues in order to responsibly understand and teach that text.

Two examples of text-critical issues involved will be noted here. Certain Hebrew letters differ by only a small stroke (ד and ר; ב and כ;

---

49. A convenient way to do this is to use a Bible software program, since they often come with a number of translations. See Appendix 1 on computer resources.

50. Several useful guides for understanding the information in BHS are listed at the end of this section.

51. See Appendix 1. The Web address for this is netbible.org.

52. For Job, the most helpful commentaries with respect to textual criticism issues are Dhorme and Clines (see full references at the end of this chapter). For Proverbs, Waltke is the particularly helpful. Longman and Fox are also helpful, though Fox tends to be more open to conjectural emendations. Both Longman and Garrett discuss these issues for Ecclesiastes and Song of Songs.

ʾ and ו; ב and כ; ה and ח), and such letters can be easily confused.[53] A possible example of this occurs in Proverbs 9:1, which reads in the MT:

חָכְמוֹת בָּנְתָה בֵיתָהּ חָצְבָה עַמּוּדֶיהָ שִׁבְעָה
Wisdom has built her house; she has hewn her seven pillars

While the MT is not unclear or confusing, "hewn" seems like an unexpected parallel to "built" in the first part of the verse, and the Septuagint, several **Targum**s, and the Syriac versions all read "erected" rather than "hewn." The difference between these readings and the MT is the difference between ה and ח in the consonantal text. It is possible that the scribe wrote חצבה "hewn" instead of הצבה, "erected."[54] In this instance external evidence from the ancient translations supports what seems to be the preferred reading, "erected," and it is easy to see how the scribe could have confused the two letters or simply written one letter carelessly. Thus the MT can be appropriately corrected with some confidence.

Sometimes a scribe heard a word but wrote a similar sounding word instead,[55] and a possible example of this is found in Job 13:15. The translation of the verse in ESV is "Though he slay me, I will hope in him; yet I will argue my ways to his face." NRSV[56] presents a very different translation: "See, he will kill me; I have no hope; but I will defend my ways to his face." The consonantal text used by the Masoretes has the negative particle לֹא (lōʾ), giving rise to translations like NRSV and reflecting the loss of hope on Job's part. On the other hand the scribes were aware of a tradition that presupposed the reading לוֹ (lô), "for him," or "in him," which leads to the more positive and hopeful translation of KJV, ESV, NIV and others. In such instances[57] the Masoretes preserved both "what is written" (the **ketib**) and "what is to be read" (the **qerʾe**). In this case there is external/textual evidence (**LXX**, the Syriac, and Qumran) supporting the qerʾe. Many scholars, however, feel that this is insufficient for deciding between the two readings, and as most recognize, it is the reader's understanding of the context that will determine which

---

53. Hebrew writing before the Babylonian exile used a different script than the Aramaic characters that have been used since the exile, and textual critics must also be aware of the letters that were easily confused in the earlier writing.

54. See Bruce Waltke, *Proverbs 1–15*, NICOT (Grand Rapids: Eerdmans, 2004), 426, n. 1.

55. A practice known as **homophony**.

56. Along with many other modern translations.

57. In most of these instances the distinction was between the consonantal text (what was written) and the traditional way the text was supposed to be read. The Masoretes were careful to preserve both traditions.

reading is preferred.[58] Longman, Walton, and others see in Job's previous words a deep skepticism and even despair, and so argue that the MT preserves the best reading.[59]

Andersen, on the other hand, sees the trajectory of Job's speeches as hopeful and moving toward a deeper faith and concludes that his words reflect hope not despair. He says Job "expects to be vindicated. A positive meaning is absolutely required."[60] While I generally agree with Andersen about Job 13:15, it is important to recognize the uncertainty surrounding this familiar verse. An awareness of such difficulties can be frustrating, but it does alert us to the importance of caution in exegesis and proclamation. Setting doctrine or practical application on the foundation of an unclear text is dangerous. Carefully studying the texts in Hebrew along with appropriate resources plays an important role in avoiding this danger.

The Hebrew Text of the Wisdom Books

A text as difficult as the Hebrew text of Job creates numerous opportunities for scholars to emend the text and change it into something that makes sense to them. Many scholars today conclude that the Hebrew text of Job is among the worst preserved in the Hebrew Bible, and that textual problems constitute a significant part of the difficulty in translating and understanding the book.

The book of Proverbs contains a number of proverbs that are cryptic and obscure, and as we move farther away from the context in which they originated and were used, that obscurity increases. Thus a number of biblical proverbs are less than transparent. It is difficult to know the degree to which this reflects problems with the Hebrew text or if our inability to understand them results from our limited knowledge of ancient Israelite images and culture. It is unclear whether the issues in this book are interpretive or textual.

The Hebrew texts of Ecclesiastes and Song of Songs are without major textual problems. Difficulties in translating and interpreting these books usually result more from unusual words and the subject matter of the books than from textual issues.

---

58. Robert Gordis, *The Book of Job: Commentary, New Translation, and Special Studies* (New York: Jewish Theological Seminary of America, 1978), 144. He notes that in the second century AD, the rabbis were aware of both readings and the issue was a matter of debate.

59. Tremper Longman, III, *Job*, BCOTWP (Grand Rapids: Baker, 2012), 208; John Walton, *Job*, NIVAC (Downers Grove, IL: InterVarsity, 2012), 178–79.

60. Francis Andersen, *Job*, TOTC (Downers Grove, IL: InterVarsity, 1974), 166.

Basic Resources for Textual Criticism

Brotzman, Ellis R. *Old Testament Textual Criticism*. Grand Rapids: Baker, 1994.

Kelley, Page, Timothy Crawford, and Daniel Mynatt. *The Masorah of Biblical Hebraica Stuttgartensis: Introduction and Annotated Glossary*. Grand Rapids: Eerdmans, 1998.

McCarter, P. Kyle, Jr. *Textual Criticism*. Philadelphia: Fortress, 1986.

Tov, Emanuel. *Textual Criticism of the Hebrew Bible*. 3rd edition. Minneapolis: Fortress, 2012.

Wegner, Paul. *A Student's Guide to Textual Criticism of the Bible: Its History, Methods and Results*. Downers Grove, IL: InterVarsity, 2006.

Würthwein, Ernst. *The Text of the Old Testament*. Revised and expanded by Alexander A. Fischer. Translated by Erroll F. Rhodes. 3rd edition. Grand Rapids: Eerdmans, 2014.

TRANSLATION AND DEVELOPING A SENSE OF THE CONTEXT

It is essential to become familiar with the text that will be the focus of teaching or preaching. Ideally, this will involve making a translation from Hebrew, which will then serve as the basis for a more detailed exegetical study. Multiple readings of the text will allow the interpreter to get a feeling for the text to more easily identify literary patterns and word plays and to recognize grammatical and syntactical peculiarities. Since understanding context plays such a critical role in interpretation, the preliminary reading should include surrounding material, not just the passage that will be the basis for teaching or preaching. This means that preparation for teaching material from Job, Ecclesiastes, or Song of Songs would involve reading the entire book, while teaching from Proverbs 1–9 would require reading at least that portion of Proverbs. Proverbs 10–31 lacks an easily determined context or the logical development of thought, but reading the entire book several times before focusing on a smaller unit or topic would be useful in helping the interpreter gain a better sense of the context by understanding the author's major points and arguments.

It is helpful to outline the book or at least the major sections and summarize the contents in your own words. Sharpen the focus on words and phrases that recur throughout the material and on words that seem particularly important for understanding the author's message. Identify words and phrases that seem ambiguous or unclear. Note the difficulties and issues on which the interpretation hinges. As your understanding of the basic teaching of the passage develops, identify the major teaching of the section and the key points made in the literary unit. Do as much of this reading as possible from the Hebrew text, but familiarity with the passage may have to be developed by reading it multiple times using several different English translations, including some that reflect different translation philosophies. This is preliminary to doing a detailed study of the pericope, but it plays an essential role in accurately understanding the message the biblical author is teaching. Key words, syntactical features, and the central issues on which the interpretation of the passage depend can be identified, and these will then become the focus of a more in-depth study.

Resources for Translation and Exegesis

Concordances
Using computer concordances is much faster than using a print concordance and allows an exegete to secure a great deal of information about word usage, grammatical features, and syntax easily. The major Bible software programs include this feature.[61] The best print concordances are these:

Even-Shoshan, Abraham, ed. *A New Concordance of the Old Testament*, 2nd ed. Introduction by John Sailhamer. Grand Rapids: Baker, 1989.

Kohlenberger, John R. III and James A Swanson. *The Hebrew-English Concordance to the Old Testament*. Grand Rapids: Zondervan, 1998.

Language Tools
These intermediate-level resources are designed for students who have completed a study of beginning Hebrew.

Arnold, Bill T., and John H. Choi. *A Guide to Biblical Syntax*. Cambridge: Cambridge University, 2003.

Beckman, John. *Williams' Hebrew Syntax: An Outline*. 3rd ed. Toronto: University of Toronto, 2007.

Joüon, Paul. *A Grammar of Biblical Hebrew*. Corrected 1st ed. Trans. and rev. by T. Muraoka. 2 vols. Pontifical Biblical Institute, 1993.

---

61. See the discussion on computer resources by Austen Dutton in Appendix 1.

Kautszch, E., ed. *Gesenius' Hebrew Grammar.* 2ⁿᵈ English ed. Rev. by A. E. Cowley. Oxford: Clarendon Press, 1910.

Van de Merwe, Christo H. J., Jackie A. Naudé, and Jan H. Kroeze. *A Biblical Hebrew Grammar.* Sheffield: Sheffield Academic Press, 1999.

Waltke, Bruce K., and M. O'Connor. *An Introduction to Biblical Hebrew Syntax.* Winona Lake, IN: Eisenbrauns, 1990.

Lexicons
Some of these are available electronically and BDB is often included with some Bible software programs.[62]

Brown, Francis, S. R. Driver, and Charles A. Briggs. *A Hebrew and English Lexicon of the Old Testament.* Oxford: Clarendon Press, 1907. (BDB)
This was the standard Old Testament lexicon for many years until the publication of more modern (and more expensive) lexicons made it somewhat obsolete. It is difficult to use because every word is listed under the three-consonant root rather than alphabetically. The English glosses are often archaic and resemble King James English rather than modern English usage. This lexicon was published in 1907 and does not reflect recent research done on word meanings. It is often lacking when it comes to definitions of unusual words in the Hebrew Bible. At the same time the lexicon regularly lists every occurrence of many Hebrew words and so can function like a concordance in many instances.

Clines, David J. A., ed. *The Dictionary of Classical Hebrew.* 8 vols. Sheffield: Sheffield Academic Press, 1994–2011.
This multivolume work is excellent and up to date. The major drawback is its cost.

Holladay, William L. *A Concise Hebrew and Aramaic Lexicon of the Old Testament,* new edition. Leiden: Brill, 2000. An abridgement of *HALOT.*

Koehler, Ludwig, and Walter Baumgartner. *The Hebrew and Aramaic Lexicon of the Old Testament (HALOT).* 5 vols. Rev. by Walter Baumgartner and Johann Jakob Stamm; trans. and ed. by M. E. J. Richardson. Leiden: E. J. Brill, 2001.

---

62. See Appendix 1.

This lexicon is available in an electronic version as well as in a two-volume Study Edition and a more expensive five-volume version. The definitions reflect the latest scholarship. Despite the cost, this lexicon has become the new standard.

Word Study Tools

Barr, James. *The Semantics of Biblical Language* (London: Oxford, 1961).
This volume had a major impact on the way biblical studies and particularly word studies were done. It facilitated a major change from the study of words based on etymology and shifted it to word meanings based on the way words are used in texts.

Harris, R. Laird, Gleason Archer, and Bruce Waltke, eds. *Theological Wordbook of the Old Testament (TWOT)*, 2 vols. Chicago: Moody Publishers, 2003.
This is a good place to begin a study of a word of interest. The articles are well-done and deal with aspects of meaning that are relevant for pastors and teachers.

Silva, Moisés. *Biblical Words and their Meaning: An Introduction to Lexical Semantics,* revised and expanded edition. Grand Rapids: Zondervan, 1995.

VanGemeren, Willem A., ed. *NIDOTTE*, 5 vols. Grand Rapids: Zondervan, 1997. This very helpful resource provides a more through and nuanced discussion of important Hebrew words than *TWOT*.

Walton, John H. "Principles for Productive Word Study," in *NIDOTTE*, vol. 1, 158–68.

Other Resources

Chisholm, Robert, Jr. *From Exegesis to Exposition: A Practical Guide to Using Biblical Hebrew*. Grand Rapids: Baker, 1998.

Stuart, Douglas. *Old Testament Exegesis*. 4th ed. Louisville: Westminster John Knox, 2009.
This extremely useful resource covers virtually every aspect of Old Testament exegesis and identifies the major resources and tools that are available, including on line and computer re-sources. The author leads the student through every step in the process and even differentiates between what should be done for a full-blown exegetical research paper and what is sufficient and realistic for preparing a sermon.

CONSIDERING THE CONTRIBUTION OF OTHERS

It is important to do your own work with the text rather than simply pick and choose from the insights and opinions of others, but it is also essential to approach the task with **humility** and openness both to the text and to the insights of those whose work reflects strengths that we lack. Commentaries and similar resources must be used with a critical eye and with an awareness of the presuppositions of those who write them, but they are indispensable tools to complement our lack of knowledge about important issues like history and culture, philology, grammar, syntax, literary structure and even a sense of the context in which a text occurs.

Good interpretation also needs to be done in community and one aspect of that includes an awareness of tradition and opinions about the meaning of the text, both today and throughout history.

General Introductions

Bartholomew, Craig G., and Ryan P. O'Dowd, *Old Testament Wisdom Literature: A Theological Introduction* Downers Grove, IL: InterVarsity, 2011.
> While there are several good introductions to the wisdom literature, this one is one of the best in terms of its discussion of the Old Testament world and the worldview of the sages. The authors also provide helpful suggestions about the relevance of the material for today.

Brown, William P. *Character in Crisis: A Fresh Approach to the Wisdom Literature of the Old Testament*. Grand Rapids: Eerdmans, 1996.

Longman, Tremper III, and Peter Enns, eds. *Dictionary of the Old Testament Wisdom, Poetry & Writings*. Downers Grove, IL: InterVarsity, 2008.
> This is an excellent resource for almost every aspect of the wisdom books. It includes articles about each book and the major interpretive approaches throughout history. There are excellent discussions of **genre**, poetry, ancient Near Eastern background, and virtually every other topic of relevance.

Commentaries and Related Studies

Among the numerous commentaries and special studies available on the wisdom books, I have found the following to be especially useful:

Job
Alden, Robert L. *Job*. NAC. Nashville: Broadman & Holman, 1993.

Andersen, Francis I. *Job: An Introduction and Commentary*. TOTC. Downers Grove, IL: InterVarsity, 1976.

Clines, David I. *Job 1–20*. WBC. Waco, TX: Word, 1989.

_____. *Job 21–37*. WBC. Nashville: Nelson, 2006.

_____. *Job 38–42*. WBC. Nashville: Nelson, 2011.

Gordis, Robert. *The Book of Job: Commentary New Translation and Special Studies*. New York: Jewish Theological Seminary of America, 1978.

Hartley, John E. *The Book of Job*. NICOT. Grand Rapids: Eerdmans, 1988.

Longman, Tremper, III. *Job*. BCOTW. Grand Rapids: Baker, 2012.

Reyburn, William D. *A Handbook on Job*. New York: United Bible Societies, 1997.

Walton, John H. *Job*. NIVAC. Grand Rapids: Zondervan, 2012.

Zuck, Roy B., ed. *Sitting with Job: Selected Studies on the Book of Job*. Grand Rapids: Baker, 1992.
 A collection of useful studies on Job.

Proverbs

Bartholomew, Craig G. *Reading Proverbs with Integrity*. Cambridge: Grove Books, 2001.

Estes, Daniel J. *Hear My Son: Teaching and Learning in Proverbs 1–9*. New Studies in Biblical Theology. Grand Rapids: Eerdmans, 1997.

Fox, Michael V. *Proverbs 1–9*. AB. Vol. 18A. New York: Doubleday, 2000.

_____. *Proverbs 10–31*. AB. Vol. 18B. New Haven: Yale University Press, 2009.

Garrett, Duane A. *Proverbs, Ecclesiastes, Song of Songs*. NAC. Vol. 14. Nashville: Broadman, 1993.

Kidner, Derek. *Proverbs*, TOTC. Downers Grove, IL: InterVarsity Press, 1964.

Longman, Tremper, III. *How to Read Proverbs*. Downers Grove, IL: InterVarsity, 2002.

_____. *Proverbs*. BCOTWP. Grand Rapids: Baker, 2006.

Reyburn, William D. and Euan McG. Fry. *A Handbook on Proverbs*. New York: United Bible Societies, 2000.

Waltke, Bruce K. *The Book of Proverbs: Chapters 1–15*. NICOT. Grand Rapids: Eerdmans, 2004.

_____. *The Book of Proverbs: Chapters 15–31*. NICOT. Grand Rapids: Eerdmans, 2005.

Zuck, Roy B. ed. *Learning from the Sages: Selected Studies on the Book of Proverbs*. Grand Rapids: Baker, 1995.
A collection of useful studies on Proverbs.

Ecclesiastes
Bartholomew, Craig G. *Ecclesiastes*. BCOTWP. Grand Rapids: Baker, 2009.

Curtis, Edward M. *Ecclesiastes and Song of Songs*. TTC. Grand Rapids: Baker, 2013.

Eaton, Michael A. *Ecclesiastes*. TOTC. Downers Grove, IL: InterVarsity, 1983.

Garrett, Duane. *Proverbs, Ecclesiastes, Song of Songs*. NAC. Nashville: Broadman, 1993.

Longman, Tremper, III. *The Book of Ecclesiastes*. NICOT. Grand Rapids: Eerdmans, 1998.

Ogden, Graham S. *Qoheleth*. Sheffield: Sheffield Phoenix Press, 2nd ed., 2007.

_____, and Lynell Zogbo. *A Handbook on Ecclesiastes*. New York: United Bible Societies, 1997.

Ryken, Philip G. *Ecclesiastes: Why Everything Matters*. Preaching the Word. Wheaton, IL: Crossway, 2010.

Seow, C. L. *Ecclesiastes*. AB. New York: Doubleday, 1997.

Zuck, Roy B., ed. *Reflecting With Solomon: Selected Studies on the Book of Ecclesiastes*. Grand Rapids: Baker, 1994.
A collection of useful studies on Ecclesiastes.

Song of Songs
Curtis, Edward M. *Ecclesiastes and Song of Songs*. TTC. Grand Rapids: Baker, 2013.

Estes, Daniel. *The Song of Songs*. AOTC. Downers Grove, IL: InterVarsity, 2010.

Exum, J. Cheryl. *Song of Songs*. OTL. Louisville: Westminster John Knox, 2005.

Garrett, Duane. *Song of Songs/Lamentations*. WBC. Nashville: Nelson, 2004.

Gledhill, Tom. *The Message of the Song of Songs*. BST. Downers Grove, IL: InterVarsity, 1994.

Hess, Richard. *Song of Songs*. BCOTWP. Grand Rapids: Baker, 2005.

Longman, Tremper, III, *Song of Songs*. NICOT. Grand Rapids: Eerdmans, 2001.

Murphy, Roland E. *The Song of Songs*. Hermeneia. Minneapolis: Fortress, 1990.

4

INTERPRETING THE WISDOM BOOKS

The Chapter at a Glance

Wisdom Literature: General Guidelines for Interpretation

Guidelines for Interpreting Individual Wisdom Books

- Job
- Proverbs
- Ecclesiastes
- Song of Songs

WISDOM LITERATURE: GENERAL GUIDELINES FOR INTERPRETATION

EXEGESIS INVOLVES A SERIES OF INTERRELATED TASKS. There is interplay between **genre**, context, and word meaning, since each element influences the other in a sort of spiral that leads to a more precise understanding of a passage. The preparation for interpretation described in the previous chapter has laid a foundation in terms of addressing such questions as most likely form of the Hebrew text. The careful reading of the text should help identify the broader context in which the passage of interest is situated and understand how the passage functions in that context. This should clarify the key themes and the major teaching points of the pericope. Literary structure should begin to emerge along with an awareness of the key words in the passage that will require more detailed study. Such studies should shed light on the author's purpose in writing or collecting the material and the key teachings of the passage.[1]

While there are many different analytical procedures that may be useful in a particular passage, only a few especially important ones will be noted below:

- The repetition of words can alert us to points of emphasis, and the author's use of those words in other contexts can sometimes clarify the author's point. The use of words that have special significance elsewhere in the Old Testament can lead to a deeper insight into the meaning or a passage. For example, the Hebrew word הֶבֶל (*hebel*), "puff of air, vanity," is used about eighty times in the Hebrew Bible, with half of those occurrences in Ecclesiastes. A careful study of this word should begin by examining its use outside Ecclesiastes. *Hebel* is regularly used of things that are insubstantial or transient.[2] Idols and foreign nations are *hebel* because their help never materializes, but vaporizes like a puff of smoke, and trusting them is as pointless as trying to capture the wind. The word is used in Job of futile and meaningless words and arguments (Job 5:7 [Heb. 6] 27:12; 35:16). It is used in Ecclesiastes 6:11 of vows that are never kept and that never amount to anything. This gives us a general sense of what **Qoheleth** is talking about, but special attention must be given to the word's use in Ecclesiastes.[3]

- Determining the meaning of key themes like "**fear of the Lord/ God**" is important, and this will require an examination of the term throughout the Old Testament, though the particular focus needs to be on its use in the wisdom literature. As Hubbard points out, wisdom literature has its own way of looking at life, and terms like תּוֹרָה, "law," "instruction," frequently have slightly different nuances than they have elsewhere in the Hebrew Bible.[4] In this instance, additional scrutiny will need to be given to the term's

---

1. Douglas Stuart, *Old Testament Exegesis*, 4th ed. (Louisville: Westminster John Knox, 2009) and Robert Chisholm, *From Exegesis to Exposition* (Grand Rapids: Baker, 1998) provide step-by-step instruction about exactly how one should proceed in doing exegesis.

2. For example, Job 7:16 and Proverbs 31:30.

3. See the discussion "Ecclesiastes Declares That All Is *hebel*," chap. 2.

4. David Hubbard, *Proverbs*, TCC (Dallas, TX: Word, 1989), 25–26.

use in Ecclesiastes, because a few scholars argue that the term has a unique meaning in this book.[5]

- Background studies can clarify the author's social and cultural context and bring us closer to what the author's words would have meant to a reader in ancient Israel.[6] Because images were prohibited in Israel, words for "image" like צֶלֶם or פֶּסֶל would have a decidedly negative connotation to an Old Testament audience, while such words would have been heard in a much more positive way by people in Mesopotamia or Egypt, where images were a regular part of religion. A person would have great difficulty understanding the absurdity of putting "a gold ring in a pig's nose" (Prov. 11:22) without understanding the extremely negative connotations of "pig" in ancient Israel. The Hebrew word נֶפֶשׁ, "life, person," is translated "soul" in many older English translations, and this communicates something in a church context today that is very different than what was understood by the author's original audience. The same is true of words like "righteousness" or "justice." Often the Hebrew words have much broader semantic ranges than is suggested by the theological contexts to which the words are sometimes confined today.[7]

- While the first task of exegesis is to "read out" the meaning of a passage, it is also important to recognize that the text comes to us in a canonical context and is part of what the believing community has recognized as revelation from God. It is, then, true and authoritative for God's people. The Old Testament is diverse, and books sometimes stand in tension as they approach the same issue from different perspectives.[8] There is, though, a coherence that exists because the material comes from God. Sometimes matters not addressed in one passage will be addressed elsewhere, and it may be appropriate to draw from other passages to reflect the broader biblical teaching on an issue. Parallel passages must be used carefully, and it is essential to establish that the passages are actually related. A clear connection between the passages can be established through similar wording or themes or in other ways. In interpreting and teaching a passage it is important to remember the progressive character of God's revelation to his people.

---

5. For example, Tremper Longman, III, *Ecclesiastes*, NICOT (Grand Rapids: Eerdmans, 1998), 123–4.

6. See "The Importance of Ancient Near East Background in Interpreting Wisdom Literature" in chap. 3.

7. See "Word Study Tools" in chapter 3.

8. Bruce Waltke, *An Old Testament Theology* (Grand Rapids: Zondervan, 2007), 49–60.

Old Testament authors were not aware of details about Jesus or theological developments that could only be understood in the light of what Jesus did. New Testament ideas cannot simply be imported back into an Old Testament passage,[9] nor can it be supposed that Moses was aware of the prophecies of Isaiah. Earlier passages can sometimes legitimately shed light on later ones, but the reverse is seldom the case. It can though be valuable to compare early and later passages to show how theological ideas developed over time.

- It is essential to interpret each text in light of the characteristics of wisdom literature, poetry, and **proverb** that were noted in chapters 1 and 2.[10] Wisdom focuses on tiny slices of life rather than comprehensive and exhaustive discussions of life, and wisdom emphasizes the importance of living according to the order that **Yahweh** designed into the universe even as it sets before us the complexity of life in the world.

- Wisdom texts must be interpreted in the light of the major themes that permeate the wisdom books. These include things like the centrality of the fear of the Lord, his sovereignty and his providence that operate over all of life, and the responsibility of human beings to choose wisdom and live it out in the world. There is also the recognition that evil, injustice, and oppression are realities in the world we inhabit. The wisdom books do not analyze the world theologically, but we recognize the world they describe as the same fallen world in which we live.

- The sages recognized the essential importance of application and balance in living. It is important to remember that wisdom must be applied to life and that an important goal of wisdom is skill in living according to **Yahweh's order**.

GUIDELINES FOR INTERPRETING INDIVIDUAL WISDOM BOOKS

Wisdom literature is characterized by great diversity. Job is a narrative story, but consists mostly of poetry. It is, though, made up of several different genres, and includes many proverbs. The book of Proverbs is largely made up of various kinds of proverbs, though there are several

---

9. For example, the New Testament teaching about the resurrection of the body should not be imposed on Job 19:6. Job's desire for a mediator or advocate to help him in his dispute should not be understood in terms of Jesus or the Holy Spirit.

10. See "Wisdom's Genres: Poetry and Proverb," chap. 1.

different kinds of poems as well. Ecclesiastes is largely poetic, but it also includes many proverbs. Song of Songs consists almost exclusively of love poetry, though it is not clear whether the book communicates a coherent story. The poetry in each book should be interpreted in ways that are consistent with the nature and purposes of poetry,[11] and the proverbs in each book should be understood in ways that reflect the characteristics of that genre.[12]

Job

The book of Job is filled with difficulties and uncertainties.[13] Rare words and peculiar grammar contribute to uncertainties in virtually every poetic passage. The poetry impacts us with diverse and intense emotions as Job moves from points of despair and confusion to points of remarkable hope. The immense contrast between the patient Job of the prologue in chapters 1 and 2 and the Job of the poetry, who both complains to God and holds on to him in trust is striking. Despite these things, I would argue that the book of Job is a unified composition and should be interpreted essentially as we have it in the **Masoretic Text**. I think such an approach is justified because, as Greenberg points out, "the literary complexity of the book is consistent with and appropriate to the nature of the issues with which it deals."[14]

Interpret Individual Passages in the Context of the Entire Book

The narrative frame created by the prose prologue (Job 1–2) and epilogue (Job 42) sets the context for the entire book. The basic literary structure is clear and further defines the context within which the poetic dialogues must be understood. Certain givens are established for the debates as Job is described as a man who is blameless and upright and who fears God and turns from evil (Job 1:1, 8), and this assessment of Job is affirmed at the end of the book in Job 42:7–8. The prologue also sets the context for the debates as the Accuser, in Job 1:9, challenges both God and his appraisal of Job by arguing that Job's excellence reflects self-interest. He is pious only because of the blessings he receives in return for it. Job's intense complaint in chapter 3 sets the context for understanding the debates between Job and his friends in

---

11.   See "The Nature of Hebrew Poetry," chap. 1.

12.   See "The Nature of a Proverb," chap. 1.

13.   For other important guidelines for interpreting Job, see Greg W. Parsons, "Guidelines for Understanding and Proclaiming Job," *Bib Sac* 151 (1994), 393–413, and C. Hassell Bullock, *An Introduction to the Old Testament Poetic Books* (Chicago: Moody, 2nd rev. ed., 2007).

14.   Moshe Greenberg, "Job," in *The Literary Guide to the Bible*, eds. Robert Alter and Frank Kermode (Cambridge, MA: Belnap, 1987), 284.

chapters 4–27 and for Job's further comments in Job 29–31. It also sets the context for both the Elihu speeches (Job 32–37) and the Yahweh speeches (Job 38–41).

"Fearing God" is a particularly important theme in the book. The prologue makes it clear that Job's piety consists in his "fearing God and turning from evil" (1:1, 8; 2:3). The poem in chapter 28 recognizes the failure of these sages to discover why Job suffered and concludes in Job 28:28 that the essence of human wisdom does not lie in discovering answers to such questions, but in fearing God and turning from evil both in times of calamity and in prosperity.

Interpreting the individual passages in the context of the entire book is essential for keeping an appropriate balance in understanding the message of the book. I regularly encounter students in classes or churches who are only familiar with the Job of the prose prologue and epilogue.[15] As a result, the message of the book is reduced to an impressive—but sometimes discouraging—example of taking whatever life brings with patience and faith and with the confidence that everything will be restored in the end. Often, Job's struggle is not even mentioned, but this is the very point at which the book resonates with those who are having difficulty understanding how God can be good and just, given the painful and unjust things they are experiencing. As Parsons notes, "Preachers who ignore the dialogue or try to pull some principle without an awareness of the immediate and overall context are in danger of not only distorting the story of Job but also misrepresenting (however unwittingly) the message for today."[16]

Setting each passage in the context of the book can also help in evaluating what is said by Job and the friends in particular speeches. Much of the dialogue is characterized by intense emotion rather than calm, carefully reasoned discussion. Many things the friends said are generally true and cannot be dismissed out of hand as false. The problem involved their incorrect and inappropriate application of the principles to Job rather than the innate falsity of their words. Paul quotes Eliphaz (Job 5:13) in 1 Corinthians 3:19. The author of Hebrews (Heb. 12:5–11) affirms Eliphaz's points about discipline in Job 5:17 and Elihu's comments in Job 33:5–11. And not everything said by Job is true. He acknowledged that some of his pronouncements were made without understanding (Job 42:3), and he repented for those statements. He also admitted that some of his words were rash and simply reflected his pain and he insisted that such words should not be viewed as theological statements that need to be challenged and corrected (Job 6:3, 25–26).

---

15. This is also true of many sermons I have heard on Job.

16. Greg W. Parsons, "Guidelines for Understanding and Proclaiming Job," *Bib Sac* 151 (1994), 395.

Interpret the Book Recognizing That It Is Poetry

The emotion of Job's lament in chapter 3 is powerfully communicated through the poetry, and this genre enables a reader to feel more deeply his distress and pain. Job's friends were shocked by these emotion-charged words from the most pious person they knew, and initially Eliphaz's words seem designed to gently redirect Job from a path that the friends saw as dangerous. When Job refused to respond to their suggestions, the friends became increasingly agitated, and before the debate came to an end in chapter 27 they attacked him with a vengeance.

Poetry has the power to capture the emotion and the intensity of his experience. Job's descriptions of his ailments were not meant to enable the astute exegete to diagnose his malady, but to reveal the depths of his pain and struggle. His frustration, confusion and even anger can be felt in the poetry of the book, and exegesis of this material should be as concerned to capture its emotional aspect as it is to identify literary structure and explain unusual words and grammar. The goal is not to analyze the poetry and recast it into propositions that constitute the teaching of the passage. Neither is the goal to eliminate all **ambiguity** or to answer every theological or philosophical question posed by this poetic text.

Interpret the Book in Its Broader Ancient Near Eastern Context

While ancient Near Eastern parallels rarely transform our understanding of a biblical text, there are times when an understanding of the broader background can give us a richer understanding of certain features in the text. Job frequently uses legal **metaphor**s and forensic terminology,[17] and understanding ancient legal language and procedures can be useful in interpreting parts of the book.[18] It is unlikely that a legal metaphor constitutes the primary interpretive paradigm for the book,[19] but the recognition of these metaphors will impact the way words like צְדָקָה, "righteous," or "innocent," and רָשָׁע, "wicked" or "guilty," are translated in legal contexts. The innocent or acquitted party in a lawsuit was declared by the court to be צְדָקָה while the guilty party was declared to be רָשָׁע. This also challenges the idea occasionally heard in sermons that Job's claim to be צְדָקָה reflects a significant level of "self-righteousness" that God needed to eradicate from him.

Some mythological metaphors are so tied to the ancient Near Eastern context out of which they came that a modern reader would

---

17. For example, such language can be found throughout Job 9 and 13, as well as in Yahweh's challenge to Job in 40:2.

18. For an analysis of numerous legal texts from the neo-Babylonian period see, F. R. Magdelene, *On the Scales of Righteousness: Neo-Babylonian Trial Law and the Book of Job* (Providence, RI: Brown Judaic Studies, 2007) and her discussion "Law'" in *DOTWPW*, esp. 422–23.

19. Magdelene (see previous note) argues for this view.

likely never understand them apart from extrabiblical material that explicates them. Job 3:8 refers to those "who are ready to rouse up Leviathan," and the term also appears in the Yahweh speeches in chapter 41. In Job 7:12, Job says to God, "Am I the sea, or a sea monster, that you set a guard over me?" Such references occur in ancient Near Eastern texts that depict creation as a struggle between the forces of order/cosmos and those of chaos/disorder. Leviathan, Rahab, the sea (Yam), and others are the **personification** of those forces that oppose order and are intent on returning creation to a state of disorder where human life cannot exist.

While the biblical authors saw Yahweh as the Creator of all things, they and their readers were familiar with the stories of their pagan neighbors, and the texts sometimes incorporated mythological language to affirm Yahweh's sovereign power. As Futato says about similar language in the Psalms, "The poet is using language well known to ancient Israelites, language that was adapted from the creation myths of Israel's neighbors and used as a metaphor for God's work of creation. Without knowledge of these myths, modern readers will be baffled by the Bible's references to 'monsters' and to 'Leviathan.'"[20] Futato further says about this kind of language: "The biblical writers did not believe the myths themselves, but they used such language in their arguments against those who did believe in such forces and deities."[21] In the case of Behemoth and Leviathan in the Yahweh speeches (Job 40 and 41), it is likely that an actual creature is in the foreground of the text,[22] and the language effectively makes the point that while Job is helpless against creatures like Leviathan, Yahweh easily controls them. In addition, Yahweh's power extends beyond whatever animal is in view to the forces of cosmic evil that threaten life in the world and are at work trying to thwart Yahweh's order and purposes. While extrabiblical literature can sometimes be helpful in understanding biblical texts, it is important to recognize the radical differences that exist between the theology of a biblical wisdom book like Job and innocent sufferer compositions from the ancient Near East.[23]

---

20. Mark Futato, *Interpreting the Psalms* (Grand Rapids: Kregel, 2007), 44.

21. Ibid., 55.

22. Robert Alter (*The Art of Biblical Poetry* [New York: Basic Books, 2011], 133) understands the creature as a crocodile, but adds that the poet's description "involves a marvelous fusion of precise observation, **hyperbole**, and mythological heightening of the real reptile, and thus becomes a beautiful climax to the whole poem."

23. See "The Importance of Ancient Near East Background in Interpreting Wisdom Literature," especially "Significant Differences," in chapter 3.

Proverbs

Studying each proverb carefully in the Hebrew text is essential. Some biblical proverbs are unclear in Hebrew, and translators sometimes feel compelled to make a judgment call about the probable meaning of a difficult proverb or resolve the ambiguity of a proverb in their translation. The resulting translation may make a different point than was intended in the original or obscure the difficulty and uncertainty inherent in the Hebrew text. Careful analysis of the text and judicious use of the commentaries can prevent misrepresenting the point of a particular proverb.

Interpret Passages in the Context of the Book and the Fear of the Lord
The book of Proverbs is made up of several collections as indicated by the headings in 1:1, 10:1, 22:17, 24:23, 25:1, and 30:1, and there are some suggestions of organization within the book as we have it. Proverbs 1:1–7 functions as the introduction to the entire book, while 1:7 ("The fear of the LORD is the beginning of knowledge") identifies the principle that Israel saw as the essential key for acquiring wisdom. This principle is found again in Proverbs 9:10 and 15:33, and the central importance of the **fear of God**/the Lord is seen numerous times throughout the wisdom Literature. [24] The book of Proverbs concludes with the poem about the excellent woman in Proverbs 31:10–31, and the fear of the Lord is an essential component of her excellence. It is likely that the fear of the Lord in Proverbs 31:30 forms an **inclusio** with the term in Proverbs 1:7 and frames the entire book in a context bounded by that idea.

Proverbs 1–9 also reveals important principles about gaining wisdom such as the "two ways"—the way of wisdom and the way of folly—and the need to choose between these paths. The exhortations in chapters 2, 3, and 4 emphasize the necessity for commitment and diligence in seeking wisdom and the importance of the heart in the quest for wisdom. Proverbs 1–9 places great emphasis on moral and ethical values that are not always mentioned in the individual proverbs in 10–31, but the context established by Proverbs 1–9 makes it clear that the wisdom affirmed throughout Proverbs includes such things as justice, integrity and righteousness. Bartholomew says, "The rhetorical effect of these nine chapters of speeches set the context for the book as a whole by building a view of the world in which the rest of Proverbs is to be interpreted. In this way Proverbs 1–9 provides the reader with an interpretive key for the whole." [25]

A proverb usually describes the way things are rather than the way they should be. "'Bad, bad,' says the buyer, but when he goes away,

---

24. For example, Job 28:28, Eccl. 12:13, and Psalm 111, which is a wisdom psalm.
25. Craig Bartholomew, *Reading Proverbs with Integrity* (Cambridge: Grove Books, 2001), 9–10.

then he boasts" (20:14) describes a negotiating technique sometimes used to get a better price on a purchase. It explains what people do, but leaves us with no moral or ethical evaluation of the practice. The book's purpose in 1:1–6, the motto of the book in 1:7, and the values emphasized in chapter 2 (kindness, justice, and honesty) provide a basis for such evaluation. Proverbs 17:8 ("A bribe is like a magic stone in the eyes of the one who gives it; wherever he turns he prospers") read in isolation from the rest of the book, could be understood as approving the use of a bribe because it works. In light of 17:23 and the ethical values elsewhere in the book, it is clear that the use of a bribe is wrong. Sometimes other proverbs address the issue and add clarity. Sometimes the evaluation will have to come from other places in Scripture, and occasionally even from experience.

Interpret Proverbs in the Light of Genre and Wisdom's Purposes

Parallelism is found in virtually every verse in Proverbs, and the parallelism must be carefully analyzed.[26] The poetry in the book and the individual proverbs are filled with metaphors and figures of speech which must also be studied in interpreting the material.[27]

Proverbs are particularly suited for the kind of instruction seen in virtually every section of Proverbs 1–9. Over and over the **sage** exhorts the young man to listen and apply the principles he is teaching. The enterprise is not simply indoctrination but is educative in that the disciples must attend to the instruction and put it into practice as they live in the world.[28] Proverbs are often cryptic and ambiguous and a variety of possibilities for interpretation and application are left open. Such sayings require the reader to reflect on the open ended claims of the proverb and think about various options and the limits regarding meaning and application.

The Hebrew text of Proverbs 11:24 reads,

יֵשׁ מְפַזֵּר וְנוֹסָף עוֹד וְחוֹשֵׂךְ מִיֹּשֶׁר אַךְ־לְמַחְסוֹר

ESV translates the verse, "One gives freely, yet grows all the richer; another withholds what he should give, and only suffers want." The proverb contrasts two people, "one who scatters (מְפַזֵּר)" and "one who withholds what he should give (וְחוֹשֵׂךְ מִיֹּשֶׁר)." There is also a contrast in terms of the outcomes of these actions. The person who scatters increases while the person who withholds experiences lack. The basic idea of the proverb is clear, but there is also ambiguity and irony which is supposed to stimulate thinking and which plays a significant role in developing the skill that constitutes wisdom.

---

26. See "Parallelism," chap. 1.

27. See "Wisdom's Genres: Poetry and Proverb," chap. 4.

28. E.g., Prov. 4:20–29.

Given this chapter's frequent emphasis on the importance of generosity and kindness toward those in need, it seems clear that a primary application of the proverb involves being generous in contrast to refusing to help others. At the same time we have to ask whether the "scattering" or "withholding" includes more than material things? Does it extend to time and help of other kinds? There is also ambiguity in the term translated "what he should give" by ESV. Is the idea limited to situations like that described in Proverbs 3:27–28 ("Do not withhold good from those to whom it is due, when it is in your power to do it. Do not say to your neighbor, 'Go, and come again, tomorrow I will give it'—when you have it with you") or to situations like the one condemned by James 5:4, where wages that have been earned are withheld by an employer?

There is obvious irony in that the proverb claims that giving money away leads to having "more" not "less." Scattering material resources seems antithetical to the kind of frugality that normally leads to the accumulation of wealth, and the tension stimulates reflection about how this can be. Certainly one answer is that practicing generosity and kindness in the community often creates gratitude that prompts others to return the favor. Sometimes the "increase" may have to do with personal satisfaction that comes from doing what is right and from helping others. In the context of Proverbs, one obvious part of the answer is that the blessing of God brings about such counterintuitive results.

The goal of interpretation is not to reduce the ambiguity or irony to one correct option, but to encourage the kind of thought the proverb is designed to engender.

Interpret Proverbs in Light of the Book's Total Teaching on a Topic

It is important to be sensitive to the arrangement of material in Proverbs and to the way contexts created by smaller literary units in the book can impact our understanding of individual proverbs within that unit. We would argue, though, that topical studies also play an important role in understanding this material.[29] Most proverbs focus on a tiny slice of reality, and it is often useful to put these small pieces together to form a more complete picture of wisdom's teaching about a topic.

In dealing with angry and foolish people it is important to be aware that a soft answer turns away wrath (15:1). It is also advantageous to know that wisdom sometimes involves answering the foolish person according to his folly (26:5), though in other instances it is prudent to avoid doing that (26:4). As we look carefully through Proverbs, it becomes apparent that people need to know more than small bits of wisdom to deal effectively with situations in life.

---

29. See the short topical study on friendship in chapter 6.

Creating a more comprehensive picture of the wise person in Proverbs and contrasting that with wisdom's depiction of the fool can be done without distorting or disrespecting the material, and it normally gives us a more robust and balanced picture than a few proverbs taken in isolation will do. An awareness of the breadth of wisdom's teaching about a topic contributes to a balance that reduces the risk of misapplication that can result from a more narrow view.

The same is true of other topics treated at length in the book. For example, there are many warnings in Proverbs about the folly of co-signing a loan for someone else, and many conclude that this should never be done. It appears likely, however, that these warnings are part of a larger complex about the folly of rash decisions and involvements. Proverbs recognizes the importance of careful, deliberate decisions in every area of life, and becoming responsible for another person's debt, often because of pressure from a friend or relative, is one example of a foolish commitment that can—and usually does—result in disaster. Recognizing this does not reduce the seriousness of the warning but does allow us to understand the overarching point that Proverbs is making, and to recognize that circumstances might occasionally justify helping someone in this way.[30]

A second example has to do with the disappointment and guilt that parents of a wayward child often feel because of teaching about parenting that focuses exclusively on Proverbs 22:6: "Train up a child in the way he should go; even when he is old he will not depart from it." While several interpretations of the verse have been suggested that limit the point of the proverb in ways that reduce the difficulty, it seems likely that the proverb is making a general point about the importance of good parenting. Other proverbs like 19:18; 13:22; and 29:15 make it clear that bad parenting will generally result in rebellious and ungodly children. The early chapters of Proverbs identify other variables that can lead a child onto a path that will lead to disaster. Such things as the influence of sinful and wicked companions (Prov. 1:10–19) or the willful refusal of a child to heed their parents' wise teaching (Prov. 2:1–22; 3:1–12; 4:1–27) or the child's rejection of wisdom (Prov. 1:20–33) will generally result in their becoming wicked and irresponsible adults. Proverbs recognizes that the factors that determine the way a child turns out in life are far more complex than the quality of the parenting.

---

30. Derek Kidner (*Proverbs*, TOTC, 71) says that these warnings are not meant to "banish generosity: it is nearer to banishing gambling." These warnings make the point that it is rarely wise to make our financial well-being dependent on someone else's responsibility in paying a debt which we have guaranteed.

Interpret Proverbs Recognizing the Wide Diversity of Sayings in the Book

In addition to the points made about the genre "proverb" in chapters 1 and 2,[31] several additional points need to be made. Different kinds of proverbs are found in this book, and these sayings function in a variety of ways. We have regularly pointed out that proverbs are generalizations rather than principles to which there are never any exceptions because that is a point that many people who read Proverbs fail to understand, but there are other types of proverbs as well.

The following categories are not comprehensive, but they will give some sense of the wide diversity that exists within the literary genre in wisdom literature that we call "proverb."[32] An essential part of interpreting a proverb involves correctly identifying the type of proverb under consideration.

Most proverbs will fall into one of two major categories: admonitions or sayings. Admonitions are exhortations regarding behavior or attitudes. They are frequently characterized by imperatives, though sometimes in the third person[33] rather than the second person. Proverbs 14:7, which says, "Leave the presence of a fool, for there you do not meet words of knowledge," is an example of admonition. Sayings are usually characterized by the indicative mood and describe a scenario that implicitly calls for a decision of some sort from the reader. Proverbs 30:20 is one example: "This is the way of an adulteress: she eats and wipes her mouth and says, 'I have done no wrong.'" Another example is Proverbs 16:18, which says, "**Pride** goes before destruction, and a haughty spirit before a fall." Such sayings are intended to encourage those who hear them to avoid a certain kind of foolish behavior. Both the saying and the admonition can function in the ways noted below.

- Some proverbs do present absolute prohibitions

Among the many examples are the warnings against adultery and immoral sexual behavior in chapter 5, 6:20–35, and chapter 7. Proverbs 6:16–19 provides another example:

> There are six things that the LORD hates,
>   seven that are an abomination to him:
> haughty eyes, a lying tongue,
>   and hands that shed innocent blood,
> a heart that devises wicked plans,
>   feet that make haste to run to evil,

---

31. See "The Nature of a Proverb" in chapter 1 and "Proverbs" in chapter 2.

32. On this see Ted A. Hildebrand, "Proverb, Genre of," *DOTWPW*, 531.

33. The Hebrew jussive.

> a false witness who breathes out lies,
>   and one who sows discord among brothers.

- Some proverbs do express universal principles

Proverbs 3:5 ("Trust in the LORD with all your heart, and do not lean on your own understanding") expresses a universal principle that appears many places throughout the Old Testament and the rest of Scripture. The exhortations to get wisdom in Proverbs 2:1–8; 4:5–9, or to guard the heart (Prov. 4:23) are other examples. Many sayings that have to do with God and his work in the world also fall into this category. Proverbs like 29:26 ("Many seek the face of a ruler, but it is from the LORD that a man gets justice"); and 21:2 ("Every way of a man is right in his own eyes, but the LORD weighs the heart") are other examples.

- Some proverbs are simple non-moral observations

Proverbs 14:13 says, "Even in laughter the heart may ache, and the end of joy may be grief." Proverbs 10:15 ("A rich man's wealth is his strong city; the poverty of the poor is their ruin") is another example. The proverb makes the simple observation that rich people do not worry when they are confronted with unexpected expenses because their wealth protects them from financial ruin. The same situation can bring disaster to a poor person who has no extra resources to deal with the calamity. Sometimes simple non-moral observations can take on moral dimensions. Proverbs 18:11 ("A rich man's wealth is his strong city, and like a high wall in his imagination.") makes it clear that the protection that wealth provides is sometimes less than the wealthy suppose. Wealth, for all its benefits, does not reduce a person's need to trust God and can sometimes undermine it.

- Some proverbs affirm important ideals, others the consequences of deviating from the ideal

The importance of diligence and the connection between laziness and poverty are recognized in Proverbs 10:4: "A slack hand causes poverty, but the hand of the diligent makes rich." Proverbs about the sluggard affirm the same values. Many examples emphasize the importance of self-control and avoiding rash actions and words. Proverbs 18:13 says, "If one gives an answer before he hears, it is his folly and shame," while Proverbs 14:17 says, "A man of quick temper acts foolishly, and a man of evil devices is hated." Often the affirmation of the ideal and the consequences of deviating from it are contrasted in a single proverb like 13:18, "Poverty and disgrace come to him who ignores instruction, but whoever heeds reproof is honored."

The characteristics of proverbs discussed above are neither exhaustive nor comprehensive. Good exegesis requires that we correctly identify the type of proverb and understand it in the light of both its genre and its function in the culture.

Considering the Claims of Proverbs

Skepticism sometimes exists about the validity of certain proverbs in this book because they make claims that seem incongruent with the experiences of life. A soft answer does not always turn away wrath (Prov. 15:1) and sometimes even increases a hostile person's anger. The difficulty of validity is amplified when the lack of congruence involves a theological proverb. Righteous people do not always dwell in the land in peace, abundance, and good health. And there are overtly evil people who seem to fare better than some righteous ones and even inflict great injustice and harm on them. Qoheleth describes situations where righteous people are oppressed by the wicked and where the injustice continues throughout their lives.[34] In spite of what he sees in the world,[35] he insists in Ecclesiastes 3:17; 11:9; and 12:14 that God will judge the righteous and the wicked. Such tensions prompt us to ask, "Really, God will judge? When might that be, and how will it happen?"

In view of such tension between the claims of proverbial statements and the experiences of life, it is difficult not to ask, "Does the book of Proverbs promise too much?"[36] While we cannot provide a comprehensive answer to such objections, several points can be made.

Obviously, we must correctly interpret the proverb, and part of that involves understanding the circumstance presupposed by the proverb. This involves things like identifying the kind of proverb and the conditions under which the proverb is true. For example, a non-biblical proverb like "Early to bed, early to rise makes a man healthy, wealthy and wise" presupposes that a person will be diligent, organized, and focused on worthwhile goals while they are awake. It clearly does not have in view the person who gets up early to play video games all day. The truth of the proverb is contingent on certain conditions that are left unstated in the **aphorism**.

In addition, many things contribute to the complexity of reality and to outcomes in human endeavors, and people lack the ability to understand everything that determines those outcomes. Individuals make

---

34. For instance, Eccl. 3:16; 4:1–3; 7:15–17.

35. Note also his observation in Ecclesiastes 9:1–6 that there seems to be little difference between what happens to righteous people and to wicked people in the world, and he sees God's providence overseeing such outcomes.

36. On this question see Bruce Waltke, "Does Proverbs Promise Too Much?," *AUSS* 34 (1996), 319–36. See also his discussion in *Proverbs 1–15*, NICOT, 93–116, esp. 107–9.

choices that affect both what happens to them and to others around them, and as Ecclesiastes 9:18 says, "Wisdom is better than weapons of war, but one sinner destroys much good." It is a fallen world, and the pervasive effect of sin on fallen humanity has brought significant dysfunction into the created order and human experience. Many things do not work the way God designed them to work.

While the benefits associated with wise living (wealth, health, security, and general well-being) and the disasters that result from folly (violence, poverty, expulsion from the land, and disasters of all sorts) are stated in what appear to be unequivocal terms, other proverbs make it clear that the sages recognized that there are often exceptions. Sometimes the blessings of God take very different forms than money and temporal success; sometimes there are long delays before the proverbial principles are realized. Often, God's blessings can only be recognized with the benefit of hindsight;[37] and outcomes may well happen in ways that do not register with us. In the case of Job, the broader purposes of God were best served by allowing circumstances contrary to the general claims of the proverbial literature to prevail for a time. Van Leeuwen says, "In general, the sages clearly believed that wise and righteous behavior did make life better and richer, though virtue did not guarantee those consequences. Conversely, injustice, sloth, and the like generally have bad consequences."[38] He further maintains that the wisdom literature reflects the idea that "God . . . will eventually enforce his standards. The future will thus demonstrate that righteousness is better than wickedness. In the end, there will be a reversal of fortunes."[39]

Related to this are statements about judgment of the wicked and deliverance of the righteous. Experience sometimes sets before us situations like Job's description of the wicked in Job 21:13–14: "They spend their days in prosperity, and in peace they go down to Sheol. They say to God, 'Depart from us! We do not desire the knowledge of your ways." Such examples illustrate the tension between human experience and the assertions of faith. Farmer says, "One either has to give up on the idea of justice or one has to push its execution into some realm beyond the evidence of human experience."[40] Claiming that the fulfillment of these promises will take place in the future, though, leaves

---

37. The proverb in Ecclesiastes 7:8 says, "Better is the end of a thing than its beginning, and the patient in spirit is better than the proud in spirit." Sometimes it is only long after the fact that an event or experience can be seen for what it really is.

38. Raymond Van Leeuwen, "Wealth and Poverty: System and Contradiction in Proverbs," *Hebrew Studies* 33 (1992), 32.

39. Ibid., 33. Obviously this confidence is a faith assertion rather than an empirically determined one.

40. Kathleen Farmer, *Who Knows What is Good?: A Commentary on Proverbs and Ecclesiastes* (Grand Rapids: Eerdmans, 1991), 206.

us in a place where these sayings appear to be falsified by our present experience, and often this is where the wisdom literature leaves us. Van Leeuwen says "The affirmation that in the future justice will be done seems to me a hallmark of '**Yahwistic** faith,' a hope in that which is yet invisible and intangible. It is a belief in something that experience does not verify. It is a walking by faith and not sight."[41]

The authors of the wisdom books do not try to hide such realities, and sometimes set examples and counter examples in close proximity, presumably to show the complex nature of life in the world and to provoke the kind of thinking that leads to skill in living in such a world. While the book of Proverbs is seen by some as promoting a naïve and overly simplistic view of the world,[42] the reality is that it presents significant diversity on almost every topic it discusses. The tension produced by that diversity challenges us to put the various pieces together in ways that reflect reality in the world.[43]

While wisdom literature does not provide comprehensive instruction for living in the world, it does provide us with many practical principles for living wisely, and given the inspired character of this material, they are principles that God wants his people to know and apply. As Bartholomew and O'Dowd point out, this material illuminates for us the variety that exists in creation and human experience. They say, "An ordered life is one that navigates changing circumstances, dilemmas, and quandaries with wisdom. The proverbs supply basic instructions and extended metaphors to help us interpret these constantly changing events and to respond well."[44] As all the wisdom literature makes clear (Job 28:28; Ps. 111:12; Prov. 1:7; 9:10), a life characterized by wisdom must begin with the fear of the Lord and continue with that same trust in God (Ps. 111:12; Prov. 3:5–8; Eccl. 12:13).

Ecclesiastes

Debate surrounds almost every aspect of Ecclesiastes. There is no consensus about the structure of the book. The book's message includes both positive and negative elements, and it is not always clear how these elements relate to traditional Yahwistic thinking. Ecclesiastes is characterized by numerous tensions as the author says one thing but later affirms something that stands in significant tension with it. And this author raises many questions that are left unanswered in the book.

---

41. Van Leeuwen, "Wealth and Poverty," 34.

42. For a discussion of this view and an argument against it, see Peter Hatton, *Contradiction in the Book of Proverbs* (Burlington, VT: Ashgate, 2008).

43. Hatton gives numerous examples of this, though not all are convincing.

44. Bartholomew and O'Dowd, *Old Testament Wisdom Literature*, 93.

In the light of the many uncertainties, it is important to begin a study of Ecclesiastes by reading the book a number of times apart from assumptions about what the book is or what we think it should be. The goal of this reading is to get a sense of the major themes and teaching of the book as well as the purpose and general structure; it is essential to allow the content of the book to take priority over perceptions about form and structure.[45] Some ideas about literary units should begin to emerge through this reading as well.

General guidelines for interpreting the book include things like interpreting it with an awareness of similar literature from the ancient Near East and an awareness of the great diversity of literary forms used in the book.[46] It is also essential to keep the author's methodology (I sought, I built, I pursued, I found) in mind along with the limits of such self-discovery. In addition, the following guidelines are of particular importance.

Interpret Ecclesiastes as a Unified Composition

While previous generations of scholars argued that the tensions in the book reflect different sources and the activity of various redactors, scholars today are more inclined to accept the unity of the book, apart from the epilogue (Eccl. 12:9–14).[47] The epilogue stands outside the literary structure of the book, which is defined by the *inclusio* in 1:2 and 12:8, and it is written in the third person and describes the teacher, while the author typically speaks in the first person in the rest of the book. Apart from this change in perspective, there is little objective evidence to support the conclusion that the epilogue is a later addition to the book. Michael Fox argues that there is "no ideological conflict between Qohelet's teaching and the epilogue."[48] Evangelicals like Kaiser and Garrett note that there are important themes that tie the epilogue to the rest of the book and conclude that these verses are an integral part of the book as the original author intended it. Garrett says,

> Everything Ecclesiastes has affirmed up to this point—
> the sovereign freedom of God, the limits of human wis-
> dom, thoughts on the abuse of wealth and power, and

---

45. Note the comments by Greg W. Parsons, "Guidelines for Understanding and Proclaiming the Book of Ecclesiastes, Part 1," *Bib Sac* 160 (April–June), 2003, 161.

46. For a helpful summary see Greg W. Parsons, "Guidelines for Understanding and Proclaiming the Book of Ecclesiastes, Part 2," *Bib Sac* 160 (July–September, 2003), 284–90, and the bibliography in note 10, 285.

47. See Craig Bartholomew, "Qoheleth in the Canon? Current Trends in the Interpretation of Ecclesiastes," *Themelios* 24 (May, 1999), 6. Bartholomew (14), though, argues that the epilogue was part of the original text of the book and that it must be taken seriously in reading and interpreting the book.

48. Michael Fox, *Qohelet and His Contradictions* (Sheffeld: Almond, 1989), 316.

the brevity and absolute contingency of human life—all lead to the command to fear God. To excise the conclusion is to throw away that which binds together all the separate strands of the author's thought. It arises from a failure to think like the Teacher, so to speak.[49]

As Barton points out, "Before the rise of critical scholarship this juxtaposition of scepticism and moralism [that characterizes Ecclesiastes] was not, apparently, felt to be particularly puzzling or to require explanation: the mixture was simply part of the author's makeup."[50] One of the important assumptions shared by most pre-critical commentators is reflected in the opinion of Ibn Ezra who said, "even the least of the wise would not write a book and contradict his own words in his book."[51] These scholars approached the book by attempting to harmonize the conflicting positions,[52] and they saw the epilogue as a key to interpreting the book, both because it ties several themes together and because it provides an evaluation of Qoheleth and his work.[53] As Parsons suggests, "[Readers] should neither ignore the contribution of the epilogue nor superimpose the message onto the main body."[54]

Recognize the Tensions and Lack of Coherent Structure as Part of the Book's Design

These features are likely part of the author's message and teaching strategy. According to Fox, "A reading faithful to this book, at least, should try to describe the territory with all its bumps and clefts, for they are not mere flaws, but the essence of the landscape."[55] The tensions, dead ends, and enigmas described by this author confront the reader with realities that are a part of life, and the rhetorical strategies used by Qoheleth contribute to that effect on the reader. The purpose of interpretation is not to solve all the difficulties or relieve all the tensions, but to set them before our audience in ways that help them think about and come to grips with such realities.

---

49. Duane Garrett, Proverbs, *Ecclesiastes, Song of Songs*, NAC (Nashville: Broadman, 1993), 345. See also Walter Kaiser, *Ecclesiastes: Total Life* (Chicago: Moody, 1979), 13–15.

50. John Barton, *Reading the Old Testament: Method in Biblical Study* (Philadelphia: Westminster, 1984), 62.

51. Fox, *Qohelet and His Contradictions*, 20.

52. Harmonizing must be done carefully as we will note in the next section.

53. For an older Evangelical example of how the epilogue can impact the interpretation of the book see, G. Addison Wright, "The Interpretation of Ecclesiastes," in *Classical Evangelical Essays in Old Testament Interpretation*, ed. by Walter Kaiser, (Grand Rapids: Baker, 1972), 133–50.

54. Parsons, "Guidelines for Ecclesiastes, Part 1," 163.

55. Fox, *Qohelet and His Contradictions*, 28.

Qoheleth uses these tensions to develop in his pupils skills for living in the kind of world he describes. The teaching that we find in Ecclesiastes is difficult for us to follow because it reflects a type of organization that Robert Kaplan describes as "an approach by indirection." The individual units "turn around the subject and show it from a variety of tangential views, but the subject is never looked at directly."[56] The enigmatic aspects of life that Qoheleth sets in opposition to each other function in several different ways, but always to stimulate thought and reflection on the part of his readers. In Ecclesiastes 2:12–17 he contrasts wisdom and folly as he searches for a way to live that will generate a profit or advantage. His conclusion is that the advantage of wisdom over folly is like the difference between light and darkness. But then he points out another reality—death—that seems to negate the advantage that he just pointed out. Both the wise person and the fool die, and we are left with another dilemma for the budding sage to ponder. The example leaves us aware of wisdom's great advantage over folly, but also makes it clear that wisdom has its limits. And we are left wondering if there is anything past the grave, and whether there is any way to live so as to gain a profit that death cannot erase.

Sometimes the tensions seem to move us toward a more balanced understanding of life, as is the case in 7:15–18. The same is true in 4:1–12 where he explores work/achievement and what motivates it as well as the benefits of relationships. The tensions there seem focused on developing appropriate priorities as people live in the world. Sometimes the tension reflects the way things are in the world versus the way they ought to be. In 4:1, 3:16, and several other places Qoheleth describes the reality of oppression and injustice in the world and sees such evil supported by power structures that seem unlikely to change. Sometimes he resolves such tensions by appealing to faith as in 3:17 where he concludes that God will judge the righteous and the wicked. Sometimes he appeals to patience and perspective as in chapter 7 where he points out that things are not always what they appear to be on the surface.

Qoheleth wanted his readers to learn to deal with difficult issues like these and saw questions and tensions as important teaching devices. He clearly thought something important was gained through such struggles as he sought to equip people for life in a complex world.

Interpret the Book in the Light of Its Dominant Themes

Despite the tensions and absence of a clear linear structure, certain themes are prominent and should occupy a central role in interpreting

---

56.   Robert B. Kaplan, "Cultural Thought Patterns in Inter-Cultural Education," in *Readings on English as a Second Language*, 2nd ed., ed. by Kenneth Croft (Boston: Little, Brown, 1979), 406.

the book.[57] Among these are the meaning and function of *hebel* in the book,[58] the nature of the "profit/advantage" that the sage is looking for, the significance of the unanswered questions, the significance of the fear of God,[59] the meaning and significance of "**under the sun**," the exhortations "to enjoy," and the providence of God.

Seek a Balanced Understanding of All That Qoheleth Affirms

It is tempting to flatten the message of the book to a single theme and neglect other themes that stand in tension with it. Some harmonization must be done with a book like Ecclesiastes, but it needs to be done with caution. As Fox points out,

> A certain measure of harmonization is a proper and necessary part of the reading process, for a reader must attempt to construct a coherent picture of an author's thought by interpreting one statement in light of another. The goal of reading makes the reader strive to discover coherency in the text. . . . Harmonistic interpretations become objectionable . . . when they do injustice to specific passages (or perhaps we should say *too many* passages) or when they use makeshift and arbitrary explanations to achieve consistency. Excessive exegetical ingenuity may make an author consistent at the price of making him incoherent.[60]

Clearly the book has, to use Bartholomew's terminology, both "*hebel* conclusions" and "joy conclusions," and as he points out "the effect of this is to open up gaps in the reading which have to be filled in as the reader moves forward."[61] It is easy to reduce the teaching of the book to either the *hebel* pole or the joy pole and then disregard the other aspect of Qoheleth's tension. It is essential that we take seriously both emphases in this sage's teaching.

Interpret Ecclesiastes in the Broader Context of Scripture.

Parsons says, "Without the moorings of the rest of the canon, one's

---

57. See the discussion on several of these themes in "Ecclesiastes" in chapter 2.
58. And appropriate attention needs to be given to the *inclusio* in 1:2 and 12:8, which brackets the book.
59. This would necessarily include a determination of whether the term "fear of God" in Ecclesiastes has the same meaning as the "fear of the Lord" in the other wisdom books.
60. Fox, *Qohelet and His Contradictions*, 22–23.
61. Bartholomew, "Qoheleth in the Canon?," 15. I would add that this is part of Qoheleth's teaching strategy.

view of portions of Ecclesiastes can drift into the sea of subjectivity."[62] One must, of course, avoid reading New Testament ideas back into the text of Ecclesiastes, but it is important to interpret the book fully aware of its canonical context. It is also crucial to recognize the way in which the New Testament answers questions that Qoheleth asked but was unable to answer—questions about whether death is the final reality that it appears to be based on Qoheleth's methodology or whether it is possible to gain an advantage in life that death cannot completely erase. Given Qoheleth's likely allusions to the early chapters of Genesis,[63] it also seems plausible to suppose that he was aware that the world is fallen, even apart from explicit statements to that effect.

Song of Songs

It is especially important to begin a study of Song of Songs by reading the book numerous times with a view toward determining the purpose and major teaching of the book. Out of this reading the literary units should begin to emerge along with the matters that will be the focus of more detailed study. Since much of the book consists of dialogue, it is important to identify the speakers to the degree possible.[64] The question of whether the book is about God's love for his people or about human love[65] is important, as is the question about whether there is a story behind the poetry. It is also important to decide whether the poems are about an actual relationship or an ideal one. While decisions about such issues are important and constitute a basic part of exegesis, the answers for many of these questions remain unclear for Song of Songs.[66]

Commentators often suggest plausible answers to these questions and then interpret the text based on those assumptions, but it seems prudent to recognize the tentative nature of the answers and focus primarily on the things that are clear. What is clear is that these are love poems that on the surface describe a relationship between a man and a woman. It is also clear that these poems are situated in the context of Scripture. In the absence of the sort of narrative and background information that

---

62. Parsons, "Guidelines for Ecclesiastes, Part 2," 296.

63. See "Ecclesiastes Affirms the Reality of Human Limits," chap. 2.

64. This is sometimes difficult in the Song, and most translations, including ancient ones like **LXX**, provide notes to help readers identify the speakers. Reading the text in Hebrew is helpful since Hebrew differentiates between second-person masculine and feminine forms and between second-person singular and plural.

65. Or perhaps some combination of the two.

66. See "Song of Songs" in chapter 2, where these issues are summarized along with suggestions about themes and teaching.

we normally bring to exegesis, we will need to give particular attention to the poetry in the book and to the way poetry functions along with its goals and purposes.[67] A central element in learning from this book will involve listening and observing the couple as they converse and interact, and the poetry will be the vehicle through which that occurs.

Interpret Song of Songs as Poetry

For many interpreters, the first step should be a review of what poetry is and how it works.[68] It is essential to remember that a significant part of understanding and interpreting a poem involves allowing it to impact the emotions as well as the cognitive faculties, and the exegete should begin here as well. Jeannine Brown suggests that a careful, holistic study of a poem should bring the interpreter to the point where he or she "will be able to hear it and respond to it more organically than technically—as the original audience would have done."[69] The ability to experience and understand poetry is something that must be learned and cultivated much like appreciation for excellent music or art. Poetry captures the aesthetic, the emotional, and the relational much more effectively than do intellectual propositions. An interpretation that excludes the emotional and experiential dimensions of the text and fails to connect people with the experience described in the poem falls short of exegetical excellence.

Exegesis of Song of Songs Requires Careful Analysis of the Poetry

In addition to the lack of the kind of background information that is normally available for establishing the context of a passage, Song of Songs uses many words and metaphors that are strange to our ears. The enormous cultural and linguistic gap that exists between our world and that of the biblical poet makes careful analysis of every aspect of the poetry essential. Particular attention must be given to the parallelism and to the metaphors and images.[70] Metaphors and figures of speech give poetry its power to affect the one who hears or reads it, and they provide the lens through which the reader will understand the poem. We are generally familiar with pomegranates and doves and gold and jewels and fragrant oils, but when the poet compares the woman to those items, we still have the task of trying to figure out which charac-

---

67. See "The Nature of Hebrew Poetry," chap. 1.

68. For an excellent and practical discussion of this, see Leland Ryken, *How to Read the Bible as Literature* (Grand Rapids: Zondervan, 1984), 87–120. For a more extensive discussion by the same author, see *Words of Delight*, 159–289.

69. Jeannine Brown, *Scripture as Communication: Introducing Biblical Hermeneutics* (Grand Rapids: Baker, 2007), 148.

70. See "The Nature of Hebrew Poetry," chap. 1.

teristic of the metaphor the author has in mind in the comparison. Even when we encounter a familiar metaphor, we must be alert to possible connotations or symbolic elements that may have existed in the world of the poet and his audience.

There are many metaphors in Song of Songs about which we have little familiarity. We do not know what the tower of David was (4:4), nor do we know the significance of a metaphor like "a mare among Pharaoh's chariots" (1:9), and an important task of analysis involves determining what the images would have meant to the original audience. It is important that the interpreter understand the images and metaphors in the same way as the author intended them, and discovering as much as possible about the world in which the poem originated gives us our best hope for accomplishing this. This analysis can help identify which aspects of a metaphor or figure of speech the poet likely had in mind as he used concrete images to communicate something about abstract concepts like love or pain or frustration or beauty.[71]

It is especially useful to note words and phrases that are repeated several times in the Song. For example, the adjuration to the daughters of Jerusalem to refrain from awakening love "until it pleases" occurs three times in the book (2:7, 3:5, and 8:4). Not only does this repetition suggest the unity of the book, the words are set in some sort of context that may provide clues for understanding larger interpretive issues.[72] The word כֶּרֶם, "vineyard," occurs several times in the book and the meaning shifts from the concrete to the metaphorical in interesting ways. In 1:6 the woman complains that her family has required her to tend the vineyards, obviously the concrete meaning, and because of that she has neglected her own "vineyard." The point is that her complexion has suffered because of exposure to the sun. The proverb in 2:15 probably reflects the concrete meaning but obviously it becomes their relationship in the application. In 7:10–12 "going into the vineyards" takes on another dimension as she says, "There I will give you my love." The shifting meanings of "vineyard" may then provide a clue to understanding 8:11–12, arguably one of the most cryptic sections in a notoriously difficult book. In 8:11 "Solomon's vineyards" may represent both his grape-growing vineyards and his harem. In 8:12 the woman's vineyard probably represents her and her sexuality—something that she freely chooses to give to her beloved in a relationship that she would not trade for all of Solomon's wealth.

Attention to the metaphorical significance of "garden" can add dimensions to the understanding of 6:2. The word plays on the Hebrew

---

71. Material from the ancient Near East can often be helpful in this analysis, as can parallel passages in the Bible.

72. For example, are these warnings related in any way to 8:6–7, which many see as the thematic high point of the book?

root רעה can provide insight as well. Two different homonyms are reflected in the same Hebrew root. One indicates either what a shepherd does as he tends the flock or what the sheep do as they graze or feed in the pasture. The second word is related to "friend," "neighbor." The man normally uses a form of the second root, רַעְיָה for the woman, and, in this context it is probably a term of affection like "darling." In 6:2–3 the woman says, "My beloved has gone down to his garden . . . to graze in the gardens . . . he grazes among the lilies." The word plays, the repeated use of these metaphors, and the context make it clear that the young man is "both a shepherd who grazes his flock and a lover who 'feeds' on the delights of his darling."[73]

While analysis is critical, it is not the goal of interpretation, and can sometimes have the same impact as "explaining a joke," which usually destroys its point. The analysis involves taking the poem apart and examining its component parts, but the meaning of the individual parts do not constitute the meaning of the poem any more than the flute or violin component of a symphony constitutes the essence of a musical composition. It is only when all the parts are functioning together that the "meaning" of the piece becomes apparent, and the poem will need to be put back together for it to have the impact on a reader that it was designed to have. The goal of exegesis is not to take the poem apart, analyze the pieces and then reframe it into a series of propositions. The poet chose words and put them together in particular way; he designed the poem to function in a certain way. The structure and even the aesthetic aspects of a poem contribute to its meaning, and interpretation should bring out those dimensions along with the cognitive. Good interpretation should also equip and encourage others to experience the text as the author intended it to be experienced.

The images in Song of Songs often leave possibilities open ended and ambiguous. The goal of interpretation is not to eliminate the ambiguity by identifying the one correct answer. Rather it is to guide readers by explaining possibilities and steering them toward plausible and likely options. Such interpretation should encourage others to engage the text for themselves and explore possibilities for application that are relevant for their particular situation and needs.

---

73. Greg W. Parsons, "Guidelines for Understanding and Utilizing the Song of Songs," *Bib Sac* 156 (1999), 407.

5

PROCLAIMING THE
WISDOM BOOKS

The Chapter at a Glance

The Value of Proclaiming Wisdom

Preparing a Sermon

- Gaining Familiarity with the Passage
- The Importance of Context and Literary Analysis
- Organizing the Presentation

General Guidelines for Proclaiming Wisdom Literature

- The Nature of Wisdom
- The Realities of Life **under the Sun**
- The Goals of Wisdom and the Importance of Application
- The Potential of Wisdom
- The Power of Rhetorical Devices and Examples

Guidelines for Proclaiming Individual Books

- Job
- Proverbs
- Ecclesiastes
- Song of Songs

PREACHING FROM THE OLD TESTAMENT is relatively rare in most churches, and when it is done, it is seldom the wisdom literature that is the focus of the message. Many Christians seem to think that there is little reason to focus on *Old* Testament when we can study *New* Testament instead, and people often find the wisdom literature somewhat off putting. But the questions with which this part of Scripture deals are important ones—how to deal with undeserved suffering, marriage, parenting, attitudes toward money, priorities, and how to find meaning and fulfillment in life. Admittedly, though, wisdom often leaves important questions unresolved, and it puts much of its instruction in proverbial forms that are not absolutely true in every circumstance. Ecclesiastes is filled with tensions that reflect a different kind of teaching than we normally encounter. Perhaps worst of all, these books regularly seem devoid of theological and spiritual topics and confront us with ambiguous and secular-sounding advice.

Many people in the church seem to feel that general truths, common sense and straightforward practical principles are somehow beneath the dignity of spiritual minded people. As Ellen Davis says about the **aphorism**s in Proverbs, "Proverbial wisdom seems at the opposite end of the literary spectrum from 'the revealed word of God,'"[1] and based on that many think, "Why then should we bother with such mundane material?" In addition the meaning of many of the **proverb**s seems so transparent that no special training is needed to interpret them. According to Davis, "Proverbs does not seem to require that the preacher or teacher have command of a large literary and theological tradition in order to get started. All one needs to have is some life experience, and all one has to do is slow down over the proverbs, savoring their words, as with any good poem."[2]

The seemingly secular character of much of this material and apparent simplicity of the principles, no doubt, deter some from studying and teaching this body of material. There are, however, many important reasons for teaching wisdom, not the least of which is that Jesus often patterned his teaching—in terms of both method and content—on this literature. This part of Scripture can be particularly beneficial in helping people navigate the tensions between the values that dominate our culture and those affirmed in God's Word. It can also play a significant role in bridging the gap between theological theory and practice in the lives of God's people.

A note I received from a student several years ago illustrates a problem that plagues the church in the twenty-first century:

---

1.   Ellen Davis, "Surprised by Wisdom: Preaching Proverbs," *Interpretation* 63 (July 2009), 264.
2.   Ibid., 265.

Ecclesiastes reminds us that there are consequences to our actions and that we are ultimately accountable to God. This has significance to me because I am continually pressured by my culture and surrounding environment to live for myself and seek personal, immediate happiness. I am warned by Christian leaders and by my Christian friends to live for God and make his purposes my purposes, but at the same time all that I see and observe is different than what they say.[3]

While evangelicals affirm the value and authority of Scripture at a confessional level, many appear to have a different commitment at a functional level. They seem to have adopted the view of the broader culture that while the Bible has many interesting and even useful things to say, it is not capable of dealing with the complexities of life in the modern world. Many believers deal with the Bible and theology in the same way that they manage the vast amounts of information with which they are bombarded regularly. It is stored away in the brain or relegated to the internet where it can be retrieved if it ever seems relevant or useful. It is interesting, but it remains disconnected from the way people actually live their lives.

THE VALUE OF PROCLAIMING WISDOM

Wisdom literature has a remarkable power to address the disconnect between confession and life, and when people teach this material, they are often struck by how readily people relate to proverbs and the rest of this literature. It gets into a person's mind and provokes thought, and it provides a unique interface between the world of ancient Israel and today precisely because it deals with experiences that are the common lot of people living in the world. People deal with inexplicable suffering and loss and often struggle as Job did. They wonder whether life has any meaning and whether anything they do really matters. They experience the delights and challenges of relationships; they struggle with injustice and with government systems that often support oppression rather than seeking to eliminate it. While the circumstances in which these challenges are set change with time, place, and culture, the basic struggles remain essentially the same.

Davis talks about her own experience of meditating on Proverbs during a personal crisis and how it changed her view of the importance of this material in the Bible. She says, "What I discovered in meditat-

---

3. These "quotes" are paraphrases that capture the essence of what was said but protect the identity of the student.

ing on Proverbs is that my experience had been anticipated within the pages of the Bible; my personal story had a place within the larger experience of the faith community persisting through generations."[4]

Wisdom has a remarkable ability to connect God's truth with our own lives, and this gives it great potential for evangelism as it shows people a way to think and live that is radically different from the path commended by the world. These books also challenge believers to more seriously engage in pursuing wisdom as it calls them to actually apply God's truth to life and experience the difference this makes. Choosing the way of wisdom in the simple, common sense areas addressed by the wisdom literature rather than continuing on the path of folly can often be an important catalyst in deepening faith and moving a person toward spiritual maturity.

Application of this material in practical ways sometimes produces unexpected outcomes as people discover that the experiential knowledge that comes from applying God's truth to life has the power to inform and energize a person's spiritual life. This is reflected in the comments of three students in various wisdom literature classes.[5]

> All my life I have heard people talk about wisdom, trust, and the like and I was told that I should live my life based on these virtues. The problem is that these were such abstract concepts that they meant little to me. Studying Proverbs has helped me to finally understand those concepts. This class has given me a tool box with some important tools to use as I live my life. I have actually been using some of these tools during the semester, and they have worked perfectly! I am amazed at what this study of Proverbs has done for me. Thank you for encouraging us to change our hearts and not just our actions. I had never understood what it means to be wise until I began to study the Scriptures and ask questions. Thank you for the tool box!

> Throughout my life in the church there have been things that have encouraged me and also things that have been very repetitive and less than helpful to my Christian walk. This class on Proverbs has been one of those ex-

---

4. Davis, "Surprised by Wisdom," 266.

5. The comments could be multiplied many times over. The comments capture the actual content of the students but they have been paraphrased to protect the privacy of each student. For more examples and a broader discussion of these issues, see Edward Curtis and John Brugaletta, *Discovering the Way of Wisdom* (Grand Rapids: Kregel, 2004).

periences that has truly affected me and has marked a great learning encounter in my faith. I have gained a new understanding of what it means to transform my life into one characterized by wisdom and knowledge. My study of Proverbs has been one of the most beneficial studies of my life, and the practical lessons I have learned will have a positive effect on me for the rest of my life as I continue to be molded into the person God wants me to be.

Coming into this class I never expected that I would learn such practical truths from the book of Job. As a Bible major, my intentions were to learn more about wisdom literature as a whole and to better understand the book of Job. I never anticipated coming away from the class as a new person because of what I learned, but that has actually been my experience. The class has helped me immensely in terms of giving me a better understanding of wisdom and revelation, increasing my appreciation for "renewing my mind," and growing in my faith, as I came to know God through a deeper awareness of His power and His goodness.

Few would think that a person would come to understand faith and trust more clearly from studying Proverbs or Job, but seeing what trusting God looks like in practice caused the light to come on for these students and showed them its practical dimensions. These outcomes resulted not from a focused plan that was devised to change these students' lives, though it is regularly emphasized that biblical wisdom always begins and must continue with the **fear of the Lord** (Prov. 1:7). In every case, it was the biblical text applied by the Spirit that brought about change in these students. Assignments and discussions were focused on connecting students with the text, and their interaction with the text brought them to see that proverbs are not just more bits of information unrelated to their lives. The experiential learning helped them see that "This is for me and it actually works." Wisdom has the power to bridge the gaps between ancient Israel and the present and between faith and practice. When that occurs, transformation regularly takes place.

PREPARING A SERMON

Gaining Familiarity with the Passage

In previous chapters we have focused on various themes and characteristics of Old Testament wisdom literature. It is now time to consider how to move from a wisdom text to a sermon. Most of the basic principles for accomplishing this have been discussed, but now we want to consider what it looks like in practice.

The first thing we must do is to choose a passage for preaching or teaching,[6] and once that is done it is essential to develop an intimate familiarity with that text. Translation of the passage from Hebrew helps in identifying structure, the limits of the passage that will be the focus of the sermon, and key words and themes.

The best way to develop intimacy with the text is to read it many, many times over a period of time—ideally, in Hebrew and in a variety of translations. While this reading should focus on the passage that will be taught or preached, it must also include the broader context in which the passage is set. Reading needs to be done slowly and reflectively and in ways that reflect the practice described in Psalm 1:2 ("His delight is in the law of the LORD, and on his law he meditates day and night") or in Deuteronomy 6:6–7:

> And these words that I command you today shall be on your heart. You shall teach them diligently to your children, and shall talk of them when you sit in your house, and when you walk by the way, and when you lie down, and when you rise.

Such reading and contemplation have the power to get the text out of the realm of just the cognitive and "write them on the tablet of your heart," as Proverbs 3:3 puts it. Beginning the study of a passage in this way lays a foundation for the sort of Spirit-empowered proclamation that brings about transformation to a class or congregation. The familiarity that comes from contemplative reading also helps identify key themes and teaching points, and often produces insights into the passage that contribute significantly to the proclamation of the text.

Normally, exegesis of a passage requires a careful study of things like relevant cultural and historical background, and date and authorship of the book. In the case of the wisdom books, such studies rarely pay significant dividends beyond illuminating a few **metaphor**s and figures of speech,[7] because the issues with which these books deal are largely human ones that are not tied to a particular time or culture. In addition the books themselves provide little definitive data to allow us to answer those

---

6. For examples of how Ecclesiastes and Song of Songs might be divided into teaching/preaching units and for suggestions about key themes and teaching points see Edward Curtis, *Ecclesiastes and Song of Songs*, TTC (Grand Rapids: Baker, 2013).

7. See "Helpful Parallels," chap. 3.

questions with certainty.[8] The values and theology of the books are clearly **Yahwistic**, but the issues that are described are not uniquely Israelite.

In the case of the wisdom books, exegetical analysis will necessarily focus on things like literary context and structure, analysis of the poetic images, meaning of key words, and **parallelism**.[9]

The Importance of Context and Literary Analysis

Recognizing literary structure can be helpful in several ways. It can help us identify the limits of individual units and often gives clarity to the passage's key ideas, themes, and thinking.

Proverbs 2

Proverbs 2 is one of a number of passages in Proverbs 1–9 that form a sort of collage around the central theme of this larger section. That central theme, found in Proverbs 1:7, says, "The fear of the LORD is the beginning of knowledge."[10] The images that cluster around this verse show us various aspects of wisdom. Proverbs 2 gives us a summary about wisdom—how to get it and what it will do for us. The chapter also has a clearly defined literary structure that makes the flow of thought obvious through the entire chapter. The chapter could be a convenient way to introduce a congregation to the benefits of living wisely, to the way one gets wisdom, and to several practical aspects of wisdom. It could also serve as an introduction to a sermon series that examines various aspects of wisdom in more detail.

The beginning of the chapter is structured around a series of "If . . . then . . . because . . ." statements that make the flow of the thought clear. The "if" statements in Proverbs 2:1–4 present what is incumbent on the disciple: receiving God's instruction and treasuring it, being attentive to wisdom and understanding, crying out for insight and understanding, and searching for it with the excitement and energy of a search for hidden treasure. The "then" statements present the results of such a pursuit of wisdom: understanding of fear of the Lord and knowledge of God (v. 5) and understanding of righteousness, justice and equity—every good path (v. 9). The "because" statements explain

---

8. Even advocating Solomonic authorship of Ecclesiastes and Song of Solomon does not markedly change our understanding of the central issues. What we know about Solomon's own experience with marriage can provide us little more than an example of how it should not be done, and this is the case irrespective of conclusions about authorship or date of the book.

9. See "Wisdom's Genres: Poetry and Proverb," chap. 1.

10. See Proverbs 9:10. For a brief discussion, see "Wisdom's Perspective and Worldview" in chapter 1 and "Ecclesiastes Affirms the Importance of Fearing God and Keeping His Commandments" in chapter 2.

why this occurs: God gives wisdom, knowledge, and understanding (vv. 6 and 10). The benefits are then described: God's providential oversight (vv. 7–8), and the benefits that come from living according to God's order: deliverance from evil people (vv. 12–19) and keeping the disciple on the right path (v. 21).

While the structure of this passage makes the author's logic clear, there are a number of words that will require further detailed study. Certainly these include fear of the Lord; wisdom, understanding, insight; sound wisdom, upright, integrity, justice, righteousness, and **discretion**. All of these terms are regularly used in wisdom contexts, but understanding more precisely what they denote is critical in bridging the gap between "then" and "now." And this is essential in proclaiming the message to a contemporary audience.

Job 28

A second example of how context and structure can guide proclamation can be seen in Job 28. The context in which the chapter is found is established by the narrative in Job 1–27. Job and his friends have been debating his situation for 25 chapters in an effort to understand what caused it and what should be done to turn things around for Job. As the third cycle of their debate comes to an end with the friends apparently having no more to say, Job 28 seems to function as something of a reflective summary of the situation. The tone of the chapter is much calmer and more serene than the intense and passion-filled chapters of the debate. Despite everything the participants have discussed and debated, no one has even come close to identifying the issues that according to Job 1–2 caused Job's suffering.

Job 28 is set in this context and begins by describing the remarkable wisdom of human beings displayed in their ability to get precious metals and gems from the depths of the earth. Their ingenuity and skill are evident as they overcome numerous obstacles like floods in tunnels and traversing difficult terrain to reach these treasures. Human wisdom is impressive. Set in this context though, it is apparent that human wisdom is entirely inadequate for explaining an issue like what has happened to Job, and so verse 12 expresses the key theme of the chapter: "But where shall wisdom be found? And where is the place of understanding?" The remainder of the chapter makes clear what the debate has already revealed—that the kind of wisdom needed to answer such questions cannot be found with people, nor can it be purchased by them. Only God has such wisdom.

The chapter ends on a very significant note both in terms of the interpretation of the book, and in terms of understanding what constitutes human wisdom. The chapter shows unequivocally that wisdom for unraveling the mysteries of the universe uniquely belongs to God.

The chapter also sets forth a different perspective on what constitutes human wisdom. It consists not in comprehensive knowledge about God and Creation, but in fearing God and turning from evil; it involves living in a right relationship with God.

The chapter makes clear the limited nature of human wisdom but does so in a way that is not dismissive of it. The chapter is also clear about how human beings are supposed to live in the light of the limited understanding that is part of the human condition. They are to live in dependence on the all-wise Creator of all things.

Again the structure of the chapter is clear, and it divides easily into two parts (Job 28:1–11 and 28:13–28), with the central idea of the passage found in the question posed in both Job 28:12 and 20. Again there are many things that can be usefully researched, such as ancient mining practices and metallurgy. There are also a number of words for gems, etc., of which the exact identity is not known, though the basic points made by the chapter, given its context, are not obscured by those uncertainties.

Organizing the Presentation

Proverbs 2

Once the basic exegetical work is done, it is important to organize these points and structure the message for a sermon or teaching session.

With Proverbs 2, a place to begin might be something like:

- What God Expects from a Disciple (2:1–4)
- What God Promises to Do for a Disciple (2:5–8)
- Practical Benefits for a Disciple (2:9–22)

Obviously, such outlines can be modified to make them more amenable to various contemporary audiences and many details can be added from the chapter itself. In addition, illustrations and examples will need to be crafted to connect with the congregation. Another benefit that comes out of an intimate familiarity with the text is that this often contributes to an intuitive sense of which examples and illustrations are relevant and useful and which, while they may be very good stories, do not capture the essential teaching of the passage. It is often useful to structure the message in ways that follow the flow of thought in the passage, and the proclamation of the text should conform to the **genre** of the passage when that is possible.

Job 28

Again, the structure of Job 28 suggests how it might be appropriately taught. The basic outline might be something like:

- Celebration of Human Wisdom (28:1–11)
- Limits of Human Wisdom (28:13–19)
- Where Is Wisdom to Be Found? (28:12, 20)
- God's Wisdom and Ours (28:20–28)

Obviously many details can be filled in from the text itself, and illustrations, application points must be added, but the structure of the passage provides a guideline for where to begin.

GENERAL GUIDELINES FOR PROCLAIMING WISDOM LITERATURE

While every passage must be understood and proclaimed on its own merits, the nature and purposes of wisdom literature must be kept in mind as the material is taught. We should also always be mindful of certain overriding themes and their role in shaping the broader context of this material. This literature explores many questions with which people struggle in life, but which are unanswerable based on the methods employed by the sages. Wisdom also sets before us numerous eminently practical principles for living successfully in the world, many of which could be paralleled in contemporary self-help books, and wisdom regularly recognizes human limits and the limits of its own efforts and methodology. Even as wisdom emphasizes the great benefit of living wisely, it also makes it clear that wisdom cannot completely protect us from all evil and folly. Proclamation of this material must strike an appropriate balance between the practical instructions that constitute much of wisdom's teaching and its more global—and often unanswerable—questions. Wisdom often describes the realities, and the central question for God's people is "How should one live in the face of such realities?" Out of the great diversity that characterizes the wisdom literature several dominant themes stand out.

The Nature of Wisdom

Old Testament wisdom literature unequivocally affirms that true wisdom must begin with the fear of the Lord (Prov. 1:7; Job 28:28; and Eccl. 12:13), and the acquisition of wisdom must always proceed in that same way. Numerous passages also make it clear that obtaining wisdom involves the diligent and persistent pursuit of wisdom.

That which people can discover about **Yahweh's order** is always limited, but bits and pieces of the principles that God designed into the world can be discovered through observation and experience. Many questions about God or morals—in any absolute sense, at least—or questions such as those pursued by Job or **Qoheleth** always elude human efforts to figure out, and can only be resolved through God's **special revelation** to his people.

It is essential to proclaim wisdom literature in ways that reflect an appropriate balance between the value of the wisdom that comes to us through **general revelation**, while also affirming the necessity and priority of special revelation. It is critical to remember that the practical principles contained in these books are a part of inspired Scripture and are an integral part of God's revelation to his people. These snippets of wisdom are not just helpful principles that will make life go better,[11] they reflect the way God designed the world to work and are essential for equipping God's people for ministry and good works (2 Tim. 3:16–17).

It is important to emphasize that gaining wisdom and the skills that flow from it is a lifelong task that requires openness to Scripture and to the wise people around us. It requires that people pay attention as they live life, and that they put into practice the knowledge they acquire. The perspective of the wisdom literature is that knowledge acquired apart from faith and trust in God is in essence folly, as is information or skill that is not applied in a timely and appropriate way. As the sages point out, even the great skill of the snake charmer does no one any good unless it is applied (Eccl. 10:11), and the farmer who never gets around to planting his seed will never have a crop to harvest (Eccl. 11:4; Prov. 20:4).

Finally, wisdom describes both the complexity of life in the world and the mysterious and overarching providence of God that pervades all of reality. We cannot know what will happen in the future, nor can we figure out the work of God and his providence, but in light of the realities that these books affirm, wisdom calls us both to live wisely and to trust God.

The Realities of Life under the Sun

The world is filled with things that we can neither fully understand nor control, and the patterns that are evident throughout life are often disrupted by dysfunction, evil, and folly. Risks attach to virtually everything a person does in life, and desired outcomes can rarely be guaranteed. Life is full of unexpected situations, and as Qoheleth says in Ecclesiastes 9:11, "Again I saw that under the sun the race is not to the swift, nor the battle to the strong, nor bread to the wise, nor riches to the intelligent, nor favor to those with knowledge, but time and chance happen to them all." Suffering and difficulty come to people in the world without commentary or explanation, and often there is little correspondence between a person's circumstances and whether or not that person is righteous or wicked.

---

11. They will often do that, and someone once described wisdom as "lubrication for life"; it reduces the friction we experience as we live in the world.

Wisdom literature also recognizes that life is full of beautiful and wonderful things. The delights of family and relationships, the enjoyment of food or drink, the satisfaction of doing what is right and good, or the fulfillment that comes from a job done well are illustrative of blessings that the sages recognized as coming to people from the hand of God.

Wisdom affirms the importance of human choices in determining outcomes but sees the providence of God as that which ultimately determines outcomes. The work of God and his purposes are beyond humanity's ability to understand. The proclamation of wisdom literature must balance these tensions and avoid the temptation to emphasize one aspect of the reality noted by the sages to the neglect of the other.

The Goals of Wisdom and the Importance of Application

Wisdom is related to Yahweh's order and gives people the skill to navigate life in a complex and challenging world. The instructions contained in this literature are of sufficient importance that God included them in his special revelation to his people. They tell us something about how God designed the world to work and enable a person to live in harmony with that. This process is analogous to the way people are trained for many professions, or as artists and craftsmen.

My mother would often cite the proverb, "Experience is the best teacher," and the proverb certainly applies broadly in terms of teaching wisdom literature, especially when it comes to applying this material to life. It is difficult to imagine a single person serving as an expert on parenting or a teenager with no experience managing even a household budget conducting a seminar on responsible financial management.[12]

A medical student cannot be trained for every possible scenario that he or she might encounter, just as a teacher cannot be trained for every situation that might arise in the classroom. Rather they are equipped with basic principles that are foundational to the discipline and trained to deal with the kinds of things they will likely face in that field. They see how the basic principles work in typical instances, and then they must develop the skills to respond to the almost infinite variety of specific situations that may confront them as they live and work in a complex world. This is why most people want a doctor or a mechanic who has many years of experience rather than one who is in the beginning stages of a career. We want someone who can deal effectively if our body turns out not to be average or typical or if our vehicle's problem provokes the response, "That's one I've never seen before!"

---

12. My observations in the church suggest that this principle is often ignored. It appears that "being on staff" brings with it everything that a person needs to be an expert on every topic—especially if they had a course in seminary or attended a seminar on the topic.

A central goal in proclaiming this literature must be to motivate and assist people in developing the skill to know the right time and the right way to apply the right principle (or group of principles) to the specific circumstances with which they are confronted. Wisdom and experience make it clear that life is far more complex than the textbook examples that we often hear in sermons and classes. Wisdom equips us with tools for navigating uncharted waters and difficulties in the world.

We must remind listeners that the only way skill is ever developed is through practice, practice, practice, and that practice makes perfect only when we do things right. Proverbs 2–4 and many other wisdom passages see applying truth to life and persisting on that course as the process that changes bad habits into good ones and ultimately produces godly character. There is no other way to become a skilled craftsman at living wisely.

While we cannot apply the principles for our listeners, we must guide them as they work at this task. Case studies and meditation projects can contribute to this goal. Contemporary examples and illustrations such as those found in newspaper advice columns can be helpful, but these examples must be rooted in life rather than involving complex philosophical dilemmas. Examples need to be wide-ranging and include topics such as finances and money management, work, words and relationships. They need to include the kinds of moral and ethical dilemmas that people regularly encounter in life.

The examples must also be related to principles in the text to reinforce the idea that wisdom and common sense are values in which God delights and which enable the people of God to glorify him in the world. We must be passionate about the necessity for living out God's truth.

There is an old story about a boy who from a young age wanted to be a fireman and unlike most young boys who dream of such a career, the urge persisted. He got all the education and training that was required and finally was accepted into an excellent firefighter training school. Because all his work was exemplary in every phase of his training, on graduation he was chosen for advanced work where he again excelled. He was sent to Europe to study with some of the greatest firefighting theorists in the world and was chosen to teach firefighting in the best firefighting school in the entire country. There he won many awards and moved through the ranks with distinction. His name was the first one people thought of when it came to the leading experts in fighting fires. After he died a note was found by his bedside. It read, "As I lie here today reviewing my life, I still remember my dream, my passion to be a fireman. More than anything else I wanted to put out fires . . . but I realized something today. I have never put out a real fire. NEVER!"

The goal of exegesis for the pastor or teacher is not accurate analysis for its own sake. Rather, it is to apply God's truth to life, first personally, and then to encourage the same in others to whom it is proclaimed. It is a tragedy when the church finds its paradigm for success in sources other than Scripture; it is equally tragic when there is broad knowledge about the Bible and theology, but where that truth is not applied to life. The perspective of the wisdom literature is that wisdom that is not applied is not the wisdom to which God calls his people; it is just folly in disguise.

The Potential of Wisdom

Although wisdom cannot protect a person from every danger, its value for living is immense, as passages like Proverbs 3:13–18 make clear. This short passage provides another example of how literary structure can be essential for understanding the key theme of a section and for appropriate proclamation of the unit. The section is part of a larger unit describing how God used wisdom to create the world and emphasizes the benefits that wisdom can bring to individuals. Verses 14 and 15 claim that wisdom's benefits exceed those generated by gold, silver and precious jewels. Verses 16 and 17 specify these benefits as long life, wealth, and honor. They also declare that life lived according to wisdom will be pleasant and characterized by *shalom*. The poem identifies one of wisdom's important goals, and this has particular implications for teaching and preaching these texts. The passage reads:

> Blessed is the one who finds wisdom,
>> and the one who gets understanding,
> for the gain from her is better than gain from silver
>> and her profit better than gold.
> She is more precious than jewels,
>> and nothing you desire can compare with her.
> Long life is in her right hand;
>> in her left hand are riches and honor.
> Her ways are ways of pleasantness,
>> and all her paths are peace.
> She is a tree of life to those who lay hold of her;
>> those who hold her fast are called blessed.

This poem begins and ends with words that are usually translated, "happy," "fortunate," "blessed," or "truly happy" (אַשְׁרֵי in v. 13 and מְאֻשָּׁר in v. 18), and this **inclusio** identifies the central theme of the section. The word אַשְׁרֵי[13] frequently introduces Old Testament beatitudes. It is translated μακάριοι in the **LXX**, and is the word Jesus used in

---

13. This noun is a construct plural and only appears in this form. Verbal forms sometimes occur (מְאֻשָּׁר in v. 18 is a pual participle).

the Beatitudes in Matthew 5:3–12. The word denotes the fortunate or happy state of a person as observed by another, and each of these Old Testament beatitudes identifies a characteristic of the person that accounts for this assessment.

In this passage the truly happy person is the one who has found wisdom and understanding (Prov. 3:13) and has seized wisdom and holds it tightly (Prov. 3:18). In other wisdom passages the people described in this way are those who keep the law (Prov. 29:18), listen to wisdom (Prov. 8:34), and keep wisdom's ways (Prov. 8:32). In Proverbs 16:20 it is the person who trusts in the Lord while in Proverbs 28:14 it is the individual who fears the Lord who is said to be "blessed." Psalm 112 is a wisdom psalm, which describes the person who fears God and delights in his commandments in this way (Ps. 112:1).

Finally, Psalm 1—another wisdom psalm—uses this term in verse 1 to describe the person who rejects the advice of the wicked and instead delights in the instruction of the Lord and meditates on it day and night. This person is described as a deeply rooted tree planted by a constant source of water. The tree flourishes and regularly produces fruit, a metaphor that describes a life that people most would prefer. In contrast, the wicked person is said to be like chaff that the wind blows away.

The qualities that characterize the blessed person are values regularly emphasized in the wisdom literature, and the claim seems to be that if one chooses the path of wisdom, it will make a difference that others will notice. This will be a basis for envy and congratulations on the part of those who observe this individual. When the people of God live in this way, God's reputation will be elevated and others will come to acknowledge and trust **Yahweh**. In addition, God's people will develop character that will make them more like the Lord in whom they trust.[14] Proclamation of this material should call people to practice wisdom in all of life and move them toward closer conformity to God's truth and character.

The Power of Rhetorical Devices and Examples

The genre of the biblical material seems to be as much a part of its inspiration as the content, and the text is designed to impart more than cognitive information. It is meant to impact readers holistically. The rhetorical devices used by the biblical authors play a major role in bringing about this result. Using similar rhetorical devices in sermons can sometimes be effective in guiding learners into personally experiencing

---

14.   This is implied in Psalm 111 which describes God and Psalm 112 which describes the person who fears God. Adjectives describing God in 111 are repeated in 112, but now to describe the person who fears God. For example, God is described as "gracious and merciful" in 111:4 while the person who fears God is described in the same way in 112:4.

the biblical text. Ryken says, "If we continually translate the images into abstractions, we distort the poem as a piece of writing and miss the fullness of its experiential meanings."[15]

The use of parallelism reinforces ideas in the text and helps readers see concepts from a variety of perspectives and enriches learning. Parallelism in Hebrew poetry slows the reader down, and helps him or her think about and experience the text in deeper and more comprehensive ways. An important goal of proclamation should be to facilitate these same outcomes.

Images, proverbs, or stories can be used to reinforce the main ideas in a text in memorable ways. When I was in graduate school, Dr. James Montgomery Boice was our family's pastor, and his use of stories and concrete images to illustrate a point was remarkable. After almost forty years we often think of stories that he told in sermons and our recall of the story or example almost always brings to mind the theological point he was making. The wisdom literature provides unique opportunities for this sort of thing. A sermon on wisdom in finances could make use of the humorous Jewish proverb, "When a fool goes to market, all the merchants rejoice," as a memorable theme throughout the sermon. It reflects an important point made by several biblical proverbs and makes it in a way that sticks in the mind long after the sermon has ended. Other rhetorical devices in the wisdom material can be used with similar effect, and examples taken from life also have the power to connect the principle to our time and place and set the principle or theme firmly into the core of our being.

Examples can help connect biblical images with life today and make the difference between a powerful and effective sermon and just another lecture. Failure to do this makes hearing a sermon or even reading the Bible like going to a museum. We see neat artifacts from the past, we leave and say, "That was great; I enjoyed it immensely," but no one's life is ever changed by the experience. When we participate in the text and experience what the author is communicating, the encounter can be transforming. Examples and stories have the power to affect the kind of experience that is pivotal in a person's spiritual life.

Proverbs and poetry have a remarkable power to penetrate into a person's heart where the ideas they express can change the way that person thinks and feels. Proverbs about God's sovereign oversight of the affairs of life[16] can, over time, change a person's worldview and provide a basis for hope and stability, as can statements affirming the importance of the fear of the Lord. The same is true of more mundane principles like the importance of civility in speech or kindness to others or the

---

15. Leland Ryken, *How to Read the Bible as Literature* (Grand Rapids: Zondervan, 1984), 90.

16. A number of these are found in Proverbs 16.

importance of justice and personal integrity. The rhetorical techniques seen throughout the wisdom literature have great potential for getting the people of God moving in the right direction and sustaining the momentum in a world that desperately needs to see what God's grace is able to do in the life of a person who lives in obedient trust in God.

GUIDELINES FOR PROCLAIMING INDIVIDUAL BOOKS

While the guidelines noted above have broad applicability, the individual wisdom books are sufficiently diverse to justify some comments that are particularly relevant to the unique issues raised in those works.

Job

Proclamation Should Do Justice Both to Job's Struggle and His Faith

Job's experience resulted in disorientation, confusion, and anger as he tried to square his experience with his understanding of God. The tensions reflected in Job's struggle are important because they mirror the responses of many who suffer. They are also important because of the questions they provoke about the nature of God.[17] Job was never told why he suffered, and this reflects the broader biblical pattern that rarely answers that question. The answers that come to Job have little to do with the specific reasons for his suffering; instead, the resolution brings him to a deeper intimacy with God. Job simply had to wait in a situation where there was no evidence that God was doing anything, and where it increasingly appeared that he would not respond. Job struggled to fit his experience into the theological categories he knew and do so in the presence of friends and family who insisted that their understanding of how God works in the world was complete.

Both Job's suffering and the questions and reactions it provoked reflect human experience that has been replicated in the lives of people throughout history, and it is at this point that the book of Job resonates with people.[18] Proclamation of this book must engage with both Job's struggle and the relational/experiential solution reflected in the final chapters.

---

17. That is, how can experiences such as Job's occur if God is just, good, and sovereign?

18. This is illustrated in the huge popularity of Harold Kushner's book, *When Bad Things Happen to Good People* (New York: Schocken, 1978). The book was on *The New York Times* bestseller list for many months. A number of conservative Christians gave high praise to the book despite its theologically unsatisfactory conclusion that God is unable to attend to everything in a complex world and so inexplicable tragedies sometimes fall through the cracks apart from God's attention. Kushner's description of the struggle resonates with people who suffer to such a degree that the problematic nature of his conclusions are hardly noticed.

Proclamation Should Reflect the Book's Poetic Genre

Poetry is particularly suited for conveying Job's pain, confusion, and anger, and it connects far more effectively with those who have experienced suffering than prose discourse or propositions ever could. At the same time, ideas and principles are communicated in the text, and these must also be understood. With the difficult poetry of Job, it will often be helpful to explain details about poetic structure, parallelism, metaphors and images,[19] and relevant details from the culture resulting from our exegetical study. As useful as it is to explain the difficult poetry and obscure metaphors, this should be done in ways that encourage listeners to experience the text for themselves, as they bring this new information to the text. A good teacher can explain many things about a text, but cannot experience it for someone else.

Proclamation Should Use Examples to Connect the Ancient Text to Today's World

It is often possible to bridge the gap between our time and place and something that was relevant for people in Israel three thousand years ago by contemporizing the setting and background of the passage. Books like Job provide opportunities for doing this easily. A pastor might read portions of Job 1 and 2 and say, "It is hard to imagine anyone having a worse day than Job, but because we live in a fallen world bad things still happen, even to people who are faithfully following God. Many in our congregation know what that is like and know the pain and confusion that often accompany such tragedy and loss." A circumstance involving someone in the congregation or community could be recounted, or someone struggling with uncertainty and pain could share their experience. People who have dealt with pain and grief in the past could talk about things that brought them comfort and helped to sustain them through those struggles. Someone might even describe how good friends and a caring community helped them and comforted them through their trial in contrast to the "comfort" provided by Job's friends.

Proclaim Job with a Broad Awareness of How People Suffer

Sensitive and appropriate application of the principles relating to suffering in Job requires experience in suffering and a broad awareness about how suffering impacts people and how they typically respond to pain and loss. People who have had little experience with suffering often relate more readily with Job's friends and their arguments than they do with Job.

Few words are more offensive to people who are desperately hurting than the words, "I understand," especially when those words come

---

19. See "The Nature of Hebrew Poetry," chap. 1.

from someone who has never suffered a significant loss or been the victim of a horrific injustice or evil act. The most effective counselors are often those who have been through the same kinds of experience as the person who is struggling.

While personal experience is the best teacher of these things, there are also other ways to expand our understanding. Good literature or movies can teach us much about the plight of people in a fallen world. Listening attentively to those who suffer or learning from those in medicine or psychology who have broad experience dealing with suffering can help us develop understanding and sensitivity to the issues that often accompany suffering. Such understanding can make us more effective and sensitive counselors and deliver us from the kind of mistakes made by Job's friends.[20]

It is also important to understand that helping people who suffer does not mean that we answer all their questions and use our vast knowledge of theology or another discipline to "solve their problems." Sometimes the most effective response is to say nothing and to show the person faithful, compassionate love in the way Job 2:13 suggests. It is important to remember that God's word has far more power to bring comfort and healing than our advice ever could.

I had a student in a class on Job who, along with her family, had experienced enormous difficulties. She told me that she took the class because she wanted to get answers about why she and her family had suffered so much. After it was over she said, "I did not get any answers to those questions, but what I do have now is peace." God's Word has a unique power to bring about such outcomes.

Proverbs

Proclamation Should Reflect the Big Picture and Recurrent Themes

Preaching Proverbs must emphasize that the wisdom that the biblical sages commend is never acquired apart from a right relationship with Yahweh, and that this same trust in God is essential for its continued development. The call to get wisdom and put it into practice in all of life should be issued with the same passion and energy as is seen in the early chapters of Proverbs, and its great value should be proclaimed in the same way. The principles should be taught in a balanced way that does justice to the broader teaching of the book on each topic.

The idea of the two ways—the way of wisdom and the way of folly— should be emphasized regularly along with the responsibility of each person to make choices that are consistent with wisdom.

---

20. See the comments on this in chapter 6.

Proclamation Should Reflect the Book's Genre

As we proclaim proverbs to a generation largely unfamiliar with them, it is necessary to present the message in ways that make it clear that proverbs are not promises or laws, but rather general statements of truth. It is equally important to make clear that this characteristic of a proverb does not change the fact that they are part of God's authoritative revelation to his people. It is also crucial to differentiate among the types of sayings in the book and identify the type of each proverb or saying as we interpret and teach the material in the book of Proverbs.[21]

Proclamation Should Emphasize the Need for Application

An individual proverb normally captures a tiny aspect of truth, and that truth is normally tied to a specific set of circumstances observed by the author. The one who hears the proverb and seeks to apply it to life must first identify the general principle and then begin to understand the broad range of specific circumstances where the idea is relevant. Skill in applying these general principles to life is critically important if wisdom's full potential is to be realized. A successful contractor knows much about construction techniques and properties of building materials, but he or she must also know when to use a particular technique or material for the specific set of circumstances demanded by a project. Likewise, appropriate application of wisdom must take into account the unique situations of the people with whom we are dealing.

Pastors should explain exegetical details and other relevant information in order to pinpoint the general principle conveyed in a proverb, and a teacher should explore with the congregation various ways of applying the principle that he or she has found useful. Teachers should also make it clear that their experiences in applying the proverbs are only illustrative examples that do not exhaust the possibilities. Each person must apply them to their own unique circumstances.

We often suppose that our observations and experiences are normative across time and culture, but that is rarely the case. Proverbs 18:17 says, "The one who states his case first seems right, until the other comes and examines him," and this principle applies much more broadly than in the legal realm. Reducing human experience to that which we have experienced or observed will likely put us in the company of Job's friends. The goal of proclamation is not to deliver definitive applications to a congregation; rather it is to equip disciples with skills and tools for applying wisdom principles across the entire spectrum of life. It must take into account the unique and diverse circumstances that confront people in the world.

The proverbial principles found in this material must often be balanced by other proverbs and appropriately matched to specific situa-

---

21. See "Interpret Proverbs Recognizing the Wide Diversity of Sayings in the Book," chap. 4.

tions. A general principle about the importance of parental training such as Proverbs 22:6 must be taken together with more specific principles about the forms training and discipline might take. Proverbs recognizes different methods of discipline such as gentle words of correction, harsh words of rebuke, and even corporal punishment. The goal of discipline is to bring about changes in attitude and behavior, and wisdom normally utilizes the least painful method that will accomplish the task.

We found that a very effective method for disciplining for our older son was to put him on timeout in the bathroom without things like books or puzzles. Often just the threat of having to sit in the bathroom for five minutes would bring about an instant change in his behavior. When we tried that with his younger brother, we would hear laughter and singing emanating from the bathroom. He found great fun in spinning the toilet paper roll, running water in the sink and shower, and playing with a bar of soap or the trash can. We had to come up with a different method of discipline that was effective for him.

The complexity of this task is brought into even sharper focus when one realizes that these principles regarding discipline must be applied to groups and individuals that are very diverse. To further complicate the matter, these truths about discipline must be proclaimed to parents who are just as diverse as their children and who bring their own issues to the table. This is especially the case in a culture where child abuse is a major problem. "Fitting" application of wisdom in a complex world requires all the resources that God makes available to his people.

Ecclesiastes

The guidelines here are meant to focus on issues and teachings of the book about which most evangelicals would agree, and they presuppose that the book, including the epilogue, is a unified composition.

Proclamation Should Do Justice to Qoheleth's Tensions

The book's tensions are almost certainly deliberate, and one reason for this is to alert people to realities about life in the world to which many turn a blind eye until circumstances force them to acknowledge such truths. Qoheleth wants to disabuse us of building a worldview around tradition or faith assertions, while failing to acknowledge disconcerting realities in the world.

This author uses tensions to show us that the world created by the infinite and sovereign Lord is complex. He also recognizes that the work of God in the world is far more marvelous and mysterious than people can ever fully comprehend. Qoheleth describes a world that is characterized by trouble, pain, and difficulty—often as a result of human folly and evil.

The limits that are innate to being human are readily acknowledged in Ecclesiastes. They are evident in things that we cannot understand or change and in questions we cannot answer. While such awareness can be disquieting and disconcerting, it often plays an important role in bringing people to the point of trusting God, which Ecclesiastes sees as the central duty of human beings (Eccl. 12:13).[22] Understanding such realities can move us away from self-dependence to dependence on God.

In proclaiming Ecclesiastes it is important not to isolate passages from the book so as to remove the tensions. Balance is essential and sensitivity to one's audience is critical, but it is important to teach in ways that preserve these tensions rather than obscure or eliminate them. Qoheleth's goal is to instill in people the skills to navigate a world that is characterized by tensions and ambiguities.

Proclamation Should Point to Further Light on Qoheleth's Unanswered Questions

The author of Ecclesiastes asks far more questions than he answers, and many of these show us that self-discovery and intellectual persistence will never produce answers to questions about the work and nature of God or the meaning of life. Many of the questions and difficulties presented by this **sage** find their answers in Jesus and ideas explicated more fully in the New Testament, and making that clear is an important part of preaching this book.

The existential tension created by inexplicable tragedy or difficulty or injustice is generally not eliminated even by the more complete revelation of the New Testament, and it is important to make that clear as we teach and preach Ecclesiastes. While Ecclesiastes must be taught and preached on its own terms rather than immediately jumping to the New Testament, it is still essential to keep reminding people both about God's purposes in history and about his purposes for individual believers today. Nothing can separate believers from God's love, nor can anything thwart God's purposes—he will ultimately fully redeem his people, judge evil, and restore his creation. In addition, Jesus made it clear that it is possible to accumulate treasure in heaven where it will not be lost or destroyed by death.

Proclamation Should Instruct God's People How to Live with Unanswered Questions

Despite Qoheleth's unresolved questions and tensions, he is unequivocal about how a person should live in the midst of the inequities

---

22. Just as the recognition that a person is hopelessly sinful and condemned before God is essential in bringing that person to accept the free gift of salvation, so recognizing the realities of life and human limits can motivate a person to a deeper dependence on God.

and anomalies that are part of life. The epilogue sums up what Qoheleth calls "the whole duty of man" (כָּל־הָאָדָם). He says in Ecclesiastes 12:13, "The end of the matter; all has been heard. Fear God and keep his commandments, for this is the whole duty of man." In this conclusion he highlights the importance of the **fear of God** throughout the book (Eccl. 3:14; 5:7; 7:18). Qoheleth also reinforces the point made in Job 1:1, 8 and 28:28 that in both prosperity and in great suffering and loss, a person's proper response is to fear God and turn from evil.[23]

Qoheleth calls people to a life centered in God rather than one centered in self. He calls people to trust God, and the basic trust in God to which he calls people is characterized by obedience to God's instruction. The New Testament teaching about discipleship includes the same elements advocated by Ecclesiastes.

Song of Songs

Proclaim Song of Songs as Love Poetry

A necessary part of teaching this material will be to explain things that are likely to be missed by a contemporary reader only minimally familiar with poetry. The goal in this is not to reframe the text into logical propositions that declare what the text means. Neither should it be to translate the poetry into a more proselike form that will be easier to understand. The genre of the poetic text is part of its inspired character as are the cognitive ideas that are communicated through it. Both the rational (cognitive) and the affective dimensions must be respected in proclaiming the text.

Proclamation Should Celebrate the Marriage Relationship between a Man and a Woman as Reflecting God's Order

Genesis 2:18–25 makes it clear that people are created for relationships and that the relationship between a man and woman is a central element in the way God designed the world to work. The story of human rebellion against God in Genesis 3 makes it clear that this relationship was impacted in a particularly negative way by sin and God's judgment. Human history is replete with evidence of dysfunction, oppression, and abuse that has replaced the harmony, respect, and mutual help implied in the "one-flesh" relationship that reflects God's order.

Song of Songs sets before us a relationship that, presumably, is functioning according to God's order and various aspects of that relationship are clearly evident. The passion and delight that characterizes this relationship is obvious in almost every verse, and while it would be a

---

23. For a more detailed discussion see above in chapter 2, and the chapter on "Fearing God" in Curtis and Brugaletta, *Discovering the Way of Wisdom*.

serious mistake to reduce the relationship to the physical and sexual, it is unmistakable that sexuality is a part of God's design and is one of his good gifts to humanity. Obviously, this is related to procreation and God's instruction to "be fruitful and multiply" (Gen. 1:28; 9:1), but it is also related to relational intimacy and delight.[24]

Proclamation Should See Song of Songs as Congruent with the Rest of Scripture

Song of Songs focuses on the relationship between a man and woman without addressing questions about morality. Given that we possess this book only in the context of Scripture,[25] it seems legitimate to assume that Song of Songs presupposes the same moral values found elsewhere in the wisdom literature and the rest of the Old Testament. This establishes an interpretive grid for discussing and proclaiming the book in a post-sexual-revolution cultural context. It also provides guidelines for discussing a number of ambiguous passages in the book.

Proclamation of Song of Songs Should Reflect Wisdom's Pedagogy

We learn from Song of Songs in ways similar to the incident described for us in Proverbs 24:30–34. There a person is walking down the road and sees the field of a sluggard. It is overgrown with weeds, the fence is broken down, and no useful crop is growing. The traveler reflected on what he saw and was instructed by the experience. He gained insight into what one should do in order to achieve success and avoid failure.

Song of Songs teaches in much the same way. We do not have a clear narrative frame in which to set the poetry. Instead we get small glimpses into the experiences of the couple and hear brief snippets of their conversations. We learn as we watch and listen. Our experience with the lovers should send us away "instructed." Obviously we must process what we see and hear through the filter of our own experiences in relationships as we seek to apply the instruction.

Our proclamation of this text should impact our audience in ways that bring about their own engagement with the text. Certain things are prominent as we reflect on these poems. There is mutuality as both the man and woman express praise and gratitude for the other, and both initiate love making. Their relationship is characterized by a mutual commitment, and both deeply value the other and express that gratitude for the one they love. They focus on the best in the other rather than on the things they wish were different. Their words build each other up rather than tear the other down. They find excitement and delight in their mate, and the enjoyment includes far

---

24. See also Prov. 5:15–20; Eccl. 9:7–9.

25. See the brief discussions above in chapter 2 and 4.

more than just the physical. It includes forays into nature and the beautiful things they see and enjoy there. They enjoy being together and delight in one another wherever they are and in whatever they happen to be doing.

Their words and actions seem to flow out of profound respect for one another. There is no self-seeking and manipulation. Song of Songs 8:6–7 suggests that deep love for one another[26] characterized this relationship.

Proclamation of Song of Songs Should Emphasize the Importance of Application

Application of this material is the ultimate goal of the text, and obviously, a pastor or teacher cannot apply it for others. A teacher must first understand, experience, and apply the text personally before exploring implications for application with others. In proclaiming these texts we must recognize that our application inevitably reflects our own experiences and circumstances, and we must avoid the assumption that our relational experiences are normative for others. Pastors and teachers must learn as much as possible by drawing from the experiences of others. Assuming that every person's experience is a mirror image of ours is naïve and can even harm others.

It is also essential to remain aware of the great diversity in terms of culture, education, and life experience that characterizes our audiences. A person who has never been in a serious romantic relationship will miss much of the potential that exists in Song of Songs. A person who reads the book before and after marriage will be astounded at the difference. People whose knowledge about marriage and relationships comes from participating in and observing healthy, flourishing marriages will read the book through radically different eyes than those who come from profoundly dysfunctional and toxic situations.

There are people who have chosen career paths that require enormous time commitments that make doing things together very difficult and others who do everything together. There are people who struggle just to survive financially while others possess an abundance of wealth. Many couples find themselves faced with significant health issues or other family difficulties. Then there is a whole continuum of personality types and emotional issues that impact relationships. There are overly sensitive people who get their feelings hurt easily; there are people who have no self-confidence and others who are over confident to the point of arrogance. A specific way to apply this material with spectacular success in one instance may make the situation even more difficult in another instance. Again, the world is complex and far

---

26. Apparently the kind of love about which Shakespeare said, "Love is not love that alters when it alteration finds."

different than the "one size fits all" approach that often characterizes Christian proclamation.

It is essential, however, that we help the people to whom we minister to begin to think as a Christian about relationships—and especially about marriage. Things like the importance of praising others and expressing thanks to them and for them, civility and kindness, concern for the well-being of one another, **humility** and loyalty to each other can always be appropriately applied and one never reaches the point where growth in such things is complete.

An important part of proclamation and application of this material is to get people to reflectively consider questions like:

- How does what I see and hear in Song of Songs apply to me in my present situation?
- What relevance might these general principles have for me, and what difference might it make if I began to live them out today?
- How might Song of Songs help me to put into practice Paul's exhortation to husbands to "Love your wife as Christ loved the church and gave himself for it"?

6

PUTTING IT ALL TOGETHER:
FROM TEXT TO SERMON

The Chapter at a Glance

Step One: Focusing on the Topic
- Proverbs and Friendship
- An Example of Friendship in Job 4–6

Step Two: Recognizing Genre and Exegetical Details
- Proverbs and Friendship
- Job 4–6 and the Practice of Friendship

Step Three: Organizing the Material
- A Topical Study on Friendship in Proverbs
- A Case Study on Friendship from Job 4–6

Step Four: Applying the Text
- Applying Proverbs to Life
- Applying Job 4–6 to Life

IN THIS FINAL CHAPTER WE WILL APPLY METHODS discussed in earlier chapters to several wisdom texts to show how a sermon might be prepared on that material. Exegesis and proclamation would normally focus on a single text and involve the sort of analysis, organization, and proclamation briefly discussed in chapter 5.[1] The second text (from Job 4–6) that we will consider fits more closely into that mold. We will begin, however, with a topical study that will be constructed largely from individual **proverb**s.

STEP ONE: FOCUSING ON THE TOPIC

Proverbs and Friendship

The widely diverse **genre**s and rhetorical methods used in the wisdom literature make it impossible to create a single universally appropriate paradigm for interpreting and proclaiming this literature. Proclamation needs to be tailored to the particular text rather than squeezing each one into a monolithic paradigm. Proverbs 1–9 contains similar principles and teaching as Proverbs 10–31, but the longer literary units found in 1–9 (and only occasionally in 10–31),[2] show evidence of coherence and design and should normally be dealt with as units. These sections lend themselves well to verse-by-verse exposition.[3]

The individual proverbs that dominate Proverbs 10–31[4] often require a different approach than the units that characterize chapters 1–9. In sections where short **aphorism**s are strung together with little indication of plan or purpose, it is often more useful to do a topical study that creates a mosaic from individual proverbs dealing with a particular subject. The goal is to piece together small bits of information provided by each proverb to gain a broader understanding of the topic. It is important to deal with the various proverbs in ways that recognize the literary arrangement of the material, but it is also the case that the individual proverbs in these units probably existed as independent proverbs and appropriately contribute to our understanding of the topics with which they deal. Thus even these proverbs can be legitimately used in topical studies to create a broader and more balanced understanding of a particular aspect of wisdom.

A topical study from Proverbs should begin by reading through the book a number of times. This will reveal certain themes such

---

1. See "Preparing a Sermon" in chapter 5, and the references in note 4 below.

2. For example, 26:1–12; the **acrostic** poem on the excellent woman in 31:10–31; the longer proverbs in chapter 30; or chapter 16, where a number of proverbs dealing with the sovereignty of God and his providence occur together.

3. Additional insight into how to do this with poetic texts can be found in Mark D. Futato, *Interpreting the Psalms: An Exegetical Handbook*, HOTE (Grand Rapids: Kregel, 2007), and Gary V. Smith, *Interpreting the Prophetic Books: An Exegetical Handbook*, HOTE (Grand Rapids: Kregel, 2014).

4. See "Guidelines for Interpreting Proverbs," chap. 4.

as wisdom and folly, the wise person and the fool, financial issues, proper speech, self-control and **discretion**, the importance of diligence and careful planning, and friendship that recur throughout the book.

If one chooses the topic of friendship for preaching or teaching, it quickly becomes apparent that this book contains more proverbs that directly address friendship and related issues than could be realistically covered in a single sermon or teaching session, and to exhaust everything that it says about this topic would likely require a series on the subject rather than a single sermon.

Even proverbs that say nothing directly about friendship sometimes deal with important matters relating to the topic. For example, fools do not make good friends for a number of reasons. You cannot depend on them to do what they say they will do (25:14); their foolish speech often leads them to betray a confidence (11:13; 20:19) or to persist in saying irritating things at particularly inconvenient times (25:20; 27:14). Their rash and foolish behavior can completely undermine a project that has been carefully planned and appropriately carried out (Eccl. 8:18–9:1).

Their impulsive behavior and lack of judgment can sometimes lead to damage that cannot be reversed by simply saying, "I am sorry. I never thought that would happen" (26:18–19). Their lack of self-control can lead to strife and disaster (12:16; 17:14), and adverse outcomes of such outbursts will often impact those who are with them (23:20–21). Fools rarely learn, and so the problems they create for those around them are often ongoing (18:2; 19:19; 27:22). It becomes clear that putting together a picture of a good friend will involve more than simply gathering together the proverbs that contain words like "friend," "neighbor," or "colleague."

An Example of Friendship in Job 4–6

We also want to do a brief study based on a text from Job. The passage is poetry set in a narrative context and will require a different approach than will be used with individual proverbs from the book of Proverbs. We will have to analyze this section aware of its poetic character and respect its function within the narrative. It is essential to allow the contours of the story to set the context, and individual sections must be interpreted within that broader context. One would never think of reducing a movie to a single scene or a novel to a single incident. It is the entire narrative that establishes meaning, not single isolated incidents. We chose a passage in Job that deals with friendship because Eliphaz contrasts radically with Job's idea of a good friend. This text has the potential to take us past superficial description and penetrate into aspects of friendship that seem relevant today. Bringing insights from both Proverbs and Job together[5] can lead to a deeper understanding of friendship and provide insight into more effectively ministering to people who are suffering.

In terms of a teaching/preaching strategy, one could easily construct a sermon based on either the material from Proverbs or from Job. At the same time the two could be combined, with Eliphaz serving as an example of what not to do as a friend.

STEP TWO: RECOGNIZING GENRE AND EXEGETICAL DETAILS

Proverbs and Friendship

Our goal is to illustrate a method for using individual proverbs in a way that respects the characteristics of the genre but also allows us to use them to bring about a broader understanding of how God designed the world to work. We will put together the tiny pieces provided by several different proverbs to build up a more detailed image pertaining to friendship.

It is important to study the original text of each proverb to identify both textual and translation issues.[6] Ancient proverbs are regularly cryptic and concise, and they use unusual words and strange (to us at least) **metaphor**s. English translations sometimes smooth out these difficulties to produce a simple translation that will make the greatest impact on the reader.[7] Problems and uncertainties in the Hebrew text should be noted so we do not base our teaching on something other than what the biblical text actually says. In addition, we must determine the type of each proverb that we use.[8] Once a topic of interest is chosen from the various subjects dealt with in Proverbs, it

---

5. Appropriately connecting texts can sometimes be done through careful reading. It is more often developed through years of familiarity with texts, and this constitutes an important part of the "art" of exegesis.

6. There are several resources that make this more manageable. The NET Bible identifies most of the major issues associated with each verse. Comprehensive commentaries like Bruce Waltke, *The Book of Proverbs Chapters 1–15*, NICOT (Grand Rapids: Eerdmans, 2004) and *The Book of Proverbs Chapters 15–31*, NICOT (Grand Rapids: Eerdmans, 2005) provide detailed discussions of most of these matters. While several of the proverbs used in this discussion contain minor uncertainties, none of them affect the meaning of the verse or significantly modify the principle expressed by the proverb.

7. See the helpful discussion by Roland Murphy (*Proverbs*, WBC [Nashville: Nelson, 1998], 251–54) on the reasons for this along with appropriate warnings about the care with which this should be done.

8. See "Interpret Proverbs Recognizing the Wide Diversity of Sayings in the Book," chap. 4.

is important to read through the book and compile a list of relevant proverbs. Then it is useful to check lists of proverbs on various topics in most commentaries to make sure that no important ones have been missed. [9]

I have found that a helpful way to do this is to use a computer program like Bible Works to print out each proverb of interest in both English and Hebrew. At this point the selected proverbs can be examined for textual issues and words or metaphors that require special study. At the same time one can begin organizing the proverbs into categories in the way that is reflected in "A Topical Study on Friendship in Proverbs."

Job 4–6 and the Practice of Friendship

In this study we will be confronted with an example of friendship gone awry. The poetry of Job is set in a narrative context, and we will need to follow the development of the story and understand each segment in the light of the larger narrative. It is also important to understand that Job is poetic material. It is not a tightly ordered and logical scientific or philosophical argument. The poetry is filled with allusions—sometimes repeated words, sometimes proverbs or other traditional sayings, but almost never quotations from the book of Proverbs or other sources known to us. The participants in the debates certainly understood the full implications of the quotations and metaphors, but these often elude us. We often have to rely on our sense of what is being said or our perception of the speaker's mood, and so commentators will disagree on many details even when they agree on the general points about the way the argument is developing.

While Eliphaz, Bildad, and Zophar have become stereotypes of bad friends, we need to note that nothing in the text suggests that their intentions were anything but noble. They wanted to comfort a friend whose life had been turned upside down by an unimaginable series of tragedies. They had heard about his loss of wealth and children and about his terrible illness. They were willing to inconvenience themselves and travel several days under difficult circumstances, to see their friend. How then could their efforts have turned out the way they did? It would appear that being a good friend, effectively showing sympathy, and bringing comfort in times of suffering and tragedy requires more than just good intentions.

---

9. Most commentaries on Proverbs list proverbs topically and a few include brief discussions of topics regularly mentioned in the book. Another useful resource is Kathy Miller, *The Useful Proverbs* (Cleveland, OH: God's Word to the Nations, 1997).

STEP THREE: ORGANIZING THE MATERIAL

A Topical Study on Friendship in Proverbs

Building Up the Image: Benefits and Liabilities of Friendship

Proverbs does not provide a blueprint for friendship, but focuses on several important principles related to this topic. Some of these have to do with the value of relationships and illustrate why the time and energy that must be invested into relationships is worthwhile. At the same time, Proverbs identifies things that make it very difficult for strong friendships to develop and flourish.

Proverbs recognizes the value of good advice and counsel from a trusted friend (15:22; 27:9; and 27:17) as well as the help that is always forthcoming from the friend who is truly committed to us (17:17 and 18:24). On the other hand Proverbs identifies things that have the power to destroy friendships in the way described in Proverbs 18:19. Such things include instantly taking offense and constantly arguing about trivialities (18:19; 12:16; 19:19), rash behavior that fails to consider potential outcomes (26:18–19; 27:14; and 25:17), and a pattern of words that hurt others (12:18).

Ecclesiastes 4:9–12 puts several of these basic wisdom principles together as it describes the importance of relationships:

> Two are better than one, because they have a good reward for their toil. For if they fall, one will lift up his fellow. But woe to him who is alone when he falls and has not another to lift him up! Again, if two lie together, they keep warm, but how can one keep warm alone? And though a man might prevail against one who is alone, two will withstand him—a threefold cord is not quickly broken.

Most of us have experienced the benefits of friendship and the help that a good friend can give, particularly in times of need and difficulty. I think of times when my wife and I struggled financially and had to watch every penny. Out of necessity, we practiced frugality in ways that I hope we never have to do again. Our whole life was structured so that our obligations could be met—as long as there were no unexpected expenses like car repairs or trips to the dentist. There was always anxiety because I kept waiting for something else to go wrong. I remember how family members and friends encouraged us and often gave us money, food, clothing, and sometimes even took us out to a nice restaurant or on a fun trip. What a difference that made.

We once bought a house that needed a lot of work, and a friend traveled 800 miles to help us. We were touched by his kindness, and many of the tasks went much better because two people were working on them. I think of friends who have gone through difficult experiences of caring for loved ones during a prolonged illness. I have seen the difference it makes when others provide support and comfort and show their love and concern in concrete ways.

Friendships do not always result in such positive outcomes. Sometimes friends disappoint us and fail to come through when we need them. Many people, who claim to be friends, do not respond in gracious and sacrificial ways but suddenly disappear when there is a significant need. Many of us know what it is like to be in a situation where we truly need help and call on a friend who has offered to provide it, only to have him or her fail to deliver. We do not want friends like the one described in Proverbs 25:14: "Like clouds and wind without rain is a man who boasts of a gift he does not give."

Building Up the Image: Friends, Relatives, and Needs

Proverbs recognizes that there are people whose friendship with others is self-serving and based on what they get out of the relationship. Proverbs 19:6 says, "Many seek the favor of a generous man, and everyone is a friend to a man who gives gifts." I grew up hearing the proverb, "A friend in need is a friend indeed." While the proverb is ambiguous and has been understood and applied in many different ways, I always heard it in contexts that related to the fact that there are people you do not see or hear from for long periods of time, but when they need things, they suddenly begin calling, coming by regularly, and acting as if they are your best friend.

Proverbs 14:20 says, "The poor is disliked even by his neighbor, but the rich has many friends." Proverbs 19:4 and 7 affirm the point but also add new insights to the picture by pointing out the strain that various needs can put on a relationship. Proverbs 19:4 says, "Wealth brings many new friends, but a poor man is deserted by his friend," and Proverbs 19:7 adds, "All a poor man's brothers hate him; how much more do his friends go far from him! He pursues them with words, but does not have them." While these proverbs articulate the need in financial terms it can take many different forms.

In a crisis, the first people to come to the rescue will likely be close relatives, and normally they will keep providing necessary resources after everyone else has gone. Long-term needs, though, can sometimes exhaust the commitment and resources of family members to the point where even they will no longer help.[10] There are friends—though not many—

---

10. These are proverbs and they are making specific points. Proverbs 17:17, "A brother is born for adversity," states the general principle that close family members will stick with you

who are loyal no matter what. Their loyalty and faithfulness persist without limits. Proverbs 17:17 says, "A friend loves at all times, and a brother is born for adversity," while Proverbs 18:24 adds, "A man of many companions may come to ruin, but there is a friend who sticks closer than a brother." Obviously, these are the kinds of friends we want—friends who are loyal and trustworthy. We do not want fair-weather friends who are with us in good times but then abandon us for greener pastures when we have needs or when we are simply no longer of any use to them.

Proverbs 27:10 adds a relevant piece to our picture of friends and friendship: "Do not forsake your friend and your father's friend, and do not go to your brother's house in the day of your calamity. Better is a neighbor who is near than a brother who is far away." The proverb likely makes three points. The first is that it is important to maintain good relationships with friends and family, and this would include helping them when it is possible and appropriate. The second point is that relationships with close family members should be ongoing and not limited to just those times when help is needed from them. The third point is to recognize that needed resources are of many sorts. Sometimes proximity and immediate availability are more important than close family relationships. It is important to maintain good relationships with all in the community, first, because it is the right thing to do, but also because you never know when their help might be needed.

Building Up the Image: Companions Can Either Build Us Up or Tear Us Down

It is important to have good, faithful, and wise friends because we will almost certainly be influenced by them and will, over time, become like them. Scripture gives us many warnings about the dangers of friendship with evil and ungodly people. Examples can be found throughout the early chapters of Proverbs, and in the proverb cited by Paul in 1 Corinthians 15:33.[11] Proverbs 22:24–25 makes the point by saying, "Make no friendship with a man given to anger, nor with a wrathful man, lest you learn his ways and entangle yourself in a snare." People who travel with those who lie and deceive as a matter of course will begin to have a compromised view of truth and appropriate behavior. People who immerse themselves in a world where loyalty is viewed as more important than truth and justice or where integrity and compassion take a back seat to making money will almost certainly find their understanding of right and wrong modified in problematic

---

through thick and thin. It does not guarantee that they will *never* abandon you. Likewise, Proverbs 19:7 does not indicate that they will *always* abandon you when the difficulty gets sufficiently extreme.

11.   "Bad company corrupts good morals."

ways. No matter how winsome and compelling such friends may be, there comes a time when Paul's instruction in 2 Corinthians 6:14–18 must be employed: "Do not be unequally yoked with unbelievers. . . . Therefore go out from their midst, and be separate from them."

Unfortunately, being in a largely Christian community does not always eliminate this problem. As Derek Kidner has pointed out, "Some sins are hidden, not because they are too small to see, but because they are too characteristic to register."[12] I am amazed at how often believers compromise biblical values for the sake of pragmatism and what works in the short term. Frequently, it is because they are surrounded by other believers who, influenced more by the culture than by biblical truth, have made those now "characteristic" values into the new standard.

On the other hand, the right kind of friends can help us grow in faith, wisdom, and knowledge of God. As Proverbs 13:20 puts it, "Whoever walks with the wise becomes wise, but the companion of fools will suffer harm." This works in many different ways including the enlightening and invigorating conversations and debates that often take place among good friends. As Proverbs 27:17 puts it, "Iron sharpens iron, and one man sharpens another."

An important, though not always appreciated, function of a friend is to give needed counsel and correction. A wise and insightful friend can recognize when we are deviating from the right path and detect areas where we need to make changes. An astute and perceptive person can offer correction, and while hearing rebuke is never pleasant, when it comes from someone we know has our best interests at heart, it is more readily accepted. Such a person will not allow us to continue on a path that likely leads to disaster because she understands that "Better is open rebuke than hidden love; faithful are the wounds of a friend" (Prov. 27:5–6), and that "Whoever rebukes a man will afterward find more favor than he who flatters with his tongue" (Prov. 28:23). The person receiving the advice will also recognize that "Whoever loves discipline loves knowledge, but he who hates reproof is stupid" (Prov. 12:1). Such interchanges in a community of people growing in wisdom play a significant role in "stir[ring] up one another to love and good works . . . encouraging one another" (Heb. 10:24–25).

Building Up the Image: Finding Good Friends

These proverbs identify several important qualities that we should look for in a friend, including things like loyalty, honesty, integrity, and commitment. Another vital quality in a friend is the sensitivity to know when to confront, when to overlook a fault, and when encouragement is a better way to help a friend.

---

12. Derek Kidner, *Psalms 1–72*, TOTC (Downers Grove, IL: InterVarsity, 1973), 100.

Proverbs does not directly address the question of how to find a faithful friend, but a few proverbs identify a principle that is likely relevant. Proverbs 20:11 says, "Even a child makes himself known by his acts, by whether his conduct is pure and upright," and Proverbs 19:19 says, "A man of great wrath will pay the penalty, for if you deliver him, you will only have to do it again." Jesus made a similar point in Matthew 7:15–20 in a discussion about false prophets. He said, "You will recognize them by their fruits" (v. 16, 20), and the principle applies more broadly than just to prophets. You can generally tell much about a person by carefully observing what they do and by listening to what they say. Values will be reflected in behavior and words.[13]

Intimate friendships do not happen overnight. They must be cultivated over time; there is no other way to build the trust that is essential in this kind of relationship. A person will demonstrate whether or not he or she is trustworthy in the way they live their lives over the long haul.

Obviously, we have a responsibility to behave wisely and appropriately in a relationship as well, and we must also be cultivating these characteristics in order to be a good friend to others. We must never take our friends for granted, and must always remain cognizant of the fact that even the best relationship can be seriously damaged by neglect or by words or actions that offend. Proverbs 18:19 reminds us that "A brother offended is more unyielding than a strong city, and quarreling is like the bars of a castle." We must be careful to avoid things that have the potential to destroy even special relationships.

A Case Study on Friendship from Job 4–6

The Prologue and the Narrative Context

The prose prologue in chapters 1 and 2 sets the context for the poetic debate between Job and his friends, and gives us important information for interpreting the passage. We learn that Job was a blameless and upright man who feared God and turned from evil (1:1, 8; 2:3). The prologue also identifies one of the book's central issues in the Accuser's[14] question ("Does Job fear God for no reason?" [1:9]) and also recounts the magnitude of Job's loss and personal suffering. We are told about the debate between God and the Accuser and are given information about Job's experience that neither Job nor his friends possessed.

The description of Job is essential in understanding the book. He was "upright" (יָשָׁר), and this indicates that he was morally and ethi-

---

13. This assumes that the person's words and deeds are congruent, that this is someone with integrity.

14. See discussion about this term in "Job Shows that People Should Serve God for Who He Is Rather Than for Benefits He Provides" in chapter 2.

cally "straight," as opposed to being crooked or perverse. He was also "blameless" (תָּם), a term used to describe Noah in Genesis 6:9. God's instruction to Abraham in Genesis 17:1 was to "walk before me, and be blameless." The Hebrew root often also conveys the idea of being complete. It does not mean that Job was sinless but rather he was a person of integrity. A rabbinic comment says that the word refers to a person "whose without is like his within." We are also told that Job feared God and turned from evil. Taken together, these terms indicate that he was a man of integrity who was wholehearted in his commitment to God. He was not a hypocrite but lived before God and others in ways that were characterized by trust, obedience, and integrity.

Job's Outburst (Job 3:3–26)

When the friends arrived, they could not believe what they saw; they did not even recognize Job, and they simply sat for seven days and nights in shocked silence. Then Job finally broke the silence and said,

> Let the day perish on which I was born,
>> and the night that said,
>> "A man is conceived."
> Let that day be darkness!
>> May God above not seek it,
>> nor light shine upon it.
> Let gloom and deep darkness claim it.
>> Let clouds dwell upon it;
>> let the blackness of the day terrify it (Job 3:3–5).

And he continued through the rest of the chapter—twenty-six verses in all—cursing the day of his birth and wishing for anything that might have prevented him from experiencing the terrible and painful tragedy that had befallen him.

Job's Experience and Contemporary Relevance

Think about the most mature and godly person that you know. Life has gone well for them, and God has blessed them with health, material abundance, an ideal family, and respect from all who know them. Suddenly there is a radical change. Their business fails through no fault of their own, and the husband is diagnosed with a painful malady for which there is no cure. A tragic accident takes both their children, and ill-founded accusations raise unjust questions about their integrity. You go to see this person to express your concerns and offer condolences. You sit with him for several hours without anyone saying a word and then he turns, looks you in the eye, and says, "I wish I had never been born; I wish I had died at birth; I wish God had taken me as a child; I wish anything had happened that would have spared me this awful pain and distress. I wish I had never even lived!"

What would you think? What would you say to your friend?

I once heard a missionary report on their work in a third-world country known for its hostility to Christianity and the gospel. He talked about the superstition and magic that was prevalent there and asked the church to pray for them. His wife then gave a more visceral and emotional report. She affirmed all that her husband said and described the oppressive evil that expressed itself in ways that she never even imagined before going to that country—and it seemed to be everywhere. She ended her report to the church by saying, "Please pray for me that when it is time to return there I will want to go back. Right now I never want to go back."

As we were leaving, I overheard a woman saying to her friend, "Why does our church support missionaries like that? I think we should use our money to support more spiritual people." This woman was obviously unable to relate to the missionary's experience or to the depth of suffering that sometimes comes to godly people engaged in doing God's will.[15] That woman, I suspect, felt comfortable with Job's friends.

Eliphaz's Response: A Resort to the Doctrine of Retribution (Job 4–5)

A recording of Eliphaz's words would be helpful since the tone of his voice would give us insight into where he was on the emotional continuum between astonishment and anger. Eliphaz was profoundly shocked at the things he heard from his friend. He never expected a godly man like Job to utter such imprudent words and was probably deeply concerned about his friend.

Eliphaz was the most civil of Job's friends, and he began, I think, with a gentle rebuke. He probably had too much respect for Job to directly accuse him, but wanted to point out things that would bring his friend back to a more appropriate state of mind. Given what he had just heard, he told Job that he was not practicing what he had preached to others in similar situations (4:3–5). He then reminded Job of a theological principle that captured the friends' perspective about how God works in the world—the doctrine of **retribution**, which says that God rewards righteous people with blessing and punishes wicked people with difficulty and tragedy. It is this principle that the friends first suggest and then finally insist is the key for understanding Job's situation.

Irony is evident in Eliphaz's response as he says in 4:6, "Is not your **fear of God** your confidence, and the integrity of your ways your hope?" The terms he uses—your fear (יִרְאָתֶךָ) and the integrity of your ways (תֹּם דְּרָכֶיךָ)—are almost identical to those used to describe Job

---

15. Examples include Jeremiah, Isaiah, and Jesus.

in 1:1. The irony lies in the fact that Job lived his life on the basis of fearing God and integrity and those values had always been the basis of his hope and confidence. The problem was that while he had not changed, his expectation had been turned upside down by his experience—something that in the theological paradigm of the friends was impossible. None of them realized that he was being used by God to prove a point to the Accuser precisely because of Job's character.

Eliphaz and Knowing What Is True

Eliphaz saw no other possibility than retribution working here, and simply followed what seemed like irrefutable logic. He said in 4:8, "those who plow iniquity and sow trouble reap the same." He insisted that innocent people do not experience such terrible things, and advised Job to seek God, commit his cause to him (5:8), and accept God's discipline (5:17). Restoration and blessing would be the inevitable result (5:18–26). Eliphaz insisted that his interpretation was true; its validity was established first by his own observation—"As I have seen" (4:8); secondly, by a vision that confirmed the principle (4:12–21); and thirdly, by the tradition of past generations ("this we have searched out; it is true" [5:27]).

Application and the Reality of Human Limits

Eliphaz was correct about the general truth of the doctrine of retribution, and his general application of the principle was correct as well—people do sometimes suffer for their sins. He was wrong in applying it to Job because his situation was not about justice at all, as the happenings in the heavenly realm make clear.

The importance of appropriate application is set in clear relief in Eliphaz's initial response to Job, and the other friends' interaction with Job will make this even more apparent.

The section also illustrates an important principle about friendship and ministering to those who are hurting. Job's friends applied the theology they knew, but went wrong in at least two ways. First of all, they assumed that their theological paradigm was comprehensive and that they knew everything about how God works in the world. They also assumed that they knew enough about Job and his experience to analyze and interpret his experience without error. In essence, they lacked the **humility** that is basic to genuine wisdom. As the debate continued, it turned into an argument that was focused more on who was right than on comforting Job.

Having all the answers is never a necessary criterion for being a good friend or for helping others; being humble and recognizing our limits is basic and essential. Job's friends had no way of knowing what he had or had not done; they had no way of penetrating to the level of motives, but they assumed that they were fully capable of doing both. Friends must sometimes trust a friend and give them the benefit of the doubt rather than immediately assuming that they know enough to pass judgment.

Defining Key Words and Allowing the Narrative to Develop

The interaction between Job and Eliphaz in Job 4–6 has relevance for understanding friendship at another point as well. In his response to Job, Eliphaz uses several words that refer to Job's attitude or emotional state. He said in 4:2, "If one ventures a word with you, will you be impatient (תִּלְאֶה)?" He tells Job that he is not practicing what he has preached to others and in 4:5 said, "now [tragedy] has come to you, and you are impatient (וַתֵּלֶא); it touches you and you are dismayed (וַתִּבָּהֵל)." Then he cites a proverb in 5:2 that says, "Surely vexation kills the fool, and jealousy slays the simple." The proverb uses two generic nouns for fool (אֱוִיל and פֹּתֶה) and two nouns to describe an attitude or state of mind (כַּעַשׂ, "vexation," and קִנְאָה, "jealousy, intense emotion"). These words describe emotions, and while they are not identical in meaning, they have semantic ranges that move from distress and frustration to vexation, anger, and more intense emotions. Job recognized that Eliphaz was offended by his words in chapter 3 and considered them to be to be rash and inappropriate.

He also understood that Eliphaz was using the proverb in 5:2 to make two points. The first was to emphasize that Job's words were inappropriate and offensive, and to point out to him that it is foolish people who are characterized by rash words. His second point was to remind Job that if he persisted along that path, it would likely lead to disaster.

Proverbs, Metaphors, and the Importance of Hesed in Friendship

While there is uncertainty in terms of the specifics of the metaphor in 6:2–3,[16] the point of Job's response seems unmistakable. He is saying, "You are right. My words have been rash, but you have misunderstood the significance of those rash words. You have concluded from them that I am a fool. What you should have concluded from them is the depth and intensity of my pain." What he says in 6:5 seems to reinforce this understanding. He cites another proverb, "Does the wild donkey bray when he has grass, or the ox low over his fodder?" and the point is that when an animal keeps crying out even though it has plenty of food, a farmer concludes that the animal's problem goes beyond hunger. Job accused his friends of failing to do even that.

In 6:14–23, Job expressed his disappointment over their failure to help him in his distress and depicts them as unreliable. The one thing that Job

---

16.   It is not clear whether both his vexation and calamity were put in one pan of the balance or whether his vexation was weighed against the magnitude of his calamity.

had hoped to receive from them is identified in 6:14, and while the verse has been translated in a variety of ways,[17] the central point is clear: what Job expected from them was חֶסֶד (*hesed*), "loyalty" or "steadfast love." Clines says, "However the verse is translated, it is clearly the friends' lack of 'loyalty' (חֶסֶד), as Job sees it, that is central, for he proceeds to describe how they have been 'treacherous' (בנד) to him, the very opposite of loyal."[18]

Hesed is used in a variety of ways, though here it clearly refers to loyalty or kindness in a relationship. We see an example of *hesed* in Ruth's kindness to her husband and in-laws while they were in Moab (Ruth 1:8; cf. 3:10) and in her returning to Judah with her mother-in-law despite the fact that in so doing she seemed to be abandoning her own future (Ruth 3:10). In contexts involving *hesed* between people, the word regularly refers to loyalty, compassion, and doing what is necessary to meet the needs of another person.

In other contexts, *hesed* involves God's loving kindness or loyal love to his people. This is seen both in his general kindness to all people and in his special kindness to his chosen people. This *hesed* is demonstrated in many different ways in nature, in history, in the lives of those who fear God, and most especially in God's "steady, persistent refusal to wash his hands of wayward Israel."[19] God's loyal love for his people becomes the basis and the pattern for the *hesed* that his people are to demonstrate toward one another.[20]

While Job did not provide a full description of what the *hesed* that he hoped for involved, he did provide some hints. It is clear from Job 6:1 and 27 that the friends were lacking the kind of relational sensitivity to understand Job's situation and provide the help and comfort he needed. In 6:15–20 he compared them to a wadi, a dry river bed that gives travelers hope that there may be water farther back in the canyon, but only disappoints those who look for it there. There may be another implication in this metaphor in that wadis are sometimes subject to destructive flash floods. Their accusatory words did additional damage to Job, their hurting friend whom they supposedly wanted to comfort.

Job seems open to instruction in 6:24 and willing to repent if they can show him where he has gone astray, though he obviously resented their

---

17. ESV translates it, "He who withholds kindness from a friend forsakes the fear of the Almighty." NAS translates it, "For the despairing man *there should be* kindness from his friend so that he does not forsake the **fear of the Lord**." NKJ translates it, "To him who is afflicted, kindness *should be shown* by his friend. Even though he forsakes the fear of the Almighty."

18. David Clines, *Job 1–20*, WBC (Dallas, TX: Word, 1989), 178.

19. Norman Snaith, "hesed," in *A Theological Word Book of the Bible*, ed. by Alan Richardson (New York: MacMillan, 1951), 136.

20. For more detailed discussions of this word see, R. Laird Harris, "חסד (ḥesed)" *TWOT*, 305–7, and David A. Baer and Robert P. Gordon, "חסד (ḥesed)" *NIDOTTE* v. 2, 211–18.

reproof and efforts to correct him and prove him wrong.[21] Most commentators take Job's words in 6:26 ("Do you think you can reprove words, when the speech of a despairing man is wind?") as a complaint that the friends have dismissed his words in chapter 3 as having no substance—they are nothing more than the emotional rantings of a distraught person.

One wonders if he is rebuking them for misunderstanding the significance of his rash words. They are cries of pain which they take to be statements of theology that need to be refuted and corrected. Job also points out that he has not asked them to risk their lives for him (rescue him from kidnappers) or to do something that would cost them money (pay a ransom on his behalf). All he has asked is that they show him loyalty and a measure of kindness that would help him in his distress. As the debate continues, it becomes apparent that the friends see this as a dispute between Job and God and are concerned that their support for Job might displease God and bring them under judgment.

STEP FOUR: APPLYING THE TEXT

Applying Proverbs to Life

Applying these proverbs to life could be done in several ways. One might structure the teaching points around the idea that a wise friend makes a good friend and then use several examples of the wisdom that cements friendships. In addition, several things have the power to disrupt friendships like gossip, a lack of self-control, or failure to carry through on commitments could also be pointed out. Almost every individual proverb that we used in this study could become a legitimate teaching point, and certainly each of the categories that we chose to use could stand as a principle for application.

Among these principles things like these stand out.

- Keep your promises and do what you say you will do for others.
- Respond to the needs of a friend even when it is costly or inconvenient.
- Trust your friends, support them, and encourage them. Do it faithfully and consistently.
- Understand the importance of mutuality and trust; do not be a fair weather friend or a self-seeking one.
- Pick your friends carefully and understand the influence they will have on you for good or for ill.
- Be aware that friendship is something you do, not just something you think about or talk about.

---

21. In part this reflects the fact that while they advise him to confess and repent, he is not aware of anything to confess and repent of, and the friends have not identified what that might be.

Applying Job 4–6 to Life

Despite many uncertainties in Job 4–6, we can determine several things that prevented these initially well-meaning friends from bringing comfort to Job by showing him *hesed*. The first of these had to do with their arrogance and lack of humility in imagining that they knew what had happened to Job and that their theological paradigms were sufficiently comprehensive to explain his experience. They obviously did not know what had gone on in the heavenly realm, and they had no evidence of any wrongdoing or unrighteous behavior on Job's part, yet they insisted that he must be guilty of something—it could not be otherwise. They were unwilling to entertain the possibility that there might be an experience that fell outside their awareness, and they were unwilling to listen to Job and even consider his claim that he might be innocent.

One suspects that those of us who have graduate degrees in Bible and theology or who have many years of teaching and ministry in the church are especially susceptible to the mistakes that Job's friends made. We assume that our experiences are wide ranging and sufficient for dealing with any experience that might be encountered. We imagine that our encounters with suffering and injustice are fully normative and that our training and ministry experience have equipped us to diagnose and fix every problem that might arise in another person's life. Such attitudes set us up to jump to wrong conclusions just as Eliphaz and his friends did.

A second point at which the friends went wrong is reflected in their failure to understand how people suffer and as a result they trivialized Job's suffering. They misunderstood his cries of pain and supposed that he was making theological statements that had to be aggressively refuted. If I am working in my yard and a large boulder falls and crushes my foot, the words I say will likely not reflect my best theology. They are simply cries of pain. The friends' error at this point changed the entire dynamics of their interaction with Job. It changed from an opportunity to mourn and offer comfort to a hurting friend to a debate about theology and philosophy. Such arguments rarely have the power to comfort and bring *shalom*. Accuracy in biblical and theological matters is essential, but those discussions normally belong much later in the experience when emotions have settled and when the pain is less intense.

The lament psalms and Jeremiah's cries of pain and frustration to God reflect the same emotional intensity as Job's cries, and Goldingay's comments about those texts are relevant. He says:

> God allows the saints to plead with him in this babbling
> manner. The Psalms are a collection of the things that

> God has been happy for the saints to say to him, prayers
> and praises that might not every time satisfy the theolo-
> gian (or the superior kind of believer), but which found
> acceptance with God because they expressed what was
> in the heart of his believing people—found such ac-
> ceptance, in fact, that he welcomed them into his book,
> and implied the recognition of the activity of his Spirit
> in inspiring these astonishing prayers and praises.[22]

The book of Job makes it clear that God accepts honest cries of pain
and frustration from his believing people—finds them more acceptable
than the misguided pronouncements of those like Job's friends. They
were rebuked for speaking about God "that which was not right" and
told to ask Job to offer sacrifices on their behalf (42:7–8). God also described what the friends did as "folly." One wonders how many times
the friends' modern counterparts have behaved much like Job's friends
did here, but then after doing the same kind of damage to a struggling
friend, have left congratulating themselves for setting another deluded
person straight about theology.

Again, it is important to note that the issues in Job are not issues like
murder or adultery where evidence is available and irrefutable. These
are matters of subjective analysis and interpretation, and none of the
parties had the necessary information to fully understand this situation.
The issue in Job is not about the toxic spread of compromise or about
the culture persistently eroding away biblical standards.

Discussions of faith, doctrine, and appropriate Christian practice
regularly deal with grey areas, and flexibility and tolerance are a necessary part of what *hesed* involves. In this instance Job's friends were
willing to sacrifice him rather than lose a theological argument. They
failed to recognize the limits of their own understanding and certainly
could not bring themselves to say, "This is the way it looks to us, but
we could be wrong about it."

His friends could not see that practicing *hesed* is a higher priority
than agreement on speculative theological matters. Nor could they
see that the two issues are not inextricably connected. Even when
we disagree with another person about basic issues, it is still essential
to respect them and treat them in ways that reflect *hesed*. No matter
how deep the disagreements may be, it is essential that we be there to
support, help, and show compassion to people in their distress. The
friends were wrong to think that they had to choose between God
and Job, and they were wrong in thinking that if Job were innocent,
then God must be guilty and unjust.

---

22. John Goldingay, *Psalms from a Strange Land* (Downers Grove, IL: InterVarsity, 1978), 66–67.

It is highly unlikely that Job ever imagined that the friends could "fix" his situation. All he wanted was for them to support him, be there for him, and hear him out without immediately declaring him guilty. They did what they did, in part, at least, in order to make God look good, and God does not need our help in that. What honors God and elevates his reputation is when his people humbly live out his truth in the world in both good times and bad.

7

APPENDIX: COMPUTER AND INTERNET RESOURCES FOR OLD TESTAMENT EXEGESIS

BY AUSTEN M. DUTTON

The Chapter at a Glance

Introduction

Using Bible Software for Searches

Downloadable Software

Online Resources

Conclusion

INTRODUCTION

THE TWENTY–FIRST–CENTURY BIBLE INTERPRETER IS BLESSED with a nearly unimaginable wealth of resources for the task of exegesis. Detailed grammatical studies that used to take months of painstaking research in printed lexicons and biblical texts can now be done in mere seconds with the click of your mouse. The power of these tools equips the interpreter with new abilities for study and dramatically reduces the time necessary for complex research. Each year the number of resources increases, and the power, speed, and ease of use of these resources grows exponentially.

Digital resources have many advantages over printed resources. When a digital resource is updated, revised, or corrected, the reader can usually download the updated revision as soon as it's available, often without additional cost. Digital resources are also extremely portable. One can carry literally thousands of books on their smartphone, tablet, or computer for handy access anytime, anywhere. Digital resources are searchable, allowing the reader to find anything in their digital library, even if they only know a few words to search. Most resources also include the ability to highlight text and record personal study notes or commentary for future study. Having digital resources allows one to copy and paste biblical text, commentary text, or personal notes into text-editing or presentation programs (e.g., Microsoft Word, PowerPoint®) for editing, printing, displaying, or saving.

Several different types of resources are available today. Some resources are designed for one particular device (e.g., computer, Kindle, iPad or tablet, smartphone) or for a particular operating system platform (e.g., Windows, Mac, iOS, Android, Blackberry, Linux), whereas other resources have versions that work on different devices so you can buy once and use them on all your devices. Some resources require you to download and install them on your device, while others are web-based and work through the Internet with any web browser. The latter kind will operate on virtually any Internet-connected device, regardless of your specific device.

USING BIBLE SOFTWARE FOR SEARCHES

The power of digital resources becomes especially evident when the user needs to perform searches. Searches for Greek, Aramaic, or Hebrew words are simply a matter of typing in the search term. More powerful searches on root or morphological (parsing) data are extremely valuable for in-depth exegesis. The user can perform these kinds of advanced searches on the morphologically tagged Hebrew or Greek Bibles available in BibleWorks, Accordance, Logos, Olive Tree, theWord, Shebanq, and others. The user can search for a specific inflected form (e.g., וַיְבָרֶךְ) with or without vowels and accents taken into account; for all occurrences of a root (also called lemma or lexeme) in all its morphological forms across Scripture (e.g., ברא which will find בָּרָא and וַיִּבְרָא and all its other forms); or for specific morphological forms (e.g., every occurrence of any Qal perfect third-person feminine verb). These searches can be performed instantaneously with just a few clicks of the mouse; or if one learns the specialized encoding format used in the morphological databases, one can perform more complex, customized searches. For example, the Groves-Wheeler database in BibleWorks and theWord uses the format: lemma@ morphology. The morphology is represented in a series of abbreviated codes, all of which are searchable. Thus, for instance, ברא@vqp3ms represents all occurrences of verbs (v) with the root (lemma) ברא in Qal (q) perfect (p) third-person (3) masculine (m) singular (s) form. BibleWorks and theWord users could then use the search expression ברא@vqp* to find all Qal (q) perfect (p) verbs (v) from root ברא with any person, gender, and number (the * is a wildcard allowing for any other morphological code following the p). By adding in special placeholder characters as wildcards (e.g., the ? placeholder stands for any one character), the user can perform even more complex searches. For example, to find all occurrences of I-Nun verbs (in all their forms) one could search נ??@v* (or ??נ@v* depending on your software). Similar searches can be performed for III-He verbs (??ה@v* or ה??@v* depending on your software), II-Vav verbs (?ו?@v*), or all Qal perfect feminine singular verbs in either second- or third-person (*@vqp[23]fs*).

Accordance users can search their morphology database with simple English terms rather than code abbreviations. For instance, they can search [VERB imperative] to find all occurrences of verbs used as an imperative, or they can search ברא@ [VERB perfect] to find all perfect verbs from the root ברא. Likewise, Shebanq users can conduct complex morphological searches in the ETCBC database, but the format of the search query for this tool is much more specialized and requires learning beforehand. Resources available in Accordance, Logos, and Shebanq also allow for syntax—or discourse—level searches for intricate research (e.g., search for every occurrence of "the LORD" as the subject of root נכה, or for every time אֱלֹהִים is used as the object of a preposition). The level of depth one can research with these exegetical tools is nearly unbelievable.

Like searching in the original languages, searches within English Bible translations are also simple and powerful. One can search for phrases (e.g., "hill country of Judah") or individual words. One can look for search results occurring within a single verse or spanning adjacent verses. Each software uses a different method of specifying your search query. For example, BibleWorks starts searches with a period (.) when searching for individual words and with a single-quote (') when searching for a phrase. Using special keywords like OR and NOT, searches can be even further customized to include variations and exclusions (e.g., "Jordan" but not "Jordan River," or "Judah OR Judea"). If words are translated differently in different translations, the user can search across multiple translations without missing any relevant results.

For example, using this method, searching for "slothful" will return Proverbs 12:24 as a result, because some translations like the KJV use "slothful," even though other translations like the NIV use "laziness" instead. Some digital resources also allow for flexible and fuzzy searching in case the exact search phrase does not match word for word. For example, flexible searching for "find" will also return verses with "found." Similarly, fuzzy searching for the phrase "out of the land of Egypt" could also find results with "out of Egypt." This makes English translation searches extremely powerful.

Searches in the original languages or in English can usually be saved and easily reused at a later time. The user can also assign limits to searches to search only within a specific book or chapter rather than across the entire Bible, and search result occurrences can be graphed for statistical analysis. Since each digital resource uses a slightly different query format, see the instructions for your specific software for how to perform searches. The advanced capabilities of digital resources make exegetical searches extremely fast and easy and can drastically reduce the time necessary for detailed research.

The following is a summary of several important digital resources for Old Testament exegesis.

DOWNLOADABLE SOFTWARE

Downloadable software is typically more powerful than website-based resources. Some downloadable software requires purchase, while others are free. Free software is generally limited to offering noncopyrighted older commentaries, dictionaries, and English Bible translations. Paid software offers more resources and has more powerful search features. Prices for base packages or premium modules range from $20–60 ($) to $500+ ($$$$). All of the downloadable software described below offer the Hebrew Bible with a morphology database and one or more lexicons (BDB, *TWOT*, premium ones like BDAG, *HALOT* for additional cost). The Groves-Wheeler Westminster morphology database by the J. Alan Groves Center for Advanced Biblical Research is available for each of the programs. Hovering over a word in the software pops up helpful information on that word, including root, morphology, and links to lexicon entries. Advanced searches in English translations are easy too. Other helpful premium modules available in Bible software include: **LXX** (Rahlfs, *NETS*), **Targum**s, Peshitta, biblical maps and photos, language grammars, Bible translations in other languages, and Hebrew and Greek diagramming to show syntactical relationships. Accordance, Logos, and Olive Tree each offer a selection of preeminent commentary series for additional cost, including: AB, Berit Olam, Brazos Theological Commentary, EBC, Hermeneia, Holman Old Testament Commentary,

ICC, JPS **Torah**, Keil & Delitzsch, NAC, NICOT, NIVAC, TOTC, and WBC. The user can search inside these commentaries and other resources too, just like in the biblical text, making research quick and easy. These add-on modules allow you to purchase additional reference works for your specialty, letting you invest only in the resources you need.

The programs below are available for Windows and/or Mac, and some offer apps for other platforms too (iOS, Android, Kindle). Most of the Windows or Mac software offerings can be run on other operating systems (including Linux) using an emulator or a virtual machine.

BibleWorks

BibleWorks (http://bibleworks.com) has been publishing Bible software since 1992 and is known for its speed and powerful capability to interact deeply with the original languages. The base package ($$$) includes Hebrew text with morphology, LXX with morphology, most major English Bible translations, Hebrew lexicons (Holladay, BDB), and a LXX lexicon. Extra modules include Dead Sea Scrolls resources and scans of Codex Leningradensis. BibleWorks' website has a very helpful series of tutorials on integrating BibleWorks into a teacher's classroom, called Classroom Tips. BibleWorks runs on Windows (and Mac thru an emulator). The base package of BibleWorks is one of the best values available in downloadable exegesis resources, especially with its powerful original languages capabilities included by default.

Accordance

Accordance (http://www.accordancebible.com) began in 1994 with software for Mac users and now is available natively for both Mac and Windows. It is best known for its speed and user-friendly, intuitive interface. It offers exceptional capabilities for interacting with the original languages. The Starter base package ($) is very limited in its offerings, but users can purchase from several additional collections for their particular specialty or by individual add-on package, including Hebrew add-on packages ($$) with morphology and a lexicon. The LXX is also available separately or with the Hebrew as part of the Original Languages collection ($$$). Special premium modules available for purchase include: *BHQ*, Mishnah, Masorah, Dead Sea Scroll manuscript images, *NIDOTTE*, **BHS** Apparatus, Samaritan Pentateuch, and Talmud. Accordance has a substantial library of resources for Old Testament and Jewish studies. Accordance has an app for iOS (iPad/iPod/iPhone) which allows the user to sync personal notes, highlights, and book resources between all the user's devices. Accordance frequently sponsors free in-person training events at local churches and colleges/

seminaries. Their website regularly offers promotional discounts, and a limited free trial version is available to download and evaluate before you buy. Accordance's library offerings, multiple platforms, and ease of use make it a great choice, especially for Mac users.

Logos

Logos (http://www.logos.com) has been offering Bible software since 1992. The user can purchase individual packages customized for their interests. Hebrew with morphology is available as an add-on ($-$$) or in the Biblical Languages package ($$$$) with many other resources, including the LXX. Logos offers a few different Hebrew morphological databases, including Groves-Wheeler, as well as their own internally developed one. The greatest strength of Logos is the size of its resource library, offering a seemingly endless amount of digital resources on virtually every Old Testament-related topic imaginable. Each of these titles is searchable and can be highlighted, annotated, or copy/pasted to another program. Special premium modules available for purchase include: Yale Anchor Bible Dictionary, Mishnah, *NIDOTTE*, *ANET*, and Masorah. Topical books are available on Egypt, the ancient Near East, archaeology, religion, inscriptions, hermeneutics, Old Testament survey, Old Testament introduction, history of Israel, and Old Testament theology. Language study works include Assyrian, **Ugarit**ic, Sumerian, and **Akkadian**. Logos works with major biblical studies publishers to offer many modern reference works in electronic form and also offers a variety of ebooks through their Vyrso store (http://vyrso.com). Logos also has apps for Kindle Fire, Android, and iOS (iPad/iPod/iPhone) allowing users to sync their library resources across all their devices. The vast library of Logos makes it a good choice for having many resources in the palm of your hand, though the investment for such a library may be considerable.

Olive Tree

Olive Tree (http://www.olivetree.com) offers a flexible package that runs on many different platforms. A Hebrew add-on module ($$) is available to add to the base package for morphology, as is a LXX module. Olive Tree works on Windows and Mac and also has apps for iOS, Android, and Kindle Fire.

TheWord

TheWord (http://theword.net) is one of the most feature-rich Bible software packages distributed for free. It has many features similar to paid software, including impressive search features. The free base package offers a few English translations, the Hebrew Bible, LXX, forty-plus Bible translations in other languages, and older commentaries and dictionaries. The Groves-Wheeler Hebrew morphology—which is the same database as in other premium software—can be added inexpensively ($) to greatly expand theWord's research functionality at a bare minimum price. With this add-on, one can run searches in the Hebrew and its morphology, similar to more expensive software resources. Like paid software, theWord offers several premium modules for a reasonable additional cost, including: BDAG, *TWOT*, NICOT, and major English Bible translations. In portable mode, a user can run theWord from a USB flash drive without installing any software. It may not replace premium commercial software for the power user, but depending on your needs, the free theWord software may be suitable for much of your basic research, especially if you invest in inexpensive premium modules. It's an extraordinary entry-level resource.

Other Software

Other free resources offer many English-focused resources with Strong's numbers and dictionaries to help with Hebrew study, including e-Sword (http://e-sword.net), Xiphos and BibleTime (http://crosswire.org/applications) (also with a Linux version), Scripture4All (http://www.scripture4all.org), and Bible Analyzer (http://www.bibleanalyzer.com).

Kindle Resources

Kindle is a growing platform, originally designed primarily for reading rather than searching. Increasingly more Old Testament-related ebooks, commentaries, and English Bible translations are available through the Amazon marketplace (http://www.amazon.com). The oldest generations of Kindle readers may not display Hebrew or Greek correctly, but newer readers can. One publisher (http://ebooks.shalomil.com) offers the Hebrew Bible (with or without linked English translation) and the Hebrew-Greek-English Bible (including the New Testament) for Kindle readers. Kindle is available as an ebook reader device, as well as an app for other Windows, Mac, iOS, and Android devices.

ONLINE RESOURCES

The world of web-based biblical resources is constantly expanding but is still limited since usually only non-copyrighted resources are available online. With the rising movement for open-source technology, we can expect to see many more resources becoming available in the near future. The blessing of online resources is that most of their content is available, generally for free, through any Internet-connected device, regardless of its operating system or platform. These resources can usually display translations in parallel and can be copy/pasted into other programs or printed. Some of these resources also publish apps for iOS, Android, or Kindle to optimize their content for your device. Most online resources require you to be connected to the Internet to work, but some downloadable apps are able to save the digital resources to your device for offline access.

English Bible Resources

Many online resources offer English translations of the Bible, Hebrew and Greek Bibles, and commentaries. For the most part, aside from basic tagging with Strong's numbers, morphological data for the Hebrew is not yet fully available. Several effective resources have the Hebrew Bible linked to a lexicon and Strong's numbers when you hover over a word. These well-featured websites are pushing the limits of what can be done in Hebrew Bible exegesis with free resources. These include StepBible (http://www.stepbible.org), BibleWebApp (http://biblewebapp.com), Lumina (http://lumina.bible.org), BibleHub (http://biblehub.com), and Blue Letter Bible (http://www.blueletterbible.org). By linking Strong's numbers to the Hebrew text, these resources allow the user to perform simple searches to find root word occurrences across Scripture for basic research.

Many other online resources focus on reading the Bible in translation without providing too many in-depth original language resources. Some noteworthy resources include BibleGateway (http://www.biblegateway.com) (also has NIVAC commentaries available), YouVersion (http://www.bible.com), eBible (http://ebible.com), Crosswire's Bible Tool (http://www.crosswire.org/study), Unbound Bible (http://unbound.biola.edu), MySword for Android (http://www.mysword.info), Faith Comes by Hearing (http://www.bible.is), BibleStudyTools (http://www.biblestudytools.com), and Crosswire's AndBible for Android and PocketSword for iOS (http://crosswire.org/applications).

Hebrew Resources

The J. Alan Groves Center for Advanced Biblical Research maintains a digital version of the Westminster Leningrad Codex (http://tanach.us). The Hebrew text with vowels and cantillation marks can be read online or downloaded as a PDF, XML, or text file. Basic (though slow) search of Hebrew words (without morphological data) is available under the Supplements>Search menu. Scans of the original WLC can be viewed through their website under the Instructions>Facsimiles menu.

The German Bible Society has the text of *BHS* (without apparatus) available on their website (http://www.academic-bible.com).

Septuagint Resources

The *New English Translation of the Septuagint (NETS)* website (http://ccat.sas.upenn.edu/nets/edition) offers free downloadable PDFs of their English translation of the LXX. The German Bible Society has the Greek LXX available on their website (http://www.academic-bible.com).

Up-and-Coming Resources

To date, the most widely used Hebrew morphology databases (Groves-Wheeler and Logos' Lexham Hebrew) are copyrighted and require the user to purchase a license to use them. This prevents them from being used online in free resources. Two important up-and-coming resources are on the verge of changing this status quo, however, and have the potential to transform scholarly research and access to Hebrew Bible data.

The Eep Talstra Centre for Bible and Computer (ETCBC, formerly called Werkgroep Informatica Vrije Universiteit or WIVU) in Amsterdam (http://godgeleerdheid.vu.nl/etcbc or http://www.godgeleerdheid.vu.nl/en/research/institutes-and-centres/eep-talstra-centre-for-bible-and-computer) has been researching the Hebrew Bible since 1977, including some involvement by Professor Talstra with the Groves-Wheeler morphology project. The ETCBC team has published the fruit of their research in a database of word-, clause-, sentence-, and discourse-level morphological and syntactical tagging called the ETCBC database. This database used to be included in Logos, and now through partnerships with the German and Netherlands Bible Societies, scholars all over the world can access their work thru free tools such as Shebanq (http://shebanq.ancient-data.org). Licensing of this database is generous for scholarly non-commercial usage. A user can perform simple or extremely complex searches thru Shebanq, or theoretically download and run the software offline (though this option is only for expert users). This database can handle the same kinds of searches as commercial Bible software discussed earlier, though Shebanq's interface may be slightly too overwhelming for the everyday user. However, advanced users can format and execute searches, and then publish and cite the search results for use in scholarly journals or books. Working with the ETCBC database on Shebanq carries a significant learning curve to understand how to format queries using a specialized search language, but more user-friendly tools to tap into the power of this database will likely be forthcoming, and the potential for research with this tool is extraordinary.

Another exciting project is still young but has enormous prospects. The volunteers of the OpenScriptures Hebrew Bible project (http://openscriptures.github.io/morphhb and http://openscriptures.org) are creating a community-built morphological database of the Hebrew Bible. Currently they are inputting parsing data and tagging words in the biblical text to entries in major lexicons. Their vision is for a generously licensed database for use in all kinds of projects. When this project is available, it will mark a significant turning point in the creation of far more robust free Hebrew Bible digital resources. Between the ETCBC and OpenScriptures projects (and others), we could not be more excited about the future of Old Testament studies with free, widely-available digital resources. These projects will truly open the door to vast new worlds of rapid, deep research for every scholar and user.

CONCLUSION

The sea of resources available is vast and, like the field of biblical studies itself, the plethora of resources probably cannot be mastered by any one individual. Therefore, we recommend that you select a small handful of good resources and become knowledgeable about those, rather than attempting to learn about all the different options out there. Try using free or inexpensive resources at first, and then you can always upgrade to premium resources if they will serve you better. In addition, occasionally reading a few good blogs will help you stay informed on new features and new programs which may be worth your investigation. Resources for staying up-to-date on the ever-evolving world of digital resources for exegesis include our own list of websites (http://www.thebiblestudent.info/p/digital-biblical-studies.html), the blogs from Accordance and BibleWorks, and the Society of Biblical Literature publications.

Using digital resources carries a few cautions. Using these powerful tools can lead to the false assumption that if a user knows how to do searches in the biblical text, then she is an expert on the biblical text. This fallacy can easily lead to bad teaching. Using exegesis tools must always be coupled with an appreciation for and understanding of the biblical languages and of the task of exegesis. Let the user be warned: digital tools can help with exegesis, but they are never a substitute for the interpreter's role in exegesis.

In addition, certain digital resources may not be appropriate for all users. Some digital resources require a substantial financial investment to get the resources one wants, and usually this digital library cannot be sold, gifted, or transferred to a different user. So when one retires from research, his library and financial investment retire as well. Also, Bible software is updated regularly, and this means you may have to purchase a new edition every few years to keep using the resources you've already purchased. Finally, many readers prefer the look and feel of reading on print, rather than on a screen. Thus, your personal study habits and preferences may factor into your decision on investing in digital resources.

But the advantages to having digital resources for biblical exegesis are manifold. They will make your teaching, preaching, and research far richer and faster. And in the coming years, we anticipate a whole new wealth of resources will be available for the next generation of exegetes.

GLOSSARY

acrostic. The biblical acrostics are alphabet acrostics in which successive lines of the poem begin with a consecutive letter of the Hebrew alphabet.

affective. This has to do with the emotional impact of a text or experience on a person.

Akkadian. The language used by the Babylonians and Assyrians. Both of these dialects were written in cuneiform on clay tablets.

allegorical interpretation. Reading and interpreting a piece of literature as if it were an allegory, irrespective of whether or not the original author intended it to be understood in that way.

allegory. A type of literature in which events and characters in one realm actually represent those in a different one. An example is Orwell's *Animal Farm*, in which interactions among animals in a barnyard actually describe events from a certain era in Soviet history.

ambiguity. A literary technique that leaves the meaning open-ended. Such techniques force the reader to think about various possibilities for both meaning and application.

aphorism. A short, pithy statement expressing a truth. Proverbs are aphorisms.

Aramaic square script. The alphabet that began to be used by the Jewish people after the Babylonian exile.

autograph. The original biblical documents, none of which are extant today.

BHS. *Biblia Hebraica Stuttgartensia* is the standard scholarly edition of the Hebrew Bible. It includes Masoretic notes about the text and a register at the bottom of each page identifying the major textual variants found in the manuscripts and translations.

chiastic order. A literary technique in which elements in a poetic line are reversed in the next line of the poem to which it is parallel. If the order in the first line is subject-object, the parallel elements would be presented in the order object-subject.

discretion. The quality of caution, restraint, and self-control that is commended throughout the Old Testament wisdom literature. It is the opposite of rash, emotionally charged words and actions.

dittography. A scribal error in which the scribe inadvertently copies a word(s) or letter(s) twice.

ellipsis. The omission of an expression in one line with that element assumed in the parallel line.

emendation. A change made to the Hebrew text. A conjectural emendation is a change made without any external (i.e. manuscript) evidence.

empiricism. This term has to do with how people know and verify what is true. Much of modern culture insists that we can only be confident about things that are verified by observation and careful scientific research—that is, by empirical methods. Such insistence often rejects faith assertions out of hand because they cannot be verified by empirical means.

Enlightenment thinking. This term describes the system of thought that resulted from the Enlightenment, which began sometime in the seventeenth century. It is generally associated with rationalism and with the idea that human experience is a poor guide to knowing truth. Truth about which we can be confident consists only in those things that are either logically irrefutable or empirically verified.

epistemology. This has to do with the way people come to know things. It deals both with the methods used and with how truth claims are validated.

external evidence. This term in textual criticism refers to evidence based on manuscripts and ancient translations of the Bible as opposed to internal evidence which is based on grammatical or syntactical considerations. See also "internal evidence."

fear of God/the Lord. The essence of piety in the Old Testament. It involves an understanding of who God is and who we are as human beings. It consists in a reverential awe of God and expresses itself in a life of obedience and trust in God.

general revelation. This term has to do with what people can know about God and reality by observing the created world and human society. See also "special revelation."

genre. A type of literature defined by its structure, style, context, etc. Love poems, historical fiction, legal contracts, and laments are examples of genres.

hebel. A Hebrew word that means a "puff of air." It is used throughout Ecclesiastes to describe the futility and lack of substance that comes when a person lives a life not centered in God.

ḥesed. A Hebrew word meaning gracious or loyal love. It is used in Job 6 to describe the kind of loyalty that Job wanted from a friend.

homoeoarcton. A scribal error involving a scribe skipping from one occurrence of a word to a second nearby occurrence and leaving out the intervening words.

homophony. A scribal error involving substitution of a similar sounding word or letter. An English example would be writing "read" instead of "red, "bare" instead of "bear," or "pedal" instead of "petal."

humility. An attitude that recognizes both our strengths and our weaknesses and limits as human beings. Humility with respect to God means that we recognize that he is the sovereign, all wise, and powerful Creator and that we are creatures made by him and dependent on him. With respect to other people, humility means that we recognize that we have both strengths and weaknesses and are willing both to help others and remain open to the help others can provide us.

hyperbole. A rhetorical device that uses exaggeration in order to emphasize a point or quality. An example of this is seen in the description of the sluggard as a door that only turns on its hinges (Prov. 26:14).

inclusio. A literary device that begins and ends a section with the same word or expression in order to enclose the section with that idea. Qoheleth, for example, begins (Eccl. 1:2) and ends (Eccl. 12:8) Ecclesiastes with the word *hebel*.

internal evidence. In textual criticism this term refers to evidence derived from the grammar, syntax, word use in the text, rather than to manuscript evidence. See, "external evidence."

ketib. This Hebrew/Aramaic word means "what is written," and the Masoretic scholars who put vowels into the Hebrew consonantal text used this designation when the oral tradition differed from the written consonantal text. In this way they preserved both traditions. It was also used in situations where the scribes believed there was a grammatical problem or inappropriate reading.

LXX. The term used for the Greek translation of the Hebrew Bible that was begun in Egypt about 350 BC. This translation is called the Septuagint, and was widely used in New Testament times.

Masoretes. The scribes and scholars who added vowels and other diacritical marks to the consonantal text of the Hebrew Bible between about 700 and 1000 AD. Scribes like this faithfully copied the biblical text through the centuries to preserve the revelation that God gave to his people, Israel.

Masoretic text. The Hebrew Bible produced by the Masoretes. It is the Hebrew text considered authoritative by both Christians and Jews.

merism. The use of two opposites or extremes to indicate everything in between.

metanarrative. A broad, overarching idea that ties together widely disparate areas of knowledge and gives coherence to it.

metaphor. A figure of speech in which something concrete is compared with a more abstract idea in order to explain it. For example, the irritating and painful effect of sending a sluggard on an important mission is compared to "smoke in the eyes" in Proverbs 10: 26.

paleo–Hebrew script. The alphabetic script used to write Hebrew prior to the Babylonian captivity.

parallelism. A characteristic of Hebrew poetry in which lines are paired together in such a way that the second line presents a slightly different perspective on the idea expressed in the first line.

personification. Attributing to an abstract entity the characteristics of a human being.

pride. An attitude that the Old Testament sees as particularly destructive. At one level it is a refusal to acknowledge God's legitimate authority, and a determination to live life independently of God. At another level it is the attitude that refuses to acknowledge a need for help or correction from others. In both instances pride is antithetical to wisdom.

proverb. A short and often cryptic saying that captures practical truths about life. These concise and memorable statements about life often become a part of the tradition of the people and are passed on from generation to generation.

qer'e. The Hebrew/Aramaic word means "what is to be read," and the Masoretic scholars who put vowels into the Hebrew consonantal text used this designation to indicate what they believed to be the more correct reading when the oral tradition differed from the written consonantal text. In this way they preserved both traditions. Occasionally this distinction was used in situations where the scribes believed that the text contained a reading that was inappropriate for public reading.

Qoheleth. The Hebrew term for the sage who is the central figure in the body of Ecclesiastes. It is probably a title rather than a name, and the exact meaning or significance of the word is unknown. Some English translations render it as "the Preacher" (or "the Teacher").

Qumran. The place in the Judean desert where the Dead Sea Scrolls were found.

Rationalism. A methodology that became dominant during the Enlightenment. It essentially maintains that every issue and question must yield to rigorous rational scrutiny. It rejects subjectivity and faith as legitimate ways of knowing truth.

retribution. The idea that righteous people will be blessed by God in proportion to their goodness while the wicked will be judged by God in proportion to their wickedness. This idea is taught many places in the Bible. It is embedded in the Mosaic Covenant; it is an important theme in Deuteronomy, the prophets and Chronicles; it is also taught in the New Testament. Retribution is one of the ways God works in the world. The problem in Job resulted from assuming that retribution was the only way God works and in insisting that retribution was the only lens through which Job's suffering could be understood.

sage. A wise man. Sages specialized in wisdom tradition. Many of them probably worked for the king and played an important role in collecting the wisdom material.

source domain/target domain. The source domain is the example or metaphor a poet uses to explain a concept while the target domain is the concept the poet is explaining. In Proverbs 25:25 the source domain is "cold water to a thirsty soul," and the concept he is trying to explain (the target domain) is "good news from a far country."

special revelation. This refers to God's revelation that goes beyond what people can discover about God through nature and human society. It is generally delivered to God's people rather than to humanity in general. It comes in a wide variety of ways: miraculous interventions into history, visions, and revelations to various prophets. The culmination of special revelation came through Jesus Christ, and Scripture provides us with an inspired record of special revelation.

Targum. Aramaic translations/paraphrases of the Hebrew Scriptures used after the Jewish people returned from the Babylonian exile.

textual criticism. The discipline that seeks to examine textual evidence in order to determine the text that most likely reflects the original reading.

theophany. An appearance of God to a person or a people, often through a dream or a vision.

Torah. The term means "instruction." It is often used more narrowly to refer to the five books of Moses.

Ugarit. A city in northwest Syria where a number of texts dealing with Canaanite mythology were found. These texts, which provided many details about Canaanite gods and goddesses, were written in Ugaritic, a language closely related to Hebrew.

under the sun. The phrase used in Ecclesiastes to indicate life as we experience it in the world.

vowel letters. Hebrew was originally written using only consonants, but certain consonants were sometimes used to indicate the presence of a particular vowel in order to reduce ambiguity in written texts.

Yahweh. The personal name for the God who revealed himself to Israel and chose them as his people. In the past this word has been inaccurately rendered *Jehovah*.

Yahweh's order. This term reflects the principles by which God designed the world to work. A goal of wisdom was to discover as much as possible about Yahweh's order.

Yahwistic. Pertaining to Yahweh. Yahwistic values and practices, and other elements of Yahwistic theology flow out of God's revelation to his people and the covenant that Yahweh made with them.